Journey with Jeremiah
Nourishment for the Wild Olive

Julie Almanrode

Julie EMA Almanrode
(3 John 1:4)

Cover photograph, View of Dead Sea from
Lower David Stream Trail, En Gedi, Israel.
All photographs © The Almanrode Family

Scriptures taken from:
The Holy Bible, New International Version ©1973, 1978;
Complete Jewish Bible, ©1998 David H. Stern;
and *The Amplified Bible.*

ISBN 10:1507756895
ISBN-13: 978-1507756898

For my wild olive shoots:
Jesse, Josi, Jacob, and Jemima

"A song of ascents:
How happy is everyone who fears Adonai,
who lives by his ways.
You will eat what your hands have produced;
you will be happy and prosperous.
Your wife will be like a fruitful vine
in the inner parts of your house.
Your children around the table will be
like shoots from an olive tree.
This is the kind of blessing that will fall
on him who fears Adonai.
May Adonai bless you from Tziyon!
May you see Yerushalayim prosper
all the days of your life,
and may you live to see your children's children!
Shalom on Israel"
(Psalm 128).

Table of Contents

**Part Two
The Ancient Paths**

Part Three
Yielding Fruit

The Journey Begins

"Stand at the crossroads and look; ask for the ancient paths, ask where the good way is, and walk in it, and you will find rest for your souls" (Jeremiah 6:16).

For my husband and I, these words didn't seem to have any value. They were spoken by God to an Old Testament prophet that had nothing to do with being a New Testament Christian. Besides, wasn't Christianity trying to remove itself from the 'ancient paths'?

When asked by a Messianic Jew nearly 25 years ago, "What is it like to be grafted into the Olive Tree of Israel?" my husband and I began to look in the Bible for an answer. Though we were attending a Bible teaching fellowship, we had never heard about the Olive Tree of Israel. In our search, we found that many of our doctrinal beliefs and traditions we adhered to were not true to the Word of God. We were exactly like those from the nations saying, *"Our fathers have inherited nothing but lies, futility and things of no profit"* (Jeremiah 16:19).

God gave Jeremiah unique instructions: *"See, today I appoint you over nations and kingdoms to uproot and tear down, destroy and overthrow, to build and to plant"* (Jeremiah 1:9). We began to see that we had to uproot and tear down kingdom ideologies that denominational divisions and anti-semitic church fathers had brought into our walk of faith. We had to repent from many manmade traditions that we thought were of God, but nullified the very commands of God. We had been drinking from empty cisterns and we were very thirsty.

"My people have committed two sins: They have forsaken me, the spring of living water, and have dug their own cisterns, broken cisterns that cannot hold water" (Jeremiah 2:13).

God also told Jeremiah to build and plant. This became the exciting part of our journey. We learned that as wild olive branches grafted into the Olive Tree with the natural branches of Israel, we have deep spiritual roots. Living water began to fill us and the Spirit of God brought light to Scriptures we had never even seen before and a new understanding to those we had misinterpreted.

We learned what it meant to have our citizenship in Israel built on the foundation of the apostles and prophets with Yeshua as the cornerstone. As family members of God's household, there were ways of worshipping Him that were different from what we were used to as 'foreigners to the covenants.' We stopped skipping over phrases like 'Jewish festivals' and learned about the Feasts of the LORD. With each one our eyes were opened to the reality of Messiah Yeshua's past, present and future work. Each celebration allowed us to touch him, see him, hear him, taste him, and smell him. More importantly, we became aware of our responsibility as non-Jewish believers to take the message of salvation to the Jewish people.

We learned that both Testaments give the complete understanding of God's plan of salvation. Without the Torah, Prophets and Writings, gentiles lose their rich spiritual heritage. Without the Gospels and Letters, the Jewish people will never know the Jewish Yeshua as their Messiah. The dividing wall, the partition that caused this separation, was literally a page in our Bible that had the words "New Testament." We tore that page out and never looked back.

When each of us stands at a crossroad in our walk of faith, we have to make a choice - keep going the same direction or look for the better way. It's difficult to stand alone and take the path everyone claims is 'obsolete.' It's not easy to tear down and uproot things that we hold dear to our hearts, but it is the only way to stop drinking water polluted with lies, lawless doctrines and anti-semitic ideologies.

Journey with Jeremiah was compiled to encourage other wild olives who are thirsty for living water. Along the ancient paths are rivers flowing with fresh water that will end years of drought and bring forth fruit from the wild olive branch.

Part One
Inherited Lies

"Adonai, my strength, my fortress,
my refuge in time of trouble,
the nations will come to you
from the ends of the earth, saying,
"Our ancestors inherited nothing but lies,
futile idols, completely useless"
(Jeremiah 16:19).

The Memorial Name of God

"Moses said to God, 'Suppose I go to the Israelites and say to them, 'The God of your fathers has sent me to you,' and they ask me, 'What is his name?' Then what shall I tell them?" God said to Moses, 'I AM who I AM. This is what you are to say to the Israelites: 'I AM has sent me to you'. God also said to Moses, 'Say to the Israelites, 'The LORD, the God of your fathers - the God of Abraham, the God of Isaac and the God of Jacob - has sent me to you. This is my name forever, the name you shall call me from generation to generation" (Exodus 3:13-15).

In Hebrew the "I Am who I Am" is יהוה. For centuries the *'Yod Hey Vav Hey'* has been considered too holy to speak and thus the actual pronunciation of God's memorial name has been lost. It was replaced in Jewish thinking with *HaShem* meaning 'The Name' or *Adonai* meaning 'Lord'. The words 'God' and 'Lord' have their vowels removed and become G-d and L-rd to show respect for God's name. Because of these historical and cultural anomalies, the Preface in most Bibles says that the divine name for God or Tetragrammaton has been changed from the יהוה to LORD with all capitals letters.

Using modern Hebrew, the יהוה or *'Yod Hey Vav Hey'* could be pronounced Yahweh or Yahveh. The Waw or Vav can be used as a hard or soft vowel sound - v or ooo - which also causes many differences of opinion for speaking these letters. It could be that the unknown sound with the Vav comes from the Spirit of God or the Ruach רוח. So the name of God could be said Yahooowaaaay breathing out deeply or Yah-way with a 'w' sounding breathy.

However the name of God is to be spoken, it will be revealed by Him in the future as prophecies come to pass. As I write, I will most often use God or LORD for the '*Yod Hey Vav Hey*' and only when I want to emphasize His name, Yahweh or YHVH. I do this to be respectful, however, being that God does have a 'memorial name forever', I believe in trying to use it to the best of our understanding especially in these last days when names of foreign gods are becoming more pronounced within our world's culture.

"I am YHVH (Yahweh); that is my name. I yield my glory to no one else, nor my praise to any idol" (Isaiah 42:8).

"Who has gone up to heaven and come down? Whose hands have gathered up the wind? Who has wrapped up the waters in a cloak? Who has established all the ends of the earth? What is his name, and what is the name of his son? Surely you know!" (Proverbs 30:4).

Hebrew Word Pictures

Each letter of the Hebrew alphabet or aleph-bet is a word picture. When word pictures are put together, unique meanings to words appear. Here are the Hebrew word pictures for the name of God: *Yod Hey Vav Hey* (Yahweh or YHVH in English).

יהוה

Yod י - A Closed Hand means 'a 'finished work'

Hey ה - A Window means 'behold or reveal'

Vav ו - A Nail means 'binding or connecting to'

Hey ה - A Window means 'behold or reveal'

The Hebrew word picture for *Yod Hey Vav Hey*: *"Behold the finished work of the binding revealed."*

God is One. He gave His divine name given to Moses, however, multiple attributes are seen in compound forms with His name throughout the Scriptures. In the beginning, יהוה did not reveal His name to the patriarchs, but His character.

Elohim - אלוהום means 'God, Judge, Creator'

"In the beginning, God (Elohim) created the heavens and the earth. Now the earth was formless and empty, darkness as over the surface of the deep and the Spirit of God (Elohim) was hovering over the waters. And (Elohim) said, 'Let there be light,' and there was light' (Genesis 1:1-3).

Some say that because *Elohim* is the plural of *eloah* used in these verses, it supports the trinity doctrine. However, the meaning is actually the singular as it is used only with singular verbs and with adjectives and pronouns in the singular.

Hebrew Word Pictures

God - *Elohim* אלהים

Aleph א - An Ox means 'first, strength'

Lamed ל - A Shepherd Staff means 'to urge forward'

Hey ה - A Window means 'reveal'

Yod י - A Closed Hand means 'finished work'

Mem מ - Water means 'large or massive like an ocean'

The Hebrew Word Picture for *Elohim*: *"Strength propels to reveal a massive finished work."*

El Shaddai - אל שדי means 'Lord God Almighty, All Sufficient One'

El is translated 'God' and can be used in conjunction with other words relating to the aspect of God's character. It refers to God completely nourishing, satisfying and supplying His people with all their needs. This is God's first revelation to Abraham, Isaac, and Jacob as to 'who' He is - The Sustainer. The Hebrew etymology for *shaddai* includes a destroyer, a mountain and a bosom.

"When Abram was ninety-nine years old, El Shaddai appeared to him and said, 'I AM El Shaddai; walk before me faithfully and be blameless" (Genesis 17:1).

"So Isaac called for Jacob and blessed him. ... May El Shaddai bless you and make you fruitful and increase your numbers until you become a community of peoples" (Genesis 28:3).

"Jacob said to Joseph, 'El Shaddai appeared to me at Luz in the land of Canaan, and there he blessed me" (Genesis 48:3).

El Elyon - אל אליון mean 'The Most High God'

This character name of God expresses the Sovereignty and Majesty of God. This is first used when Abraham returned from defeating Kedorlaomer and the kings allied with him. Melchizedek, King of Salem brings out bread and wine and blesses Abram.

"Blessed be Abram by El Elyon, Creator of heaven and earth. And praise be to El Elyon who delivered your enemies into your hand" (Genesis 14: 17-20).

YHVH Shammah - יהוה שמע means 'Yahweh is Present'

This is more than a simple statement that God is in a place. It is part of His name and a statement of His actual presence being with men and dwelling with men. YHVH wants us to know that He is with us wherever we go until the end of the age.

"The distance all around will be 18,000 cubits. And the name of the city from that time on will be: 'YHVH Shammah'" (Ezekiel 48:35).

"YHVH replied 'My shammah will go with you, and I will give you rest" (Exodus 33:14).

"Therefore go and make disciples of all nations, baptizing them in the name of the Father and of the Son and of the Holy Spirit, and teaching them to

obey everything I have commanded you. And sure I am with you always, to the very end of the age" (Matthew 28:19-20).

YHVH Roeh - יהוה רעה means 'Yahweh it the Shepherd'

"Hear the word of YHVH, you nations; proclaim it in distant coastlands: 'He who scattered Israel will gather them and will watch over hi flock like a shepherd" (Jeremiah 31:10).

"YHVH is my shepherd I shall not be in need…" (Psalm 23:1).

"But you, Bethlehem, in the land of Judah, are by no means least among the rulers of Judah; for out of you will come a ruler who will shepherd my people Israel" (Matthew 2:6).

YHVH Rapha - יהוי רפה means 'Yahweh Healer, Restorer'

"There YHVH Rapha (at the waters of Marah) issued a ruling and instruction for them and put them to the test. He said, 'If you listen carefully to YHVH your God and do what is right in his eyes, if you pay attention to his commands and keep all his decrees, I will not bring on you any of the diseases I brought on the Egyptians, for I am YHVH who heals you'" (Exodus 15:25-26).

"Praise YHVH Rapha, my soul, and forget not all his benefits - who forgives all your sins and heals all your diseases, who redeems your life from the pit and crowns you with love and compassion …" (Psalm 103:2-4).

"The moon will shine like the sun, and the sunlight will be seven times brighter, like the light of seven full days, when YHVH Rapha binds up the bruises of his people and heals the wounds he inflicted" (Isaiah 30:26).

"On a Sabbath Yeshua was teaching in one of the synagogues, and a woman was there who had been crippled by a spirit for eighteen years. She was bent over and could not straighten up at all. When Yeshua saw her, he called her forward and said to her, 'Woman you are set free from your infirmity.' Then he put his hands on her, and immediately she straightened up and praised God" (Luke 13:10-12).

YHVH Tzidkenu - צדקנו יהוה means 'Yahweh our Righteousness'

This attribute of God should bring comfort to believers for we do not have to rely on our own righteousness because YHVH is our Righteousness. Anytime we are being accused or reminded of sin in our lives, either by the enemy, other people or ourselves, we just need to remember that Righteousness is the name of our God.

"In his days Judah shall be saved, and Israel shall dwell safely: and this is his name whereby he shall be called, YHVH our righteousness" (Jeremiah 23:6).

"This righteousness is given through faith in Messiah Yeshua to all who believe. There is no difference between Jew and Gentile, for all have sinned and fall short of the glory of God, and all are justified freely by his grace through the redemption that came by Messiah Yeshua" (Romans 3:22-23).

YHVH Yireh - יראה יהוה means 'Yahweh Provider'

The Hebrew word *yireh* can also mean "will see, to be seen, to experience to be allowed to see, to understand." This verse is in reference to when YHVH provided the ram in the thicket in place of Isaac. This significance of the event on Mt. Moriah with the binding of Isaac was that Abraham might see and understand the message of God's plan of redemption through the ram.

"So Abraham called that place YHVH Yireh. And to this day it is said, 'On the mountain of YHVH, it will be provided" (Genesis 22:14).

YHVH Nissi - נשי יהוה means 'Yahweh My Banner, My Miracle'

This attribute of YHVH tells us something about God: He is in the center of the warfare of His people.Enemies attack all of us whether they are physical enemies or spiritual. We are instructed to put on the whole armor of God which in essence is our battle standard. It is under His name, His banner, that we will find victory and it is in His name that victory is won.

YHVH Nissi was revealed to Israel while wandering in the wilderness after crossing the Red Sea. Amalek came against Israel in

Rephidim. In Exodus 17:8-16 Moses calls on Joshua to lead the Israelites into battle while he stayed on top of a hill to pray. As Moses lifted his hands to pray, the Israelites prevailed in battle, but when he let his hands down, Amalek prevailed. Eventually Moses' brother Aaron and his assistant Hur sat Moses on a rock and held his hands up for him until the Israelites completely won the battle. After the battle Moses built an altar to the Lord.

"Moses built an altar and called it YHVH Nissi" (Exodus 17:15).

"So shall they fear the name of YHVH from the west, and his glory from the rising of the sun. When the enemy shall come in like a flood, the Spirit of YHVH will lift up a standard [banner] against him" (Isaiah 59:19).

"And in that day there shall be a root of Jesse, which shall stand as an ensign of the people, to it shall the nations seek: and his rest shall be glorious" (Isaiah 11:10).

"You have given a banner to them that fear you that it may be displayed because of the Truth" (Psalm 60:4).

YHVH Shalom - יהוה שלום means 'Yahweh is Peace'

Shalom is the greeting one gives to another in Israel. When Yeshua sent his disciples to the lost sheep of the House of Israel, he spoke of peace (John 10). In verse 13, he says *"If the home is deserving, let your peace rest on it; if it is not, let your peace return to you."*

"So Gideon built an altar to YHVH there and called it YHVH Shalom. To this day it stands in Ophrah of the Abierzrites" (Judges 6:24).

"The God of peace be with you all. Amein" (Romans 15:33).

"For God is not a God of disorder but of peace … " (1 Corinthians 14:33).

YHVH Mekoddishkim - יהוי קדש means 'Yahweh Sanctifies, Makes Holy'

Mekoddishkim comes from the Hebrew word *kodesh* that means 'to sanctify, make holy, or dedicate.' Sanctification is the separation of an object or person to the dedication of the holy.

"Say to the Israelites, 'You must observe my Sabbaths. This will be a sign between me and you for the generations to come, so you may know that I AM YHVH, who makes you holy" (Exodus 31:13).

"Keep my decrees and follow them. I AM YHVH, who makes you holy" (Leviticus 20:8).

YHVH Sabaoth - יהוה צבאת means 'Yahweh of Hosts; Commander of the Angelic Armies'

Sabaoth means armies or hosts. This attribute of YHVH denotes His Universal Sovereignty over the angelic armies both in heaven and on earth. YHVH *Sabaoth* is King of all heaven and earth.

"Lift up your heads, you gates; lift them up, you ancient doors, that the King of glory may come in. Who is he, this King of glory? YHVH Sabaoth - he is the King of glory" (Psalm 24:9-10).

"Woe to me!" I cried. 'I am ruined. For I am a man of unclean lips, and I live among a people of unclean lips, and my eyes have seen the King, YHVH Sabaoth" (Isaiah 6:5).

Who is Jehovah?

There IS no other name for God except the יהוה given to Moses. Though there are differences of opinion to how that name is spoken, it still remains God's Memorial Name. Still, there are those who use the name Jehovah.

The name Jehovah has an interesting history apart from it being the Latin, then Anglicized version of Yahweh. It begins with the Tetragrammaton, יהוה, or YHVH in our modern alphabet.

YHVH

Hebrew in its purest form does not have vowels. Over the centuries, vowels were created as little marks above, below or next to the letter. However, there have never been vowel points with the Yod Hey Vav Hey.

In Hebrew God is referred to as *Adonai* or the title 'Lord'. For some reason, someone somewhere decided to put the vowels from *Adonai* between the Hebrew letters for יהוה.

In English transliteration, this would make the name of God look like this:

YaHoVaH

The letter Y in the beginning was changed to an English J. This adds another interesting twist since the Hebrew alphabet has no letter J. In fact, the letter J in terms of alphabets is relatively new, only several hundred years old. This change transformed YaHoVaH into

JaHoVah or JeHoVaH.

Now, you decide if Jehovah is the name God gave to Moses. Use the same concept with your own name. Write your initials leaving space between them for vowels. Think about a title you have such as husband, father, mother, wife, brother, sister, pastor, or deacon. If you can't think of a good title, just use *Adonai*. Insert the vowels from that title between your initials. You have just created your name in the same manner as Jehovah evolved from Yod Hey Vav, Hey. What is your name? Is that the name given you at birth, used by your family and friends?

The Name of יהוה on His People

"The LORD said to Moshe, "Speak to Aaron and his sons, and tell them that this is how you are to bless the people of Israel: you are to say to them,

'Y'varekh'kha יהוה v'yishmerekha.
[May Yahweh bless you and keep you.]

Ya'er יהוה panav eleikha vichunekka.
[May Yahweh make his face shine on you and show you his favor.]

Yissa יהוה panav eleikha v'yasem l'kha shalom.
[May Yahweh lift up his face toward you and give you peace.]'

In this way they are to put my name on the people of Israel, so that I will bless them" (Numbers 6:22-27).

Name Above All Names

"But after he considered this, an angel of the Lord appeared to him in a dream and said, 'Joseph son of David, do not be afraid to take Mary home as your wife, because what is conceived in her is from the Holy Spirit. She will give birth to a son, and you are to give him the name Jesus, because he will save his people from their sins" (Matthew 1:20-21).

The English name 'Jesus' comes from a Latin transliteration of a Greek rendering of the Savior's name; however, 'Jesus' was not Greek, Latin or English, he was an Israelite. The angel refers to Joseph as a 'son of David', thus Jesus' human lineage as found in Matthew and Luke was from the Tribe of Judah making him Jewish. When Joseph took his infant son to be circumcised and named, he did not name him 'Jesus'. When his parents wanted him for dinner, they did not call him 'Jesus'. His brothers and sisters did not call him 'Jesus.' His friends and relatives in the Galilee did not call him 'Jesus.' His disciples and the Jewish leaders of the day did not call him 'Jesus.' They called him *Yeshua*.

Most Bibles have a footnote after the name of 'Jesus' directing the reader to the bottom of the page. Generally, the footnote reads something like "the name Jesus comes from a Hebrew word that sounds like Joshua and means God saves." In the Hebrew language there is no letter "J" so even Joshua would be incorrect as it would be Yoshua.

"I have come in my Father's name, and you do not accept me; but if someone else comes in his own name, you will accept him" (John 5:43)

"God saves" could be translated *Yahshua,* יהשוה, - The *Yah* coming from Yahweh and the *shua* meaning 'salvation'. This is sometimes considered a rendering of Messiah's name since Yeshua did say that he came in his Father's name. By having *Yah* in his name, however, he would have caused an even greater uprising with the Jewish rulers of his day since they had stopped using the memorial name of God. Though he was called a blasphemer and that could suggest he used his Father's name as his own, I personally believe that he respected his Father's name as well as the culture in which he lived. He did not toss יהוה around to prove he was God's Son. He used his actions and teachings.

"She will give birth to a son, and you are to give him the name Jesus, because he will save his people from their sins ... (Matthew 1:21).

A more accurate rendering of the passage in Matthew 1:21 would be *"You are to give him the name Yeshua because he will yesa his people from their sins."* Just as the character of the "I Am that I Am" is embedded in the יהוה, so too would the character of *salvation* be embedded in the Savior's name, *Yeshua.*

Using a Hebrew dictionary, the common word for 'salvation' is *yeshua.* This is the name that was most likely given to Joseph and used by all who knew God's Son while he walked on earth. This is the name and spelling that will be used in this book. There are many different ideas about the spelling of Yeshua's name, but because *yeshua* is the literal Hebrew word for salvation and found in Scripture, it is the one I will use for the name of God's Son.

"The LORD (Yahweh) is my strength and my defense he has become my Yeshua..." (Exodus 15:2).

"The LORD (Yahweh) is my light and my Yeshua - whom shall I fear?" (Psalm 27:1).

"Sing to the LORD (Yahweh) a new song, for he has done marvelous things; his right hand and his holy arm have worked Yeshua for him" (Psalm 98:1).

Throughout their generations the Israelites looked for *yeshua*. They knew that God would make provision for their salvation because they understood the binding of Isaac and the substitute ram. They knew that God and His salvation would be Himself because the Scriptures revealed God working His *yeshua* on behalf of the people. When this occurred in the physical body of Yeshua, some accepted him, many did not. Even though they had the prophecies of Isaiah 53 and Psalm 22, many struggled with the idea that the Word had actually become flesh in a man from Galilee, a Nazarene (John 1:14). His physical presence didn't match the voice they heard from the prophets. This could be compared to having a phone conversation with someone who you later meet and they don't look anything like you expected.

"The Son is the image of the invisible God, the firstborn over all creation" (Colossians 1:15).

"For God was pleased to have all his fullness dwell in him (Messiah) ..." (Colossians 1:19).

It is important to know the actual name of the Messiah given to his parents by God. There is power in his name (John 17:11, Acts 4:7). There are answered prayers in his name (John 16:23). There is protection in his name (John 17:11-12). There is life in his name (John 20:31). Repentance and forgiveness will be preached in his name (Luke 24:47). Miracles will be done in his name (Mark 9:39). There will be persecution because of his name (John 15:21). He will return when the Jews call on his name (Luke 13:35). These are all things that have been done in the name of Jesus, but with the God-given name of *Yeshua* and the acceptance of his Biblically Jewish heritage, his name may bring even more repentance, power, life, miracles, and life from the dead.

"Therefore God exalted him to the highest place and gave him the name that is above every name, that at the name of Yeshua every knee should bow, in heaven

and on earth and under the earth, and every tongue confess that Yeshua is LORD (Yahweh) to the glory of God the Father" (Philippians 2:9-11).

Philippians is clear that one day every knee will bow and every tongue will confess Yeshua, not only as Lord, but as Yahweh in the flesh. This means that everyone will confess salvation in the person of Yeshua as coming from Yahweh and no one else. Though for many centuries the name of Yeshua has been hidden away just like the name of God, the time is now for the restoration of all things and the purifying of our lips which includes the Hebrew, Jewish name of the Messiah of Israel, *Yeshua*.

Hebrew Word Pictures

Each letter of the Hebrew alphabet is a word picture. When word pictures are put together, unique meanings to words appear. Here are the word pictures for the name of Yeshua: Yod, Sin, Vav, Ayin

ישוע

Yod י - A Closed Hand means 'a finished work'.

Shin ש - A Tooth and means 'to consume.' Shin has also come to represent the Shekinah or the 'Divine Presence of God.'

Vav ו - A Nail means 'to bind or tie together, and'

Ayin ע - An Eye means 'to see and understand.'

The Hebrew word picture for *yeshua*: *"See the binding, the finished work, the divine presence of God."*

Echad or Trinity

"Hear O Israel: The LORD our God, the LORD is one" (Deuteronomy 6:4).

"I and the Father are one" (John 10:30).

Within the Christian church there is a tenet called the *trinity*. This is also known as the 'three in one Godhead.' Sometimes to explain this principle, an egg is used. It is one entity having three parts: the shell, the yolk and the white. Water is even used: solid, liquid and gas.

The Greek word *trinity* comes from a Latin word *trinitas* meaning the 'number three' or a 'triad'. Theophilus of Antioch first used this word in the second century in reference to God as God, the Word and His Wisdom. Tertullian was the first to defend the trinity in the third century.

The New Testament does not use the word *trinity* nor did Yeshua or the Apostles teach this concept of God. Though the followers of Messiah saw the power of God through the risen Savior, recognized the voice of God in the flesh as Yeshua, they did not teach three different parts or entities to God.

Nimrod

"Cush was the father of Nimrod, who became a mighty warrior on the earth. He was a mighty hunter before the LORD; that is why it is said, 'Like Nimrod, a mighty hunter before the LORD" (Genesis 10:8).

The notion of the trinity is not new. It began after the time of Noah with the son of Cush who was known as Nimrod. Nimrod was from the land of Cush, modern-day Ethiopia. He was also known as 'a mighty hunter before the LORD'. The word 'hunter' can also mean 'tyrant'. 'Before the LORD' is a Hebrew idiom for "in the face of, against, impudent, anger and battle." Thus, Nimrod was a man whose face was set against the LORD and hunted down men stealing their lives and souls. This is the ultimate spirit of rebellion and is the beginning manifestation of the the 'man of lawlessness'. Nimrod was given authority over many cities and one of them was Babel from which a great rebellion against God at the Tower of Babel.

Nimrod is known in different cultures as Molech, Baal and Zeus. Molech was the god of death and required the sacrifices of children in fire (Leviticus 20). Baal worship is mentioned throughout the Scriptures especially in the days of the prophet Elijah and the wicked queen Jezebel (1 Kings 18:19). Finally, there was the forced worship of Zeus in Israel by Antiochus Epiphanes. This was the god idol put in the Temple in Jerusalem during the days of Judah Maccabee when the Temple was desecrated (1 Maccabees).

Queen of Heaven

"We will certainly do everything we said we would: We will burn incense to the Queen of Heaven and will pour out drink offerings to her just as we and our ancestors, our kings and our officials did in the towns of Judah and in the streets of Jerusalem" (Jeremiah 44:17).

Nimrod had a wife named Semiramis. She is known through different cultural eras as Astarte, Istar and Easter. She was famous for being a beautiful woman and was worshipped as 'the queen of heaven' (Jeremiah 7:18). She was also believed to be a 'holy spirit' because she gave birth to a reincarnated son, Tammuz.

Tammuz

"Then he brought me to the entrance of the north gate of the house of the LORD, and I saw women sitting there, mourning the god Tammuz" (Ezekiel 8:14).

Tammuz was the son of Nimrod and Semiramis. In world cultures Tammuz is known as Cupid who represents modern Valentine's Day, Dagon the idol that fell over in front of the Ark of the Covenant (1 Samuel 5), and Horus and Osiris both being embraced by Egypt's worship of death.

The simple account of Tammuz is that he was killed by a wild boar and taken to the netherworld. His mother-turned-lover mourns for him for 40 days until he is brought back to life at the spring equinox. He was worshipped as his brought-back-to-life father, Nimrod.

This family unit of Father (Nimrod), Mother Spirit (Semiramis), and Son (Tammuz) became the model for the three-in-one god foundation of the *trinity* in other world religions. Each of these gods within the *trinity* was worshipped as an individual. Each of these gods had a unique purpose within the godhead. Nimrod was cruel, Semiramis was the beloved mother of the god Tammuz, and Tammuz was the murdered child who resurrected.

Early followers of Messiah did not want to adopt the *trinity*, but Constantine forced the doctrine on threat of exile. The Roman Catholic church merged this trinitarian story with Biblical accounts. Lent became the 40 day mourning period of Tammuz and Easter became the day of the child's resurrection. The mother with her baby is worshipped in the Madonna and she is called the 'mother of god.'

The Protestant church also adopted the *trinity* in spite of there being no reference to such a doctrine in the Scriptures. The worship of the three individual gods (parts) is easily recognized within different segments of Christianity. Protestant churches like the Methodist and Lutheran focus their worship on the father. The Evangelical Christian movement worships the son. Pentecostal churches exalt the spirit above all.

Returning back to the concept of the egg, accepting the *trinity* in this manner would be like choosing to worship the shell, the yolk or the white of the egg. This would not be worshipping the egg in its fullness. Nor would worshipping ice or steam be honoring water in the fullness of its created state.

The Shema

"Hear O Israel: The LORD our God, the LORD is ONE" (Deuteronomy 6:4).

This doctrine of *trinity* leads people, especially Jewish people away from the truth of the God of Israel who took His people out of Egypt from the worship of false gods and the *trinity* of Ra, Isis, and Osiris. He brought them to Mt. Sinai so they could worship Him as their God, the One true and living God. He commanded them to worship Him as One in what is known as the *Shema*, a Hebrew word meaning 'to hear or to listen.'

Hebrew Word Pictures

Hear - *Shema* שמע

Shin ש - A Tooth means 'consume' or Shekinah, 'the Divine Presence of God'

Mem מ - Water means 'come down from, immense'

Ayin ע - An Eye means 'to see or understand'

In Hebrew word pictures *shema*: *"Understand the immense divine presence of God."*

The word 'one' in this passage is *echad* and means 'one, single.' God is telling the people He redeemed from Egypt that He is ONE SINGLE GOD. This was probably a new concept to these people as they had seen the multitude of gods in Egypt worshipped as trinities and other diverse ways. The *Yod Hey Vav Hey* is ONE God, the only entity to be worshipped as the Eternal God, the *Elohim*.

Hebrew Word Pictures

One - *Echad* אחד

Aleph א - An Ox means 'strength, first'

Chet ח - A Fence means 'inner room'

Dalet ד - A Door means 'pathway'

The Hebrew word picture for *echad*: *"The first inner room pathway."*

Though *echad* has the nuance of 'diversity', this doesn't mean God is a trinity. It means that God can, did, and does reveal Himself in diverse ways: a bush that didn't burn, the man who ate with Abraham, the pillar of fire, the cloud of glory, a still small voice, a hand on the wall, and wind blowing where it will.

The Creator

"Do you not know? Have you not heard? The LORD is the everlasting God (Elohim), the Creator of the ends of the earth" (Isaiah 40:28).

We know that *Elohim* was the Creator; and according to John chapter 1, so was Yeshua. This makes Yeshua *echad* with Elohim because *'he was with God and was God'*. Through Yeshua all things were made because all things were spoken into existence by *Elohim*.

"In the beginning was the Word, and the Word was with God, and the Word was God. He was with God in the beginning. Through him all things were made; without him nothing was made that has been made" (John 1:1-3).

Spoken Word

"This day I call the heavens and earth as witnesses ... and that you may love the LORD your God (Elohim), listen to his voice, and hold fast to him" (Deuteronomy 30:20).

We know that Elohim spoke to Noah and told him to build an Ark. Elohim spoke to Abraham and gave him His promises. Elohim spoke to Moses from a burning bush and told him to deliver His people. Elohim spoke to the Israelites when He brought them to Mt. Sinai and gave them His Words. Elohim spoke through the prophets preparing Israel for the Messiah.

"The Word [of God] became a human being and lived with us, and we saw his glory, the glory of the Father's only Son, full of grace and truth" (John 1:14).

The voice of *Elohim*, His spoken words became a human being in the flesh of Yeshua. Yet, Elohim remained *echad*. His voice was not separate from Himself; His voice only did the things He told it to do. As God's Word in the flesh, Yeshua made it clear that he and His Father were 'one' or *echad* in John 10:30. The Greek word 'one' in in that verse is *heis* and is used to signify 'one in contrast to many, and in union with.' Yeshua also said that he only says what he hears his father tell him to do.

"For I have not spoken on my own initiative, but the Father who sent me has given me a command, namely, what to say and how to say it" (John 12:49).

The Spirit

"In the beginning God created the heavens and the earth. The earth was unformed and void, darkness was on the face of the deep, and the Spirit of God hovered over the surface of the water" (Genesis 1:1-2).

In Hebrew the word for Spirit is *ruach* and means 'breath, air, and wind.' In the beginning the *breath* of *Elohim* hovered over the waters. This *breath* was not separate from Him, but part of his existence as the 'living God' who created all things.

"For I will pour water on the thirsty land, and streams on the dry ground I will pour out my Spirit (breath) on your offspring, and my blessing on your descendants" (Isaiah 44:3).

Elohim *breathed* into the nostrils of Adam and gave him life (Genesis 2:7). He put His *breath* into Bezalel from the Tribe of Judah and gave him the ability to do artistic works with silver, gold and bronze for the Tabernacle. Joshua was filled with the *breath* of wisdom because Moses had laid hands on him. King David, when anointed by Samuel to be King over Israel, was filled with the *breath* of God. When Elizabeth heard Mary's greeting she was filled with the *breath* of God and her baby leaped in her womb. The *breath* of God descended like a dove on Yeshua when he was immersed in the Jordan River. Believers in Messiah are called the Temple and filled with *breath* of God manifested in gifts and fruits. Zechariah prophesied that the rebuilding of the Temple in the Millennial Kingdom will not be by [human] power but by the power and *breath* of God (Zechariah 4:6).

"Again Yeshua said, 'Peace be with you! As the Father has sent me, I am sending you.' And with that he breathed on them and said, 'Receive the Holy Spirit" (John 20:21-22).

The most powerful testimony of Elohim and Yeshua being one in Spirit occurs after the resurrection when Yeshua breathes on his disciples. The very holy *breath* of Elohim comes out of him, from his mouth, enters the disciples and empowers them to be sent forth to the world as he was sent - forgiving sins and being witnesses of the resurrection.

Even though the Scriptures reveal a Creator, His Word and His Spirit, this doesn't mean that they can be separated like a yolk, white and shell of an egg and called separate persons. If they are, they lose their uniqueness as being *echad* and are easily torn apart and used as means to their own end and misrepresenting *Yod Hey Vav Hey*, the I Am that I Am.

Church Fathers and the Trinity

"Therefore go and make disciples of all nations, baptizing them in the name of the Father and of the Son and of the Holy Spirit, and teaching them to obey everything I have commanded you" (Matthew 28:19-20).

Some may say that Yeshua's 'great commission' in Matthew to make disciples involved immersing them in the 'name of the Father and of the Son, and of the Holy Spirit'; however, those words are not in the original manuscripts. They were added sometime after the Council of Nicea in A.D. 325. This council which was convened by Constantine to primarily deal with the issue of Yeshua's deity and his oneness with God. Earlier church fathers like Origen, Tertullian, Polycarp, Ignatius, and Justin Martyr had come up with the idea of a 'divine trinity,' but adding the Holy Spirit to the 'divine three' was not completed until the Council of Constantinople in 360 A.D. (wikipedia)

A better explanation of the 'great commission' is found in Luke. In 'his name' repentance leading to forgiveness of sins was to be proclaimed to the world beginning in Jerusalem. Disciples were to be made through his teachings and commandments which were the same as His Father's and not something new or different.

"Then he [Yeshua] opened their minds, so that they could understand the Scriptures telling them, "Here is what it says: the Messiah is to suffer and to rise from the dead on the third day; and in his name repentance leading to forgiveness of sins is to be proclaimed to people from all nations, starting with Jerusalem" (Luke 24:45).

Elohim's Arm

"A psalm. Sing to the LORD a new song, for he has done marvelous things; his right hand and his holy arm have worked salvation for him" (Psalm 98:1).

The word 'salvation' in this verse is the Hebrew word *yeshua*. This means that Yeshua is God's right hand AND His holy arm. Yeshua was and is not a separate entity from *Elohim*. He was part of Him: His breath, His words, His right hand and His holy arm.

When God put His Spirit into Mary (Miriam) for her to conceive His Son, she knew it was salvation or *yeshua* for Israel. When the Jewish people saw the Word in the flesh, though they weren't able to accept the voice in the body, they knew Yeshua spoke with authority and wisdom. When God gave His only begotten Son to the world, they saw His holy arm reaching down and His right hand bringing them *yeshua*.

Elohim is not a three-part Godhead nor three gods known as a *trinity*. *Elohim* is not an egg or water that we should separate Him into the parts that we choose to use or worship. *Elohim* is *echad*. God is One. We must worship Him in the fullness of who He is as Yeshua said: in Spirit and in Truth. We must honor Him as the Creator of the Universe whose words and voice became flesh, whose arm worked salvation and whose breath of life empowers us to be witnesses to the world.

Chapter Photo: Our family's *mezzuzah* meaing 'doorpost'. Inside the *mezzuzah* are the words to the Shema in Deuteronomy 6:4-9). It is touched when entering or exiting any place that has one on the door frame to honor the central tenet to faith in the God of Israel, *echad*.

The Bible: Inspired or Expired?

"Do not add to what I command you and do not subtract from it, but keep the commands of the Lord your God that I give you" (Deuteronomy 4:2).

"And if anyone takes words away from this scroll of prophecy, God will take away from that person any share in the tree of life and in the Holy City, which are described in this scroll" (Revelation 22:19).

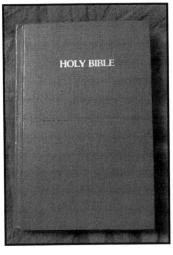

Recently I read all of the *Statements of Faith* from each the churches I have attended in my life to see how they defined the Bible. Every church, and I attended many different denominations, included one or several of the words inerrant, infallible, inspired or authoritative in their statement. One church even went so far as to say that if something isn't in Scripture it cannot be part of the faith. So, my question became, "Why, if the Scriptures are inerrant, infallible and inspired, does the church observe doctrines that aren't and discourage those that are?"

Infallible: incapable of making mistakes or being wrong

Inerrant: incapable of being wrong

Inspired: of extraordinary quality, as if arising from some external creativity

Authoritative: best of its kind, unable to be improved upon

According to the definitions of these words, each church believes that the Bible is incapable of having mistakes, being wrong or being improved upon. This means that the Bible is always right and not subject to being changed because somewhere, at some time, someone made an inspirational mistake.

It is important to remember that Yeshua and the Father are *one* and not *two* different voices. Yeshua is the Word of the Father revealed in the flesh of a man. Their words cannot be divided into denominational thoughts (John 1:1-2, 14, John 10:30).

Advent Lutheran Church

"Our congregation accepts the canonical Scriptures of the Old and New Testaments as the inspired Word of God and the authoritative source and norm of its proclamation, faith, and life."

I grew up attending this liturgical-based church which at the time was the Lutheran Church in America (LCA) and is now the Evangelical Lutheran Church in America (ELCA). This is where I learned about God and received my first Bible. I was a faithful attendee and never missed any service or activity with my family. I did not; however, learn about having a personal relationship with Jesus in this church as this was not a doctrine they supported. I did learn how to have a relationship with church. Though I was given a Bible in third grade, I never took it with me nor was I encouraged to open it. This is not to say that I didn't read my Bible as a child, I did. I just never read it in church.

Church of the Brethren

"The central emphasis of the Brethren is not a creed, but a commitment to follow Jesus in simple obedience, to be faithful disciples in the modern world. We hold the New Testament as our guidebook for living, affirming with it the need for lifelong study of the Scriptures."

A Brethren church is Anabaptist in doctrine, similar to the Amish and Mennonite faiths. I attended this church only for a few short months as my parents took a 'break' from the Lutheran church due to divisional issues about how to spend money. This was the *only* church in my youth where I actually opened a Bible. My Sunday school teacher gave me a verse to read to my fifth grade class. It was an Old Testament Scripture, not a New Testament one, that led to a lifelong study of the Word: *"The grass dries up, the flower fades; but the word of our God will stand forever"* (Isaiah 40:8).

LIFE Fellowship

"The Scriptures, both Old and New Testaments, to be the inspired Word of God, without error in the original writings, the complete revelation of His will for the salvation of men and the Divine and final authority for Christian faith and life."

This is the church I attended soon after I was born again. It was evangelical in scope, met in a movie theater, and the pastor had serious concerns about psychology in the church. He taught me the difference between a humanistic world view and a Biblical world view. It was at this church that I first raised my hands in worship and called myself a 'born again Christian.' This pastor also made a stand against living together and marriage between a believer and unbeliever. This convicted me as I lived with my future husband and he was, at that time, not a believer.

Little Church in the Pines

When I attended Little Church in the Pines, the pastor was from a Mennonite Anabaptist background. Here is a link to their entire position on the Bible since it is quite involved: http:// www.anabaptists.org/clp/just4you/jfy277.html

This is the church where I was married and attended for two years after. I don't remember much about reading the Bible, but it had wonderful fellowship and I made lifelong friendships within the community of believers. It was in this church that I was introduced to Hebraic dancing and my heart for the Jewish people began to blossom. This church [building] has now become an historic monument to the mining days in Salina in the foothills outside of Boulder, Colorado. It is considered a spiritual center where anyone can meet and follow whatever spiritual direction they choose. It no longer has a statement of faith.

Rocky Mountain Christian Fellowship

"We believe the Bible to be the inspired, the only infallible, authoritative Word of God, inerrant in the original writings" (Psalm 19:7, 2 Timothy 3:16, 2 Peter 1:21).

This church is where my husband and I went with our two young children. We attended this church for five years. At this church we had excellent new testament teaching that gave us an apostolic foundation. We were taught that we needed to obey the commands of God, but then were given vague concepts to what that obedience looked like. When I once asked the pastor how we are to look different from the world, he responded, "All we need is Jesus." I knew there was more than 'Jesus' in my Bible. According in John 14:6, Jesus said *"I am the way and the truth and the life. No one comes to the Father except through me,"* I knew there was a Father that I needed to know more intimately.

When my husband and I began to search the Scriptures for ourselves in order to 'build on Jesus', we quickly learned such building was discouraged from anything that remotely looked different from New Testament theology. Any form of worship apart from what the worship team considered acceptable 'non-denominational' was also discouraged. A small dance group that had begun and brought some much-needed intimate fellowship, disbanded.

It was during our time at this church that my husband and I went to a concert at Roeh Israel in Denver. It was at this concert that *in the twinkling of an eye* our spiritual lives changed. Many questions I had been having about the Bible and my faith since childhood were answered from Jews and gentiles worshipping together to women wearing head coverings. We continued visiting Roeh Israel when possible and the Messianic Jewish pastors connected the dots between Old Testament prophecy, the Messiah, Israel, and the Jewish people in an authentic New Testament way.

Church of the Nazarene

"We believe in the plenary inspiration of the Holy Scriptures, by which we understand the 66 books of the Old and New Testaments, given by divine inspiration, inerrant revealing the will of God concerning us in all things necessary to our salvation, so that whatever is not contained therein is not to be enjoined as an article of faith" (Luke 24:44-47; John 10:35; 1 Corinthians 15:3-4; 2 Timothy 3:15-17; 1 Peter 1:10-12; 2 Peter 1:20-21).

We attended this church for three months. While attending I had a molar pregnancy and the pastor's wife was very encouraging to me in the hospital. I do not remember any Scripture I was taught in this church as I was sick most of the time. I do know they were not afraid of all 66 books as stated because I was invited to teach Hebraic dancing to the children at their Vacation Bible School.

Dayspring Christian Fellowship

We attended this elder-directed church for a couple of years while it searched for a pastor. During these two years, I made the communion bread. While kneading it every week, I prayed that they would hire a Messianic Jew. A Jewish man was eventually chosen from several possibilities and soon after, they began to celebrate Passover. Dayspring is no longer a church, but a type of school that includes counseling services. I'm sure they believed in the inerrant, infallible, inspired Word of God when we attended; however, one of the elders made it very clear to me and my husband that God doesn't care about the 10 Commandments while another one attacked me personally about our legalistic views of Sabbath and the Biblical Holy Days. This Messianic Jewish man is now pastoring Cornerstone of Boulder (aka Rosh Pinah b'Boulder), a congregation that is Messianic in vision.

Calvary Chapel

"We believe that the Bible is God's authoritative and inspired work. It is without error in all its teachings. As Christians we must submit to its divine authority, both as individuals and as a corporate body."

We went to this church when we heard the Lord tell us our mission was complete at Dayspring. We spent a short time in this church where the people were very loving, but struggled with the lack of true Biblical leadership. An 'all you need is love' Beatles doctrine combined with some camouflaged catholicism allowed sin to run rampant. At times there were blatant teachings that went against Scripture, but were rationalized into today's lifestyles along with unBiblical tolerance. Rather than being transformed by the Word, the Word was transformed to support and encourage sinful immoral lifestyles.

Way, Truth, Life, Fellowship

We attended this church for nine months before we moved to Nebraska from Colorado. This was the closest example of a Biblical gathering that we had ever encountered. The pastor had willingly, and at the cost of membership, put aside many church traditions for teaching Biblical Truth - i.e. no more Christmas and Easter, but the Feasts of the LORD. This church did not have a statement about the Bible per se, but used Acts 2:42 as their foundation, *"They devoted themselves to the apostles' teachings, to fellowship, to the breaking of bread."*

The Old Testament was used along with the New to reveal numerous types and shadows of Messiah from prophecies including the difference between the Body of Messiah and the 'rib portion' becoming the Bride and the coming Temple of the Lord. There was a healthy view of obedience to the Law and the dietary commands were followed during meal time. After table fellowship, the pastor had a question and answer time that offered many opportunities for me to ask lifelong questions and receive sound Biblical answers. He was the first pastor who, along with his covered wife, encouraged me to wear my head covering all the time.

Assemblies of God

"The Scriptures, both the Old and New Testaments, are verbally inspired of God and are the revelation of God to man, the infallible, authoritative rule of faith and conduct."

We attended this church for only a few months. Speaking in tongues was more important to the pastor than verbally speaking the written Word of God. Eventually the pastor of this church sent me a letter about some discipleship I was doing with another woman. He called me a 'heretic' and asked that I never step foot in his church again. The 'heresy' he claimed actually came from the New Testament; he just didn't like that the woman was Scripturally challenging his man-ordained authority.

Foursquare Church

"We believe the Bible is God-inspired" (2 Timothy 3:16,17).

We attended this church for a very short time. After the pastor met with us so we could explain our view of Sabbath, he began calling Sunday the Sabbath. God will not be mocked. We could not accept such duplicity so we made our final and last cut from the institutional church into a walk of sanctification led by the Spirit and the Truth of the Word of God. We have never attended another 'Bible believing church' for it became apparent that their statements of beliefs contradicted their actual living out those beliefs.

God-Breathed Inspiration

"Every Scripture is God-breathed (given by His inspiration) and profitable for instruction, for reproof and conviction of sin, for correction of error and discipline in obedience, [and] for training in righteousness (in holy living, in conformity to God's will in thought, purpose, and action). So that the man of God may be complete and proficient, well fitted and thoroughly equipped for every good work" (1 Timothy 3:16-17 Amplified Bible).

I believe wholeheartedly that the Bible is inerrant and there are no mistakes written in the words. After all my first memory verse came from Isaiah 40:8 that the *word of God stands* forever. I also believe that, because the Bible was inspired by God, it doesn't or can't change for if it does, then that means God changes as well. This opens the door for the way of salvation through faith in Messiah Yeshua to change and makes everything we believe nothing but vain imaginings.

"God is not a man, that he should lie, nor a son of man, that he should change his mind" (Numbers 23:19).

"I YHVH do not change" (Malachi 3:6).

".Messiah Yeshua is the same yesterday, today and forever" (Hebrews 13:8).

The Fourth Commandment and the Church

"Remember the Sabbath day by keeping it holy. Six days you shall labor and do all your work, but the seventh day is a sabbath to the Lord your God. … the Lord blessed the Sabbath day and made it holy" (Exodus 20:8, 11).

Every church that I attended along with millions of similar church branches across the nation claims that the Bible is without mistakes because it was inspired by an unchanging God. The Ten Commandments are part of the inerrant, unchanged Word of God, so why is it that none of these churches keep the Fourth One: 'Remember to keep the Sabbath day holy?' This was one area where pastors and other well-meaning Christians confronted us with 'legalism'. Is it 'legalism' to obey a commandment given by the Creator Himself, to remember Him and His Creation?

Answers varied from "it was changed," to "Sunday is a memorial to the resurrection," to "Sabbath can be any day I want it to be." Each of these responses suggest that "God changes," "the Word changes," or "the Bible is fallible as I interpret it." One pastor recently told a friend that 'No one changed the Sabbath and the Ten Commandments are still in effect." If that is true, then why doesn't this pastor teach about the Sabbath? By neglecting the seventh-day Sabbath, what leaders are really saying is that God is *not* the inspiration of the Scriptures, we are. Or, God doesn't or can't remember what He said from one prophetic generation to the next. Or, God changes.

Several of the churches I attended state that the Bible is the final authority on life and faith. One church claimed the Bible is a guidebook for life. Another makes the statement that anything that is *not* contained in the Scriptures is *not* part of the articles of faith.

All of these church statements would imply that Sabbath, because it is in Scripture, should be the guide for a weekly lifecycle; and Sunday, because it's not in the Bible, should not part of the faith. Yet every church that I attended met on Sunday mornings - even the one that taught the types and shadows for the Feasts of the LORD. ALL of them. Not one ever mentioned the seventh-day Sabbath because they wrongly divided the Word of Truth. Their two-edged sword cut their Bibles in half and called the seventh-day, the Jewish Sabbath and the first day, the Christian one. Of course there was that one elder who believed that God doesn't even care about the Sabbath because it's part of the done-away with Ten Commandments.

Every one of these churches chose the doctrines of church fathers over the inspired, infallible Word of God contradicting their own statement of faith. Even the churches that said we must submit to Scriptural authority made excuses for why that authority no longer has a hold on their lives. They used a *grace doctrine* of *freedom from the law* which is nothing more than a *lawless* doctrine that encourages *everyone do what is right in their own eyes.* Remember the time of the Judges?

Somewhere along the line, most obviously church history, conviction for sin, correction of error, discipline in obedience, training in holy living by conforming to God's will has been put aside and called 'legalism.' Believers are no longer proficient in the Word, equipped for good works, and they are not receiving the gospel message in its entirety.

Institution or Kingdom

As I look back over my church experiences, the only consistent consistency is the hypocrisy of saying one thing and doing another. Love God, but don't ask Jesus into your heart for a personal relationship. Here's a Bible, but don't open it. If you do read the Bible, only read the New Testament. Read the Word, but only so you can sword stab some unbeliever with the name of Jesus. Our cornerstone of faith is Jesus Christ, but ignore his Jewishness. Build your faith on the apostles and prophets, but don't include anything spoken of my Moses for those are his laws. Preach the Word in season and out, but most of it is not really for our time or culture. All Scripture is inspired and useful for rebuke, correction, teaching and training in righteousness except the Old Testament even though those were the Scriptures Jesus used. The Old Testament is for the Jews and contains 'old laws' that were burdensome; we're under the grace of the New Testament. Above all, make sure you don't look anything like the Jewish people because they rejected Jesus, even though all of the first followers and believers in the resurrected Jesus were Jews and it was Jews who wrote the New Testament.

It is solely divine intervention that I have the understanding I do of the God of Israel through the Messiah of Israel because it didn't come through any church, pastor or statement of faith. It came because I wanted the the never-changing Word of God to correct my errors. I was willing to accept the authority of Scripture , but had to fight against double-minded manmade authorities who tried to stumble me with their foolish arguments. I learned by myself through the power of God's Spirit that simple obedience to the infallible Word would guide me into all Truth even while I endured accusations of being a Judaizer, a heretic, a legalist, and a Pharisee. I never questioned the inspired Word of God because I felt it challenge my thoughts and attitudes and change my spiritual direction. It was only the infallible, inerrant, inspired, authoritative Word of God that transformed my life from a Sunday pew sitting church attender with hundreds of questions to a vibrant born again member of the Kingdom of God ruled by the King of Kings, Yeshua.

Now, it's your turn. Make a list of the church or churches you have attended in your life and decide for yourself if they really believe in in the Inspired or Expired Word of God.

When Was Jesus Born?

"For to us a child is born, to us a son is given, and the government will be on his shoulders. And he will be called Wonderful Counselor, Mighty God, Everlasting Father, Prince of Peace. Of the greatness of his government and peace there will be no end. He will reign on David's throne and over his kingdom, establishing and upholding it with justice and righteousness from that time on and forever. The zeal of the Lord Almighty will accomplish this" (Isaiah 9:6-7).

Most Christians realize that Jesus (Yeshua) was not born on December 25 in the middle of winter. Yet few people realize that Yeshua's birth is outlined in the Bible if they could unravel some of the clues given to them in the gospels and referring back to the Hebrew Scriptures. The account of our 'reason for the season' begins in the book of Luke chapter one when Zechariah was in the Temple at Jerusalem burning incense to God. The time of his Temple service is the key to understanding the timing of the birth of his son, John, as well as Yeshua.

1. Zechariah was a Levite priest in of the lineage of Abijah, a descendant of Aaron (Luke 1:5, Numbers 3:2).

"In the time of Herod king of Judea there was a priest named Zechariah, who belonged to the priestly division of Abijah; his wife Elizabeth was also a descendant of Aaron" (Luke 1:5).

"The name of the sons of Aaron were Nadab the firstborn, and Abihu, Eleazar and Ithamar" (Numbers 3:2).

2. Abjiah was eighth in line for Temple duties. This means that as a descendant of Abijah, Zechariah was eighth in line for his Temple duties (1 Chronicles 24:10).

"With the help of Zadok ... David separated them [the descendants of Aaron] into divisions for their appointed order of ministering. ... The first lot fell to Jehoiarib ... the eighth to Abijah .... This was their appointed order of ministering when they entered the Temple of the LORD according to the regulations prescribed for them ..." (Numbers 1:1-19).

3. All Levitical priests, including Zechariah, were required by God to serve in the Temple during Passover, Pentecost (Shavuot), and Tabernacles as well as two weeks extra per year according to their family lineage (Deuteronomy 16:16).

"Three times a year all your men must appear before YHVH your God at the place he will choose: at the Feast of Unleavened Bread, the Feast of Weeks (Shavuot/Pentecost) and the Feast of Tabernacles" (Deuteronomy 16:16).

4. Zechariah would have served during the week of Passover and Unleavened Bread in the Temple.

Note: The Biblical calendar is not the same as the Julian/Gregorian calendar we use today. Passover is near April, Shavuot near June, Tabernacles near September. The Scriptures utilize a Biblical calendar beginning the year with the first month in which Passover falls (Exodus 12:2).

5. Zechariah would have returned to the Temple for his two week duties as part of the lineage of Abijah. This would have fallen in mid June during the the Feast of Weeks, Shavuot (Pentecost).

6.   An angel of the LORD appeared to Zechariah during his duties in the Temple at the Altar of Incense.

It is at the Altar of Incense in the Most Holy Place of the Temple that intercessory prayer is made by the priesthood. The angel of the LORD met Zechariah at this specific place and time. He told him he was going to have a son who he was to name John.

"… your prayers have been heard. Your wife Elizabeth will bear you a son, and you are to give him the name John" (Luke 1:13).

Because of his unbelief, Zechariah is made mute by the angel until the time of his son's birth.

7.   Zechariah returns home after his Temple duties. He and Elizabeth conceive a child. Elizabeth remains in seclusion for five months.

"When his time of service was completed, he returned home. After this his wife Elizabeth became pregnant and for five months remained in seclusion" (Luke 1:23-24).

8. One month later, *"when Elizabeth was in her sixth month,"* the angel Gabriel visited Mary (Luke 1:26).

Some people question whether this was the sixth month of the year or the sixth month of Elizabeth's pregnancy. With the wording of Elizabeth being in seclusion for five months and then "in the sixth month," it would seem that the months are contiguous and based on Elizabeth's pregnancy. Also, the angel tells Mary *"Even Elizabeth your relative … is in her fifth month"* giving a witness to the timing of the angel's visit (Luke 1:36).

9. Mary conceives a child by the Holy Spirit and immediately goes to visit Elizabeth.

"At that time Mary got ready and hurried to a town in the hill country of Judea, where she entered Zechariah's home and greeted Elizabeth" (Luke 1:39).

When Mary greets her cousin, the baby in Elizabeth's womb leaps. According to the time of Elizabeth's seclusion, this most likely would have been the first contact she had with another woman and maybe even the first time she felt the movement of her child. It is apparent that her son knew the blessing on Mary. The meeting of these two pregnant women had such profound significance that Luke recorded it with details. Elizabeth's baby leaps for joy at six months recognizing the newly conceived Messiah of Israel.

"As soon as the sound of your greeting reached my ears, the baby in my womb leaped for joy" (Luke 1:44).

Six months after Zechariah's Temple service in mid-June would be about mid-to-late December. The Feast of Dedication or Hanukkah occurs at this time as a memorial to the rededication of the Temple after it was defiled by the Greeks (John 10). It is also called the Festival of Lights because of the significance of being able to once again light the Temple Menorah after the desecration. Was it during this time of dedication that the Spirit of God came upon Mary and she conceived Immanuel, God with us, the Light of the World?

Mary's song in Luke 1:46-55 not only has prophetic significance about her baby, but is quite the declaration of humble 'dedication' (Hanukkah) regarding the 'light of the world.'

Verse 46-49 *"My soul glorifies the Lord and my spirit rejoices in God my Savior, for he has been mindful of the humble state of his servant. From now on all generations will call me blessed, for the Mighty One has done great things for me— holy is his name."*

10. Mary stays with Elizabeth for about three months.

"Mary stayed with Elizabeth for about three months and then returned home. When it was time for Elizabeth to have her baby, she gave birth to a son" (Luke 1:56-57).

Mary leaves Elizabeth very close to the time Elizabeth would deliver her baby. The timing for the birth of Elizabeth's baby would be mid-March/April, or near Passover.

11. On the eighth day after the baby's birth, he is circumcised and named.

Because of the Biblical timeline, Zechariah's son would have been born right before Passover.   This means that Zechariah would have gone to the Temple for his regular service and while there, he names his son, John, in the presence of astonished people.   This is the first time he has spoken since the angel visited him months before at the Altar of Incense (Luke 1:64).

12. From the information given about the conceptions and pregnancies of Mary and Elizabeth, it can be calculated that John (Yochanan) and Jesus (Yeshua) were born six months apart.

Six months after Passover in the spring would be the fall, the time of 'ingathering' or fall harvest of the Feast of Tabernacles. The Feast of Tabernacles also falls approximately nine months after the Feast of Dedication (Hanukkah) in December.

All the rooms in the inns were full due to the Roman census being taken by Caesar Augustus.   All native born Israelites (specifically men) were required to live in booths or sukkot for the week of Tabernacles. Women and children who were with their husbands filled in the inns to capacity.

"Live in booths (sukkot) for seven days: All native-born Israelites are to live in booths so your descendants will know that I had the Israelites live in booths when I brought them out of Egypt" (Leviticus 23:42).

Under these conditions, Mary gives birth to a son. The baby was born in a *temporary dwelling* in Bethlehem because all the rooms in the inn were full. The baby was placed in a feeding trough (Luke 2:4-7).

" ... And she gave birth to her firstborn, a son. She wrapped him in cloths and placed him in a manger (sukkah) ..." (Luke 2:6).

Being consistent with the rabbinical definition of a temporary dwelling, booth or sukkah, a stable would have been an acceptable sukkah. Because of the timing of Yeshua's birth during the Feast of Tabernacles, many people believe that it was not a literal stable, but a sukkah or booth. The Greek word for 'manger' in Luke 2:7 is *phatne* and can mean 'cattle stall' just like what Jacob built for his livestock (Genesis 33:17). The equivalent Hebrew word for 'manger' would be the singular *sukkah*.

According to the command in Leviticus 23, the Israelites were to live in a *sukkah* for seven days. Putting this information into the timeline that Yeshua was born on the first day of the Feast of Tabernacles, he would have lived in the sukkah for the first seven days of his life until he was circumcised and named on the eighth day. Whatever the specific accommodations, Joseph fulfilled God's requirement to live in a booth during Sukkot and so did Yeshua who was the first-born son of God.

13. The angels rejoiced because 'The Word became flesh and made his dwelling among us...' (John 1:14, Luke 2).

The Greek word for 'dwelling' in this verse is *skenoo* and has the meaning of 'spread his tent' among us. As a booth or *sukkah* is a temporary dwelling like a tent, this verse could read, *"The Word became flesh and spread his tent (tabernacle) among us"* making a direct allusion to Yeshua being born at the Feast of Tabernacles.

14. On the first day of the Feast of Tabernacles, the priests in the Temple would wave large branches of several different trees in the Temple.

These branches were called *lulavs* and represented the different nations. Hundreds of priests waving larges branches from the willow, the palm and the the myrtle, would have created an enormous sound like a 'rushing wind' as they walked toward the Temple mount. In Hebrew, the word for God's Spirit is *ruach* and means 'wind.' As the priests were waving these tree branches as a shadow of the Spirit of God, they were unaware of the birth of Yeshua. They had no idea that the salvation of Israel, through the Spirit of God and a humble woman, had come to make its dwelling in a little baby.

"So beginning with the fifteenth day of the seventh month... celebrate a festival to the LORD for seven days .... On the first day you are to take choice fruit from the trees, and palm fronds, leafy branches and poplars, and rejoice before the LORD your God for seven days" (Leviticus 23:39-41).

15. There were shepherds in the hills outside of Jerusalem (Luke 2:8-15).

The shepherds in the hills near Bethlehem, a short distance from Jerusalem, were special shepherds. They camped at the Migdal Eder and raised the sheep for the Temple sacrifices. According to a prophecy in Micah, the Jewish people believed that the Messiah would be revealed at the Migdal Eder, "the tower of the flock."

"As for you, O watchtower of the flock, O stronghold of the Daughter of Zion, the former dominion will be restored to you; kingship will come to the Daughter of Jerusalem" (Micah 4:8).

There was an actual military watchtower that was used to protect Bethlehem above the hills. This tower also was used to guard the Temple sheep from robbers. It was from these sheep that came the Passover lambs. These shepherds would have completely understood the meaning of the message given to them by the angels because they were at the exact location for the prophesy of Messiah's birth to be fulfilled.

16. Eight days later, it was time for the baby's circumcision and naming (Luke 2:21).

The father of a son always named the baby at the circumcision because the mother would still be in her time of purification and could not enter the Temple area. Joseph takes his baby son to

Jerusalem and names him *Yeshua* because that was what the angel told him to do. *Yeshua* means 'salvation'.

"Yosef, son of David, do not be afraid to take Mary home with you as your wife; for what has been conceived in her is from the Holy Spirit. She will give birth to a son, and you are to name him Yeshua, [which means 'the LORD saves,'] because he will save his people from their sins" (Matthew 1:21-22).

Rejoicing in the Torah - *Simchat Torah*

The Feast of Tabernacles is celebrated for seven days. The following day, the eighth day, is a special celebration called *Simchat Torah*. In Hebrew this means 'Rejoicing in the Torah'. As Yeshua was being named by Joseph, crowds were dancing, singing, and rejoicing in the Torah. In their midst, without their knowledge, the living Torah had just been named 'salvation.'

"On the eighth day, when it came time to circumcise him, he was named Yeshua, the name the angel had given him before he had been conceived" (Luke 2:21).

17. Mary's Purification Completed

"When the days of her purification for a son or daughter are over, she is to bring to the priest a year-old lamb ... and a young pigeon or dove.... He shall offer them before YHVH ... and she will be ceremonially clean from her flow of blood. ...If she cannot afford a lamb, she is to bring two doves ..." (Leviticus 12:6-8).

Forty days after Yeshua's birth, after Mary's time of purification was completed, she and Joseph took Yeshua to the Temple for the Redemption of the Firstborn according to the Torah command in Leviticus 12:8. It was at this time, they offered the sacrifice of the doves for her purification.

"When the time of her purification according to the Torah of Moses had been completed, Joseph and Mary took him to Jerusalem to present him to the Lord (as it is written) ..." (Luke 2:22).

There were two prophets in the Temple who knew and expected the Word to become flesh. Simeon and Anna (the witness of two) spoke prophetic fulfillment over Yeshua in the presence of his parents.

"Now there was a man in Jerusalem called Simeon, who was righteous and devout. ...There was also a prophetess, Anna, the daughter of Phanuel, of the tribe of Asher" (Luke 2:25,39).

18. At this time, a sign appeared in the heavens (Matthew 2:1-2).

Every kingdom in the known world had astronomers who studied and understood the signs in the heavens. Each culture, but more specifically, the Jewish culture, looked to the heavens for the fulfillment of prophecy. Constellations, planets and stars moved to tell God's story as well as to set His appointed times. Other cultures studied the Hebrew concepts and understood their connection to the people of Israel.

Astronomers from the east (probably from what is modern day Iraq/Iran) saw this "sign" and began their journey toward Jerusalem to bow down and worship the King of Kings and Lord of Lords. The word 'star' in Hebrew is the same word as 'angel' or 'messenger.' Thus, the men from the east were actually led by an angel; not a moving star (Matthew 2).

19. The magi or wise men arrived in Bethlehem.

The journey of 'the wise men' (number unknown) took a long time as they were on foot and most likely came from Iraq which is over 500 miles. They finally arrived when Yeshua was a child or at least under two years old. They visited him in his home and gave him gifts. They returned home by a different route because Herod was angry and eventually had all baby boys under the age of two in and around Bethlehem murdered (Matthew 2:13-18).

"On coming to the house, they saw the child with his mother Mary, and they bowed down and worshiped him" (Matthew 2:9).

This is how the conception, birth, and dedication began for Yeshua. According to the information given in the Torah, Prophets, and Gospels, Yeshua was born in the 'season of our rejoicing', on the first day of the Feast of Tabernacles in a sukkah. The shepherds knew from the angelic hosts that 'peace on earth and good will toward men' had come as the 'lamb of God.' While all Israel rejoiced in the Torah given by God, the living Torah, the begotten Son of God was circumcised and named 'salvation.'

Chapter Photo: The display of the Dead Sea Scroll of Isaiah, Shrine of the Book, Jerusalem, Israel.

Sign of Jonah: Three Days and Three Nights

"For as Jonah was three days and three nights in the belly of a huge fish, so the Son of Man will be three days and three nights in the heart of the earth" (Matthew 12:40).

Many people wonder about the three days and three nights of Yeshua's death, burial and resurrection. Let's face it, Friday night to Sunday morning is NOT three days and three nights no matter how you interpret the days, the hours, the times, the kingships or even the traditions. Yet, Yeshua's own words prophesied that he would be in the grave three days and three nights, no less, no more.

Creating a Timeline

Using Scripture along with the Feasts of the LORD is the perfect way to determine when Yeshua died, was buried and rose from the dead. To create the timeline, it may be more effective to work backwards from Yeshua's Resurrection and the Sabbath, to Unleavened Bread, to Passover in order to understand the timing of the events. All 'days' go from evening to morning as established by God in Genesis' days of creation. The sunset time of 6:00 p.m. is an arbitrary time that I chose to make my timeline and may not have been the actual time of sunset in the year that Yeshua died and rose from the dead.

The Resurrection - The Feast of Firstfruits

"The LORD said to Moses, 'Tell the people of Israel, 'After you enter the land I am giving you and harvest its ripe crops, you are to bring a sheaf of the firstfruits of your harvest to the priest. He is to wave the sheaf before Adonai, so that you will be accepted; the priest is to wave it on the day after the Sabbath" (Leviticus 23:9-11).

The timing surrounding the resurrection is recorded in Matthew 28 and Luke 24. On the first day of the week, after the Sabbath, before dawn, some women found Yeshua's tomb empty. It wasn't until AFTER the Sabbath that the women found the grave empty because they rested according to the commandment regarding the Sabbath day. Only the seventh day Sabbath command comes before the 'first day of the week.'

"After Sabbath, toward dawn the first day of the week, Miriyam of Magdala and the other Miryam went to see the grave" (Matthew 28:1).

"On the Sabbath, the women rested, in obedience to the commandment; but on the first day of the week, while it was still very early, they took the spices they had prepared, went to the tomb, and found the stone rolled away from the tomb!" (Luke 24:1).

Before the light of day on the first day of the week, Yeshua must have risen from the grave because he was not there. In other words, during the hours between Saturday's sunset (ending of Sabbath) and Sunday's sunrise, Yeshua rose from the dead. There is no specific time given for his resurrection so for sake of explanation, let's say the seventh-day Sabbath (Saturday) ended at a 6:00 p.m. sunset. It is possible that at 6:01 p.m., the beginning of the first day of the week, Yeshua rose from the dead.

"But the fact is that Messiah has been raised from the dead, the firstfruits of those who have died" (1 Corinthians 15:20).

Paul says that Yeshua is 'the firstfruits of those who have died' using the same terminology as the Feast of Firstfruits found in Leviticus. The Feast of Firstfruits involved the waving of a sheaf of grain on the 'day after the Sabbath' or the first day of the week

(Sunday). In agreement with the LORD's appointed times, the evidence in the gospels, and the explanation in Paul's letter to the Corinthians, Yeshua rose from the dead as a firstfruits on the day after the Sabbath, during Unleavened Bread.

Sabbath: Big 'S' or little 's'

In Leviticus 23, when Yahweh gave His 'appointed times' to the Israelites, the first festival mentioned is Sabbath. It is the only day or 'appointed time' that Yahweh called 'Sabbath' as He gave all of the other festivals specific names: Feast of Unleavened Bread, Feast of Firstfruits, Feast of Weeks, Feast of Trumpets and Feast of Tabernacles. Though several of the festivals commanded 'no regular work' like the seventh-day Sabbath, Yahweh did not call them 'Sabbath'. It is only when Yahweh's 'appointed times' became designated as 'sabbaths' that confusion with days and times began.

For example, Leviticus 23:15 outlines the timing of the Feast of Weeks or Pentecost, *"From the day after the Sabbath, the day you brought the sheaf of the wave offering, count off seven full weeks."*

If the context of this verse is read with the Sabbath being the seventh-day weekly Sabbath given only 12 verses earlier, then the counting would begin on the 'day after the Sabbath' or 'the first day of the week' (Sunday). Counting this way would allow for Feast of Firstfruits to consistently fall on a 'first day of the week' which has tremendous prophetic significance for the Resurrection.

However, the counting becomes very confusing when the first day of a festival like Unleavened Bread is referred to by traditional Judaism as a 'sabbath'. Depending on which day of the week the Unleavened Bread 'sabbath' falls and the 'day after that sabbath', counting off seven weeks changes yearly and gives no recognition to the Feast of Firstfruits. Also according to tradition, some 'sabbaths' are rated 'higher' than others; some weekly Sabbaths more important than others when they fall during a festival week. Though these delineations may not be departing from God's commands to keep the appointed times, it does cause confusion and disunity between the Jews and the Body of Messiah regarding timing especially when it comes to celebrating the resurrection of Yeshua of Nazareth.

Yeshua followed many traditions of men because he lived among men. However, whenever those traditions nullified the commands of God, he refuted them and taught the correct view of the command. It would follow that if a tradition nullified the 'appointed time' of a feast, Yeshua would celebrate it correctly.

Three, Two, One - Unleavened Bread

"In the first month ... on the fifteenth day of the same month is the festival of matzah (Unleavened Bread); for seven days you are to eat matzah (unleavened bread). On the first day you are to have a holy convocation; don't do any kind of ordinary work. Bring an offering made by fire to Adonai for seven days. On the seventh day is a holy convocation; do not do any kind of ordinary work" (Leviticus 23:6-8).

Counting backwards from the time of the Resurrection, we need three nights and three days for grave time. Once again, let's use 6:00 p.m. as the beginning time for each day. Day 1 would be 6:00 p.m. Saturday evening to Friday evening (Sabbath, Day 3 Unleavened Bread). Day 2 would be 6:00 p.m. Friday evening to Thursday evening (Day 2 Unleavened Bread). Day 3 would be 6:00 p.m. Thursday evening to Wednesday evening (Day 1 Unleavened Bread). From this timeline, Yeshua would have been put in the grave sometime BEFORE 6:00 p.m. Wednesday evening which began the first of the prophesied three nights and days in the tomb. (Note: By being put in the tomb before 6:00 p.m., three days and three nights would have him rise just before the Sabbath day ended rather than after which is still Biblically sound.

The first day of Feast of Unleavened Bread was and is considered 'a sabbath day'. In the year of Yeshua's death, this Feast would begin, according to the three days outlined above, on Wednesday evening at 6:00 p.m. Before it began at sunset, the day was called the Preparation Day. It was on Preparation Day that Yeshua's body was removed from the cross. He needed to be buried before the start of the Feast of Unleavened Bread, 'a special sabbath' which began at sunset, the 15 day of the first month.

Yeshua was buried as the 'unleavened bread from heaven' that he spoke about in John 6. He was wrapped in linen and put in the tomb of a rich man from Jerusalem. He was in the tomb for the first three nights and days of the Feast of Unleavened Bread.

"There was a man named Joseph, a member of the Sanhedrin. He was a good man, a righteous man, and he had not been in agreement with either the Sanhedrin's motivation or their action. ... This man approached Pilate and asked for Yeshua's body. He took it down, wrapped it in a linen sheet, and placed it in a tomb cut into the rock, that had never been used. It was Preparation Day, and a Sabbath was about to begin" (Luke 23:50-54).

Passover

"In the first month, on the fourteenth day of the month, between sundown and complete darkness, comes the Lord's Passover" (Leviticus 23:5).

According to the timeline being developed, the Lord's Passover on the '14 day of the month' would begin at 6:00 p.m. Tuesday evening and last until 6:00 p.m. Wednesday evening when Unleavened Bread began. After sunset, between twilight on Tuesday evening and complete darkness, the Passover memorial meal would be celebrated.

"He [Yeshua] replied, "Go into the city to a certain man and tell him, 'The Teacher says: My appointed time is near. I am going to celebrate the Passover with my disciples at your house'" (Matthew 8:29).

According to Luke 22:15, Yeshua had a great desire to celebrate his last Passover seder with his disciples. This Passover was an 'appointed time' in Yeshua's life and he had to fulfill its purpose.

It is important to remember that the Passover celebrated by Yeshua was only a memorial to the Passover that occurred in Egypt. No one was putting on sandals and carrying staffs. No one was preparing for a great flight into the wilderness. No one was outside their door sacrificing lambs and putting blood on their doorposts. Israel was no longer a people enslaved by Egypt and they celebrated their freedom with a traditional meal called a seder.

The Passover seder included four cups of wine and unleavened bread. During this seder Yeshua would turn the focus from the past to the present and future. He used one cup of wine to offer a marriage covenant to his disciples. As they shared the cup of wine together, they became his betrothed bride. With the second cup of wine, he took the unleavened bread and explained the bride price would be his broken body and blood. His death would be 'the death of the firstborn' and his blood would bring in the new covenant promised by the prophet Jeremiah.

Matthew records that *'when evening came Yeshua reclined with his disciples'*. He talked with his disciples and his words are recorded in Matthew 26, Mark 14 , Luke 22, John 14-16. After the meal, they went out to the Mount of Olives. Yeshua prayed. He asked that the final cup of Passover be removed, but submitted to the will of His Father. While his disciples slept, he prayed for all who would believe in him through the testimony of his followers. Soldiers arrive in the darkness with the high priest. They arrest him, take him to the Sanhedrin and to Pilate. Before sunrise, Peter denies Yeshua three times. The crowds want him crucified. Yeshua is beaten, bruised, mocked, and condemned to death. He goes to Golgotha where he is nailed to the cross and dies quickly without having any of his bones broken.

The events of the fourteenth day of the first month, (Tuesday evening to Wednesday evening) were completed. Yeshua gives up his spirit with the words "It is finished." The Passover's final Cup of Completion, the death of the Lamb of God, was poured out at the exact same time the priests were offering the last Passover sacrifice at the Temple.

"At that moment the curtain of the temple was torn in two from top to bottom. The earth shook, the rocks split and the tombs broke open. The bodies of many holy people who had died were raised to life" (Matthew 27:51-52).

A Little More Confusion

"On the first day of the Festival of Unleavened Bread, the disciples came to Jesus and asked, "Where do you want us to make preparations for you to eat the Passover?" (Matthew 26:17).

Though this verse suggests that Passover and Unleavened Bread start at the same time, Yeshua would have celebrated the actual dates and appointed times of Passover and Unleavened Bread no matter what the traditions. Even though unleavened bread was eaten at Passover, the two 'appointed times' have different timings and purposes.

The LORD's Passover was the fourteenth day of the first month. It began in the evening at twilight and lasted until the next evening. Historically, the Israelites did not kill the Passover lamb and then suddenly leave Egypt. They had to wait throughout the night for the 'death of the firstborn' until the next day when they prepared to leave Egypt. On the fifteenth day, Israel left Egypt.

"Celebrate the Festival of Unleavened Bread, because it was on this very day that I brought your divisions out of Egypt. Celebrate this day as a lasting ordinance for the generations to come. From the evening of the fourteenth day of the first month until the evening of the twenty-first day, you are to eat matzah" (Exodus 12:17).

There are those who say that Yeshua could not celebrate Passover AND be the Passover sacrifice at the same time, however, there were evening, morning and afternoon sacrifices every day. At the evening sacrifice of Passover, he celebrated the seder with his disciples. By the morning sacrifice, he had been arrested, judged and condemned to death. By the afternoon sacrifice, he had walked to Golgotha, been nailed to the cross and died. He was quickly buried before the evening sacrifice that began the Feast of Unleavened Bread.

Because our calendar differs from the Biblical calendar, Passover falls on a different day each year. This means that there needs to be a way to figure out when to celebrate the most significant event of all time, the Resurrection of Messiah on the Feast of Firstfruits. Obviously, the Feast of Firstfruits must come after Passover and, according to Scripture, it has to fall on a 'first day of the week' after the weekly Sabbath. So, if Passover falls on a Thursday, the following Sunday will be the Feast of Firstfruits because there is a weekly Sabbath between the two. If Passover falls on the Sabbath, an entire week must pass before celebrating Feast of Firstfruits.

The Three Days and Three Nights Unfold

In the year that Yeshua died, was buried and then resurrected, he celebrated the Passover (fourteenth day of the first month) with his disciples on a Tuesday evening. Tuesday, during the night, he prayed for his disciples and those who would believe in him through their testimony. He sweat drops of blood and submitted himself to death. He was arrested before sunrise, beaten, hung on a cross and died in late afternoon Wednesday at the exact time of the final Passover sacrifice. He was buried before the sun set while it was still the preparation day for Unleavened Bread, a sabbath.

Wednesday evening to Saturday evening, the first 'three nights and three days' of Unleavened Bread, his followers mourned. A Roman centurion pondered why he felt the earth shake and knew at that moment that Yeshua was truly the Son of God. Mockers who had seen the sign, "The King of the Jews" were wondering why many who had died were walking around Jerusalem. Peter and John and the rest of the disciples went into hiding for fear of their own lives. The women who followed Yeshua went home grieving. They prepared spices knowing they had to wait until after the Sabbath to prepare Yeshua's body. The soldiers anxiously guarded the tomb hoping no one would steal the body. All Israel rested on the seventh-day Sabbath day according to the command. For the followers of Messiah, it was a long three days and nights. It seemed like an eternity.

After resting on the weekly Sabbath, before dawn on the first day of the week, as the time for waving the sheaf in the Temple approached, several women went to the tomb. They carried spices and walked through a garden wondering who would roll away the huge stone. They could hear the whoooossssshhhhhhh of the sheaves being waved back and forth by the priests at the Temple in the distance. It was the Feast of Firstfruits. After a long, confusing, heart-wrenching week of Passover, and then a seemingly endless Sabbath, could they endure another 'appointed time' of God?

"Yeshua said to her, "Woman, why are you crying? Whom are you looking for?" Thinking he was the gardener, she said to him, "Sir, if you're the one

who carried him away, just tell me where you put him; and I'll go and get him myself" (John 20:15).

"Yeshua said to her, "Miryam!" Turning, she cried out to him in Hebrew, "Rabbani!" (that is, "Teacher!")

"Stop holding onto me," Yeshua said to her, "because I haven't yet gone back to the Father. But go to my brothers, and tell them that I am going back to my Father and your Father, to my God and your God" (John 20:15-17).

The sorrow of the women turned to joy at seeing Yeshua risen and alive. They were so excited they wanted to touch their Rabbi, but he needed to return to his Father. The women obeyed his command and went to the disciples with the amazing news that 'He is Risen'. While the priests in the Temple waved the firstfruits grain offering, Yeshua went to his Father and offered himself as the firstfruits of those who are raised from the dead. The counting of the weeks began. What could possibly happen on the Feast of Weeks?

Chapter Photo: Sign to the ancient seaport of Jaffa, Israel.

Yeshua's Last Week Diagram

In the year Yeshua was crucified, buried and rose from the dead.

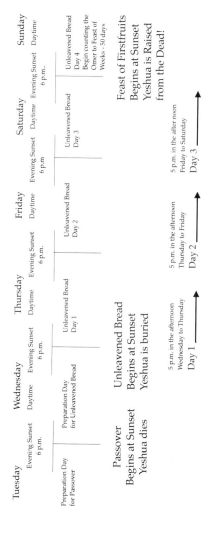

Yeshua's disciples prepared for and celebrated the Passover seder on Tuesday and Tuesday evening. Afterwards, they went to the Garden of Gethsemane on the Mount of Olives. Yeshua was arrested, taken to the Sanhedrin and judged before sunrise. He was then taken to Pilate and condemned to die by the crowds later in the morning. By the afternoon on Tuesday he was on the cross. He died at the third hour or about 3 p.m. in the afternoon at the time of the final Passover sacrifice. He was taken off the cross and put in the tomb before Unleavened Bread began at sunset on Wednesday. This probably took some time making the hour he was placed in the tomb between 4 and 5 p.m. still before sunset. He was in the tomb three days and three nights as per the 'sign of Jonah.' Sometime before sunset on the 'third day', he rose from the dead as the Firstfruits offering. Thus, Yeshua fulfilled these spring 'appointed times.'

The 'Law' of Sin and Death

"The Lord God took the man and put him in the Garden of Eden to work it and take care of it. And the Lord God commanded the man, "You are free to eat from any tree in the garden; but you must not eat from the tree of the knowledge of good and evil, for when you eat from it you will certainly die"(Genesis 2:15-17).

One of the biggest misconceptions within Christianity is that the old testament 'law' has been done away with and Christians are no longer 'under the law'. Though I cannot be sure from where this doctrine originated, I'm going to guess it developed from quoting only half of this sentence in Romans:

"For sin shall no longer be your master, <u>because you are not under the law, but under grace"</u> (Romans 6:14-15).

In this verse, the word translated 'law' is the Greek *nomos*. This Greek word can mean anything from general principles of law to the first five books of the Bible known as the Torah. It's such a general word that *Strong's Concordance* actually says that the meaning of the word *nomos* must be derived from the context in which it is used.

Within the context of the word *nomos* is the word 'because'. *Because* is used to introduce a word or phrase that gives an explanation or reason. To just say "I'm not under the law, I'm under grace" is not giving the reason *why*. The reason *why* in this verse has to do with sin no longer being the master of one's life.

Law and Justice

According to the dictionary, *law* is defined as "the system of rules that a particular country or community recognizes as regulating the actions of its members and may enforce by the imposition of penalties." From a Biblical perspective, it would be necessary that the Kingdom of God would have a system of rules that regulates the actions of its citizens. When one of the citizens breaks the *law*, they receive justice for doing so.

This is what happened in the Garden of Eden, the eternal paradise, our first glimpse at the Kingdom of God. Adam was given one rule. He couldn't eat from the tree of the knowledge of good and evil. If he broke the rule, the penalty was death.

"The Lord God took the man and put him in the Garden of Eden to work it and take care of it. And the Lord God commanded the man, "You are free to eat from any tree in the garden; but you must not eat from the tree of the knowledge of good and evil, for when you eat from it you will certainly die" (Genesis 2:15).

Adam was given the command before the woman, Eve, was made. It was his responsibility to pass the one command on to his wife. However, because she was deceived by the serpent, she ate the fruit and gave some to Adam who committed the sin of disobedience. They realized their sin in their nakedness and tried to cover it up.

"When the woman saw that the fruit of the tree was good for food and pleasing to the eye, and also desirable for gaining wisdom, she took some and ate it. She also gave some to her husband, who was with her, and he ate it. Then the eyes of both of them were opened, and they realized they were naked; so they sewed fig leaves together and made coverings for themselves" (Genesis 3:6-7).

God was not fooled by their fig leaves. He knew their hearts. He saw their sin. He cursed the serpent who deceived Eve. He gave Eve pain in child bearing and made her desire her husband. He cursed the ground from which Adam was made so that Adam would toil all the days of his life for food. He proclaimed His justice on Adam's sin: death.

"By the sweat of your brow you will eat your food until you return to the ground, since from it you were taken; for dust you are and to dust you will return" (Genesis 3:19).

Because of Adam, everyone sins. Because of Adam, sin and death entered the world. Because of Adam, everyone was kicked out of the Kingdom of God.

Going Beyond God's Boundaries

Some time ago, my son invited a friend to spend the weekend. This friend was not a Christian, did not even believe in God. However, he had questions he wanted answered. Starting with the basics, I asked him to define sin. He thought deeply for a few minutes and said, 'doing bad things'. Of course, my response could only be, 'Who determines what things are bad, or good for that matter? He replied, "Good question." If someone puts their faith in God, it should be God, not mankind, who makes that determination. The foundation was laid.

As Creator of the Universe, God gave one *law to* Adam. After the flood, God gave more *laws* to Noah for mankind. To Abraham, God gave *laws* for him and his descendants. Through Moses, God gave 613 *laws* to Israel outlining how to love and worship Him, and how to live in a community and love your neighbor. All of these *laws* from Adam to Israel have one thing in common - they are *God's laws*. In Hebrew, the word *law* is *torah* and means "teachings or instructions' of God. Sin is nothing more and nothing less than breaking God's *torah*, His teachings and instructions.

"Everyone who sins breaks the law; in fact, sin is lawlessness" (1 John 3:4).

God as the Ruler of the Kingdom of Heaven defines *sin* as breaking *His law* or *torah*. Sin is ultimately disobeying His instructions and going beyond the bounds of His established desire for our behavior. The consequences for sin, as Adam learned, is death (Romans 6:23).

In Hebrew, the word for 'sin' is *chata*. It means 'to miss or go wrong.' In Greek, the word for 'sin' is *hamartia* and means 'to miss the mark'. This is exactly what Adam did. He went beyond the boundaries that

God established for him in Paradise, disobeyed God's one instruction, and missed the mark. As a result, everyone sins (Romans 3:23). Everyone. There is no exception to the 'law of sin and death.'

God's Grace and Sin

"What then? Shall we sin because we are <u>not under the law but under grace</u>?" (Romans 6:15).

"We're under God's grace" is no excuse to continue breaking *torah*. What if Adam and Eve's conversation went something like this:

"God loves us. He created this Paradise for us. We named all these animals. We walk and talk with him every evening. He has given us all the trees in the garden from which to eat except this one. He won't kill us if we just taste the fruit. Besides what does 'death' mean anyway?" Just look at the Tree of Life. It's full of fruit."

Oh, yeah, those were the serpent's words. Adam and Eve had no understanding of God's grace, the power of His grace to overcome sin and the desire to sin. However, because of their sin, God's grace abounded to Adam and Eve. He removed the leaves and covered them with garments of skin. In order to make the garments, blood had to be shed. Animal blood. This set up the *torah* of blood for the forgiveness of sins (Hebrews 9:22). His incredible grace did not stop them or their children from sinning. After all, Cain did kill Abel.

The incredible grace of God was probably something they told and retold their children, grandchildren and great-grandchildren. They probably spoke often about how they sinned against God, how He promised a Redeemer, and how He shed the blood of an innocent animal to cover their sin. God's grace did not remove them from the *law of sin and death* nor did it change the fact that they had to live out God's judgments for their lives in a fallen world. God's grace kept them alive, kept them walking in the hope of a Redeemer. God's grace empowered them to put the past in the past and press on toward the goal, the higher calling of God's promised Seed that would restore all things to the way they were in the Garden, but an even better promise, the power to overcome sin and death (Philippians 3:14).

Victory Over Sin and Death

"Because the Torah of the Spirit, which produces this life in union with Messiah Yeshua, has set me free from the law of sin and death ...
(Romans 8:2).

The *law of sin and death* brought on by Adam's disobedience to God's *one instruction* was destroyed by the Seed of woman, the second Adam, the Messiah Yeshua. Through his death, his blood atoned for sin and brought universal forgiveness. Through his resurrection, he destroyed the power of death. When Yeshua ascended into the heavenly realm, his Father poured out His Spirit in order to begin the restoration process. Those who are born again of the Spirit of God re-enter the His Kingdom with the power to overcome sin and disobedience to *torah* - the same power that resurrected Yeshua from the dead. They no longer live as slaves to sin and disobedience to *God's laws*. They no longer live under condemnation because they are *set free from the law of sin and death* by faith in work of Messiah Yeshua. They are now free to live out the *Torah of the Spirit* or the spiritual Torah written on their hearts.

"In fact, "No one who is born of God will continue to sin, because God's seed (the Spirit) remains in him; he cannot go on sinning, because he has been born of God" (1 John 5:18).

Is Sinless Perfect?

"Be perfect therefore as your heavenly Father is perfect" (Matthew 5:48).

Not long ago I read a letter in the newspaper written by a local pastor. In the letter the woman commented several times that she was 'not perfect' as an excuse for rationalizing things that were less than virtuous and honorable in her life. I wanted to laugh, if it wasn't so sad.

"Perfect" in the the Greek is *teleios* which means 'mature and adult'. So, in essence when this pastor wrote "I'm not perfect" what she really said was, "Please excuse the sins in my life. I'm not behaving maturely and acting like an adult." What a sad commentary on the power of God in her life.

Most of the world and even people in the church think of 'perfect' in the same way this pastor does - incapable of sinning. Consequently, they just muddle along rationalizing their disobedience and never experience the victory of God in their lives. As a pastor who should be teaching and guiding a flock of God's people, her words mock the Father who is perfect, and Yeshua who told us to *"be perfect as our heavenly Father.'*

Of course, sinning and 'falling short' are inevitable in life, but that is not the same as being and acting immature. We must learn from those mistakes be transformed into maturity and not make excuses for our immaturity.

Biblical Maturity

"We do, however, speak a message of wisdom among the mature, but not the wisdom of this age or of the rulers of this age, who are coming to nothing" (1 Corinthians 2:6).

Maturity involves **wisdom** that is not of this world and does not act in the ways of this world.

"Brothers, stop thinking like children. In regard to evil be infants, but in your thinking be adults" (1 Corinthians 14:20).

Maturity involves **the way a person thinks in regards to evil**.

"When I was a child, I spoke like a child, thought like a child, argued like a child; now that I have become a man, I have finished with childish ways" (1 Corinthians 13:10-11).

We are to **put away childish behavior** and act like adults.

"Anyone who lives on milk, being still an infant, is not acquainted with teaching about righteousness. But solid food is for the mature, who by constant use have trained themselves to distinguish good from evil" (Hebrews 5:13-14).

Maturity involves **growing up spiritually, eating solid food, being trained in righteousness** so good from evil can be discerned. Again, there is a reference regarding evil so evil must be important concept when growing into maturity. (For the milk or elementary teachings, read Hebrews 6:1-3).

"Epaphras, who is one of you and a servant of Messiah Yeshua, sends greetings. He is always wrestling in prayer for you that you may stand firm in all the will of God, mature and fully assured" (Colossians 4:12).

Maturity means being *fully assured* **that you are in God's will** and you **stand firm.**

Noah

"This is the account of Noah. Noah was a righteous man, blameless among the people of his time and he walked with God" (Genesis 6:9).

The Hebrew word in this verse for blameless is *tamim* and means 'perfect, blameless, sincere, whole, complete." This word carries with it the idea of being free from objectionable practices.

Tamim is also used in reference to the people of God being called to avoid the idolatrous practices of the Canaanites (Deuteronomy 18:13). Though there are no Canaanites today, there are many idolatrous practices that the people of God should be avoiding, but instead they lack the discernment that maturity provides and sin.

Tamim also implies that a person externally meets all the requirements of God's law or *Torah*. In other words, there is nothing in a person's outward activities that are odious to God. Because of the inward condition of their heart, they meet the requirements of God's Torah.

According to Genesis, Noah walked with God and *tamim* describes his relationship to God. Noah was a mature man. He used wisdom in a corrupt world and his maturity to discern good from evil. He took no part in the idolatrous activities going on around him; he remained separate and his life exemplified this separateness. He stood firm in God's will to build an ark while the world around him went from bad to worse and mocked his faith in an unseen God. Noah had the correct internal disposition of heart and therefore walked externally blameless or *perfect* before God.

Did Noah sin? Of course he did. He planted a vineyard, got drunk, and lay naked in his tent. He was shamed by Ham. However, his sin did not affect his *maturity* in the sight of the Lord.

Abraham

"When Abram was ninety-nine years old, the Lord appeared to him and said, "I am God El Shaddai; walk before me faithfully and be blameless" (Genesis 17:1).

Abraham left Bablyon and its idolatrous ways. He lived in tents with his family apart from the rest of the world. He obeyed God's commands, even to the point of being willing to sacrifice his son Isaac on Mount Moriah. He is called the 'father of faith' and was given the sign of circumcision. He is also *tamim,* mature and blameless.

Did Abraham sin? Of course he did. Twice, he lied about Sarah not being his wife. However, his sin did not affect his *maturity* in the sight of the Lord.

King David

"For David had done what was right in the eyes of the Lord and had not failed to keep any of the Lord's commands all the days of his life—except in the case of Uriah the Hittite" (1 Kings 15:5).

David had faith in God like no other Israelite soldier. He trusted in God when he stood before Goliath with only a few stones and a slingshot. When Goliath was killed, he credited God for delivering him from the hands of the Philistines and certain death. As a warrior David cleansed the land of Israel from idolatrous people through war. With skillful hands David led the armies of Israel. As a King, he shepherded the people of Israel with integrity of heart (Psalm 78:72).

Did David sin? Of course he did. He sinned when he cut off the tzizit of King Saul, God's anointed king. He sinned when he had Uriah the Hittite killed. He sinned when he committed adultery with Bathsheba. However, his sin did not affect his *maturity* in the sight of the Lord. He was called *tamim*, blameless and a 'man after God's own heart' (1 Samuel 13:14).

Zechariah and Elizabeth

"Both of them were righteous in the sight of God, observing all the Lord's commands and decrees blamelessly" (Luke 1:6).

Both Zechariah and Elizabeth were called *tamim*. As a descendant of Aaron, Zechariah did his Temple duties as prescribed for his lineage through Abijah. Elizabeth was barren. They desired a child. An angel comes to Zechariah and tells him he is going to have a son. He doesn't believe the angel and is rendered mute until the boy is born.

Did Zechariah and Elizabeth sin? There is nothing in Scripture that says they did; however they were human beings. Perhaps Zechariah not believing the angel could be considered sin, and if it was, it didn't change Zechariah's or Elizabeth's *maturity* in the sight of God.

The Body of Messiah

"You must be blameless (perfect) before the LORD your God" (Deuteronomy 18:13).

"You, therefore, must be perfect [growing into complete maturity of godliness in mind and character, having reached the proper height of virtue and integrity] as your heavenly Father is perfect" (Matthew 5:48, The Amplified Bible).

"We proclaim Him, admonishing and teaching everyone with all wisdom, so that we may present everyone perfect in Messiah" (Colossians 1:28).

We must be *perfect* before God just like Noah, Abraham, King David, and Zechariah and Elizabeth. We are commanded to be so. As born again believers in God's Kingdom, we have been given the Spirit of God that empowers us have victory over sin and death and live blameless lives in a world as corrupt as 'the days of Noah'. We must keep ourselves spotless from the corruption of the world and mature in discerning good from evil. In order to do this, we must live according to the Spirit of life that is found in the divinely inspired teachings and instructions of God called the Law, the Torah. "I am not perfect" is no excuse for sinful behavior any more than being 'under grace, not law' should give us the freedom to disobey God's commandments and sin. When we do, we put ourselves back 'under the law of sin and death,' and forfeit the same amazing grace of God that was given to Adam and Eve.

Chapter Photo: Jewish graves on the Mount of Olives, Israel.

The Heart of the New Covenant

"I will give them an undivided heart and put a new spirit in them; I will remove from them their heart of stone and give them a heart of flesh. Then they will follow my decrees and be careful to keep my laws. They will be my people, and I will be their God" (Ezekiel 11:19-20).

For many people, the new covenant is believed to be the 26 books of the Bible known as the New Testament. For others, the new covenant replaces something 'old' they refer to as the 'the law' for a something new they call 'grace.' Often times, it is taught that the old covenant was God's law (Torah) and the new covenant is the removal of the Torah from a believer's life. What do the Scriptures actually teach?

The Original Covenant with Israel

A covenant, according to dictionary.com is, *an agreement, usually formal, between two parties to do or not do something specified.* What was the 'old, formal agreement' that constituted the 'old' covenant? How was it made? Who were the two parties? What were the formalities?

"Moses went up to God, and the LORD called to him from the mountain saying, 'Thus you shall say to the House of Jacob and tell the sons of Israel: 'You yourselves have seen what I did to the Egyptians, and how I bore you

on eagles' wings, and brought you to Myself. Now then, if you will indeed obey My voice and keep My covenant, then you shall be My own possession among all the peoples, for all the earth is Mine; and you shall be to Me a kingdom of priests and a holy nation.' These are the words that you shall speak to the sons of Israel…. When Moses went and told the people all the LORD's words and laws, they responded with one voice, "Everything the LORD has said we will do" (Exodus 19:4-5,8).

With this positive affirmation from the people, Moses goes up onto the mountain. God writes the specifics of the covenant with His own finger. Moses goes down from the mountain with two stone tablets on which are written The Ten Commandments. He reads all the words of the covenant that God made with his people.

Covenants are formally sealed with blood and this unique covenant between God and Israel was no different. Moses sacrificed bulls and sprinkled the blood on the altar and on the people. Through the blood, this original covenant with Israel was instituted and they entered into a covenant relationship. A second time, the people respond that everything God has commanded in the Book of the Covenant, they will do.

"He [Moses] got up early the next morning and built an altar at the foot of the mountain and set up twelve stone pillars representing the twelve tribes of Israel. Then he sent young Israelite men, and they offered burnt offerings and sacrificed young bulls as fellowship offerings to the LORD. Moses took half of the blood and put it in bowls, and the other half he sprinkled on the altar. Then he took the Book of the Covenant and read it to the people. They responded, "We will do everything the LORD has said; we will obey."

"Moses then took the blood, sprinkled it on the people and said, "This is the blood of the covenant that the LORD has made with you in accordance with all these words" (Exodus 24:3-8).

Broken Covenant

Then, the worst happened. Within a short time, these very same people broke their part of the covenant with God by taking His name in vain and worshipping idols. They made a golden calf, dedicating it to Him, and worshipping it as they would have in Egypt with drunkenness and immorality (Exodus 32).

Angered by several instances of their faithlessness, God punished those who came out of Egypt and their offspring for an entire generation. He forced the Israelites to wander in the wilderness for 40 years.

At the end of the 40 years before entering the Promised Land, Moses spoke the commandments of God again to a new generation of Israelites. He tells them to fear God, walk in His ways, love Him, serve Him and *circumcise their hearts*.

"And now, O Israel, what does the LORD your God ask of you but to fear the LORD your God, to walk in all his ways, to love him, to serve the LORD with all your heart and with all your soul, and to observe the LORD's commands and decrees that I am giving you today for your own good? To the LORD your God belong the heavens, even the highest heavens, the earth and everything in it. Yet the LORD set his affection on your forefathers and loved them, and he chose you, their descendants, above all the nations, as it is today. Circumcise your hearts, therefore, and do not be stiff-necked any longer" (Deuteronomy 10:12-16).

Imagine being one of these second generation Israelites. After wandering in the wilderness and watching your parents and grandparents die as the penalty for disobedience, you now need to circumcise your heart. What did that mean? How did one do such a thing? The task must have seemed confusing and unattainable.

Moses gives them hope. He promises that God will circumcise their hearts which will cause them to love Him with their whole being. In other words, he promises that God will not only hold up His side of the covenant, but make it possible for them to keep their 'I do'.

"The LORD your God will circumcise your heart and the heart of your descendants, to love the Yahweh your God with all your heart and with all your soul, so that you may live" (Deuteronomy 30:6).

Even with the all of the lessons that a whole new generation of Israelites had learned while being refined in the desert, the covenant still had a problem. The people constantly disobeyed. It wasn't God's Torah that had the problem, it was the hearts of the people.

*"For if there had been nothing wrong with that first [covenantal agreement] no place would have been sought for another. **But the LORD found fault with the people and declared I will make a new covenant** ...."*(Hebrews 8:8).

Because God found fault with the people, something had to be done. He could not change His Torah, the standard for His holiness and the essence of Himself. He could not remove the Torah because it will exist until there is a new heavens and new earth (Matthew 5:17-19). He could, however, as Creator, modify His creation. After all, He is the potter and the people were His clay. The change He made would have to enable His people to return to Him in faithfulness. The change He made would have to 'renew' the covenant relationship that had been broken.

Nothing New 'under the sun'

In Hebrew, the word 'new' is *chadashah* - חדשה. *Chadash* or a form of it is also used in the terminology for the beginning of each new month, Rosh *Chodesh*. *Chadash* is an interesting word to use with the moon. Does the earth actually receive an entirely new moon each month? Does the old moon fall out of the sky and become replaced with a completely new one? Of course not, and herein lies a nuance of the word 'new' in the Hebrew. It also means 'renew'. Thus, every month as the moon goes through its lunar cycle, it is 'renewed'.

The same word *chadashah* is used for 'new' when referring to the new covenant or *Brit Chadashah*. It is not a completely 'new' covenant where something old is thrown away to be replaced by something completely new. It is a 'renewal of the covenant' that would deal with the *fault of the people*.

Prophets and the Re-Newed Covenant

After Moses' prophecy in Exodus, God used other prophets, especially Jeremiah and Ezekiel, to elaborate on the *renewed covenant*.

"The days are coming,' declares the LORD, 'when I will make a new covenant with the House of Israel and the House of Judah. It will not be like the covenant I made with their ancestors when I took them by the hand to lead them out of Egypt, because they broke my covenant, though I was a husband to them,' declares the LORD. This is the covenant I will make with the House of Israel after that time," declares the LORD. I will put my law in their minds and write it on their hearts. I will be their God, and they will be my people. No longer will they teach their neighbor, or say to one another, 'Know the LORD,' because they will all know me, from the least of them to the greatest' declares the LORD. 'For I will forgive their wickedness and will remember their sins no more" (Jeremiah 31:31-34).

These verses in Jeremiah prophesy of the *renewed covenant* specifically with the House of Israel and the House of Judah. Renewing the original covenant with Israel became necessary because it was the Israelites as a nation who had broken the original covenant. According to Jeremiah, in God's eyes, breaking this covenant was the same as breaking the "I do" marriage contract between a Husband (Himself) and a wife (His people).

Even after all of Israel's faithlessness and idolatries, God still desired that Israel be His treasured possession, His wife. Because of His lovingkindness, mercy and grace, God promised to renew the covenant that His people had broken. He promised to *renew* the 'marriage contract' also known as a *ketubah*.

"I will vindicate the holiness of My great name which has been profaned among the nations .... I will take you from the nations, gather you from all the lands and bring you into your own land. Then I will sprinkle clean water on you, and you will be clean; I will cleanse you from all your filthiness and from all your idols. Moreover, I will give you a new (renewed) heart and put a new (renewed) spirit within you; and I will remove the heart of stone from your flesh and give you a heart of flesh. I will put My Spirit within you and cause you to walk in My statues and you will be careful to observe My ordinances" (Ezekiel 36:24-27).

The *renewed covenant* was more than just forgiving Israel's wicked, lawless ways and forgetting the sins they committed. God was going to gather His chosen people from the nations where He had dispersed them and bring them back to the Promised Land. He was going to sprinkle clean water them and cleanse them from their filthy idols. More importantly, He was going to change their hearts. Instead of just having an outward flesh circumcision, the foreskins of their hearts would be cut and removed.

The Hebrew word for 'cutting' is *brit*. It means to 'seal a covenant through cutting.' It is most familiar in the *brit milah*, the terminology used for a baby boy's circumcision when he is eight days old and his foreskin is cut. The child enters into the *covenant of the word*. *Brit* is also used in the Hebrew rendering of the 'new covenant' or *Brit Chadashah* meaning the *new cutting (circumcision)*. The *new circumcision* would be done by God's Spirit and change the stoney heart of a rebellious people into a heart of flesh bringing obedience and life.

This prophecy was not just good news, it was great news. Whenever God instituted the *new circumcision,* the House of Judah and the House of Israel would no longer have to struggle to obey the commands. God would cause them to walk in His ways and uphold their side of the marriage *ketubah* through a *circumcision of their hearts*.

Salvation and the New Circumcision

In Luke chapter 22, Jesus celebrates a Passover seder with his disciples. He lifts a cup of wine and says, *"This cup is the new covenant in my blood, which is poured out for you."* Can you imagine how these men would have received those words knowing in the context in which they were spoken? They were the Jews waiting for the prophecy of Ezekiel. They were the Israelites wondering when the prophecy of Jeremiah would happen.

In Greek the word 'new' is *kainos*. It means 'unprecedented and unheard of.' To have the Rabbi you have followed for three years lift a cup of Passover wine and and proclaim it to be the *cup of the new covenant* was definitely unprecedented and unheard of!

The disciples understood mediation of covenants. Moses had been the mediator of the original covenant with blood from animals. Now Jesus would be doing the same thing; however, there were differences. The blood would not be of bulls or calves, but the blood that flowed in his veins. The blood would not be sprinkled, but poured out. Jesus, whose Hebrew name is *Yeshua* and means 'salvation' was the promised one to bring redemption to Israel. He was renewing the broken covenant and bringing reconciliation between a Husband and His Wife.

With Yeshua's death on Passover, followed by his resurrection three days later on Feast of Firstfruits, the *new circumcision* became a living hope in the disciples' lives. Forty days later at his ascension, Yeshua tells them to go to Jerusalem and wait for the promise. They knew what that promise was. He told them on that Passover evening: *"If you love me, keep my commands. And I will ask the Father, and he will give you another advocate to help you and be with you forever — the Spirit of truth"* (John 14:15). They obeyed.

Ten days later on the day of Pentecost, on the memorial day of the giving of the original covenant, God poured out His Spirit on the the House of Judah and the House of Israel. As Jewish people from all over the world gathered in Jerusalem, a violent wind came from heaven and filled one of the areas in the Temple. The disciples who were gathered there saw what seemed to be tongues of fire that separated and came to rest on each of them. They were all filled with the Spirit of God and began to speak in other languages as the Spirit enabled them (Acts 2). Through the flames of a refining fire, God transformed the hearts of 3000 Jews and Israelites on that day from stone to flesh. Through the violent wind of His Spirit, God forgave their wickedness and forgot their generations of sinfulness. The *new covenant* promised to Israel had become reality. The *new covenant of circumcision* instituted by Yeshua had begun ... with Israel.

Peter tells the crowd of gathered Israelites from every nation, *"God has raised Yeshua to life, and we are all witnesses of it. Exalted to the right hand of God, he has received from the Father the promised Holy Spirit and has poured out what you now see and hear"* (Acts 2:32).

Those Who Are *Far Away*, Peter's Perspective

On the day of Pentecost when Peter is speaking to the crowd in Jerusalem, he says *"The promise (of the Holy Spirit) is for you and your children and for all who are far off - for all whom the Lord our God will call"* (Acts 2:39).

Peter acknowledges two different types of people who would receive the Spirit of God: those Jews who were standing there in Jerusalem and those Jews who made up the scattered tribes of Israel who didn't have the means to trek all the way to Jerusalem. Those who were in the city, whose hearts had been transformed by the Spirit, would take the message of redemption to all the Jewish people living in the surrounding nations.

I don't believe Peter was referring to the gentiles as *far off*. I don't believe he was thinking in that moment that the Spirit of God could move Philip from one place to another where there was an Ethiopian eunuch reading the book of Isaiah. I don't believe he was thinking about a Pharisee named Paul who would first persecute and murder Messianic Jews before becoming born again on the road to Damascus. Peter's understanding of *far off* had to do with proximity with the Land of Israel and the Jewish people in the surrounding nations. It wasn't until many years later when he had the vision of unclean animals in the sheet that he understood the message of salvation going to the gentiles.

Far Away Another Perspective

There is a serious ramification for non-Jewish people if the *renewed covenant* spoken of by Jeremiah is only given to the House of Israel and the House Judah. If you were not Jewish or did not know from which Tribe of Israel you hailed, then you were one of the nations, gentiles by birth. The message of the *new covenant* that the Jewish people around you were excitedly talking about was not for you. It was not made with you, a gentile, or with the nations in which you lived, or even so-called Christians because there was no such group of people.

"Therefore, remember that ... you who are gentiles by birth and called 'uncircumcised' by those who call themselves 'the circumcision' (which is done in the body by human hands) - remember that ... [you are] separate from Messiah, excluded from citizenship in Israel and foreigners to the

covenants of the promise, without hope and without God in the world... (Ephesians 2:11-13).

What if those who were *far away* weren't the Jews, they were the gentiles, the people of the nations who were uncircumcised in the flesh? As gentiles, they were without the God of Israel. They had no understanding of the covenants between God and Israel because they were foreigners to the promises and covenants. Everything about Jewish life in Israel was strange in concept and action. Being *far away* meant that they could only look at a distance at these chosen people who had a God that made promises and kept them.

Though gentiles may have wanted to have a relationship with the God of Israel and worship Him, there was one huge barrier. In the Temple it was called the 'wall of partition'. They could not pass that wall and draw near to God unless they went through something called a ritual conversion to become a legal Jew. If they did not choose to become legally Jewish, they had no hope for receiving a *renewed covenant* because they never had an *original* covenant.

That didn't mean they didn't break God's commands and sin. It didn't mean they felt no guilt when they wronged another person. It didn't mean they didn't hope that their sacrifices to their gods, surrendering of their children to the fire, would somehow appease their gods and set them free from a cycle of death.

Then, a Jewish man named Paul began traveling through their cities telling them that peace with the God of Israel was being offered to *them*. This peace would bring *them* near to all those things they desired, but didn't know how to receive. This peace would bring reconciliation between them and their Creator. This peace would bring forgiveness and their guilt would go away. The 'wall of partition' that separated them from the promises and covenants of Israel would be removed and they could worship the God of Israel with the Jewish people, like the Jewish people. The best part of this news of peace - it was not *hostile,* it did not require the ritual of cutting the foreskin of their flesh. This peace came by faith.

"He [Yeshua] came and preached peace to you who were far away [gentiles] and peace to those who were near [the Jews]" (Ephesians 2:17-18).

Faith, Abraham and His Children

"For we maintain that a person is justified by faith apart from the works of the law [ritual conversion through circumcision]. Or is God the God of Jews only? Is he not the God of Gentiles too? Yes, of Gentiles too, since there is only one God, who will justify the circumcised [Jews] by faith and the uncircumcised [gentiles] through that same faith" (Romans 28-30).

Abraham was promised by God in Genesis that all nations would be blessed through him. What was so special about Abraham that God would bless in in such a powerful way? He had faith in God and God's promises.

"Therefore, the promise comes by faith, so that it may be by grace and may be guaranteed to all Abraham's offspring—not only to those who are of the law [circumcised] but also to those who have the faith of Abraham [uncircumcised] . He is the father of us all. As it is written: "I have made you a father of many nations. He is our father in the sight of God, in whom he believed—the God who gives life to the dead and calls into being things that were not" (Romans 14:16-17).

"Understand, then, that those who have faith are children of Abraham. Scripture foresaw that God would justify the Gentiles by faith, and announced the gospel in advance to Abraham: "All nations will be blessed through you." So those who rely on faith are blessed along with Abraham, the man of faith" (Galatians 3:7-9).

A gentile enters the *new covenant* the same way as Abraham, by putting their faith in God and his plan of salvation demonstrated on Mount Moriah. They have to believe that Yeshua is the Promised Seed, the One who became a substitute sacrifice for us like the ram that took the place of Isaac. Like Abraham they have to believe that God is the giver of life and can resurrect people from the dead as He did Yeshua and 'figuratively' did with Isaac. Like Abraham and his physical descendants through Isaac and Jacob, they have to put their faith in the blood of the one called the 'Lamb of God'. They have to believe Yeshua is the Messiah of Israel and that salvation to the nations comes through the Jews (John 4:22).

Two Covenants or One?

"For if there had been nothing wrong with that first covenant, no place would have been sought for another. But God found fault with the people..." (Hebrew 8:7).

This verse is often ignored when the *new covenant* from Jeremiah is reiterated in Hebrews. The reason for a *new covenant* had nothing to do with *abolishing* an old one, especially when 'the old one' is considered God's teachings and instructions. This is a gross misunderstanding of prophetic Scripture and the *new covenant* itself. The problem of sin was not God's Torah, the problem of sin was in the hearts of mankind. Their stoney, rebellious, hearts kept them from obeying God's *original covenant*.

Paul says in Romans 3:23 that *"all have sinned and fall short of God's glory."* Everyone, whether Jew or gentile, needs a new heart in order to leave their rebellious ways and idolatrous lifestyle contrary to God's commands. Just like Israel, when gentiles enter into the *new covenant* by faith in Yeshua, they receive the Spirit of God which transforms their hearts from stone to flesh. It is on these new hearts that the God of Israel writes His laws, the same laws found in the Torah He gave to Israel.

"Consequently, you are no longer foreigners and strangers, but fellow citizens with God's people and also members of his household, built on the foundation of the apostles and prophets, with Messiah Yeshua himself as the chief cornerstone. In him the whole building is joined together and rises to become a holy temple in the Lord. And in him you too are being built together to become a dwelling in which God lives by his Spirit" (Ephesians 2:19-22).

One of the most over-looked aspects regarding gentiles coming to faith in the Messiah of Israel is their becoming members of God's household and part of the commonwealth of Israel. Faith brings more to the life of a gentile than just 'being saved' from the 'law of sin and death'; it brings a whole new identity within a holy nation that is united by a Sovereign King and His commandments. Through faith in Yeshua, gentiles are grafted into the Olive Tree of Israel and receive the same life *nourishing sap from its roots* as do the Jews (Romans 11:17).

According to Romans 11, if the *gentile* branches which are grafted into the Olive Tree of Israel by faith become arrogant over the *Jewish* branches, as has been the case for most of church history, they will be cut off, lose their nourishment and die. Gentile believers in Yeshua must always make sure that they have not become arrogant over the natural branches because a holy root supports them both.

Gentiles need to accept their Biblical heritage within the Hebrew Scriptures and be at peace with Yeshua's Jewish brothers and sisters. They are not to put up a *new covenant wall of partition* that excludes God's chosen people by abolishing that which established them as God's covenanted people. Gentiles must remember that adoption into God's family as children was given to Israel first. God revealed His glory to Israel. All of the covenants, the Torah, the Temple services, the priesthood, and the promises of a world to come were given to Israel. Through Abraham, Isaac, Jacob, Judah and King David is traced the human ancestry of our salvation, Messiah Yeshua (Romans 9:4).

When gentiles understand that the *new covenant* is not a set of 26 books found in the backs of their Bibles, it is not a new religion called Christianity started by a man named Jesus, and it doesn't just contain one verse from the gospel of John, they will come into their fullness as citizens in the commonwealth of Israel. When gentiles understand that God wants to write His Torah filled with His promises, covenants, and outline for living a set apart life for Him, there will finally be peace in God's household. When gentiles understand the all-inclusiveness of the *renewed covenant* instituted by Yeshua's blood on the cross, they will finally put to death the hostility between their two religious systems and become the *one new covenant man* they are supposed to be. The Torah will be written on their hearts of flesh as it is on the hearts of Jews and, will one day be written on the hearts of all Israel.

"For he himself [Yeshua] is our peace, who has made the two groups [Jew and gentile] one and has destroyed the barrier, the dividing wall of hostility [in Temple worship],by setting aside in his flesh the law [of ritual conversion] with its commands and regulations. His purpose was to create in himself one new humanity out of the two, thus making peace, and in one body to reconcile both of them [Jew and gentile] to God through the cross, by which he put to death their hostility [their religious differences]" (Ephesians 2:11-16).

The Big Ten and the New Testament

"The commandments, 'Do not commit adultery,' 'Do not murder,' 'Do not steal,' 'Do not covet,' and whatever other commandment there may be, are summed up in this one rule: 'Love your neighbor as yourself" (Romans 13:9).

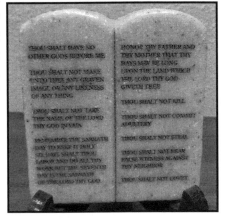

Contrary to the teachings of the modern-day church, all of the Ten Commandments are reiterated in the New Testament. None have been removed, abolished, or changed. In Exodus 20, the commandments are the summary to the complete Torah given to Israel by God on Mt. Sinai. Yeshua and the apostles throughout the new testament refer to this 'Table of Contents' summary when they talk about the commandments. They never negate any of the teachings and instructions in the Torah with only the two greatest commandments or even the supposed 'one new commandment'.

"Teacher, which is the greatest commandment in the Law?"

"Yeshua replied: 'Love the Lord your God with all your heart and with all your soul and with all your mind.' This is the first and greatest commandment. And the second is like it: 'Love your neighbor as yourself.' All the Law (Torah) and the Prophets hang on these two commandments'" (Matthew 22:36-40).

Yeshua said the Torah (and Prophets) is 'summed' up in two commandments: love God and love your neighbor. Yeshua's words come from Deuteronomy 6:4-8, words given by Moses to the children of Israel known as the *Shema*.

"Hear, O Israel: The Lord our God, the Lord is one. Love the Lord your God with all your heart and with all your soul and with all your strength. These commandments that I give you today are to be on your hearts. Impress them on your children. Talk about them when you sit at home and when you walk along the road, when you lie down and when you get up. Tie them as symbols on your hands and bind them on your foreheads. Write them on the doorframes of your houses and on your gates."

The ten commandments are only a summary of the Torah and the Prophets, not the complete Torah and Prophets which outlines righteous living within God's kingdom both physically on earth as well as spiritually within our hearts.

Some pastors teach that the Torah was only given to Israel suggesting that believers in Yeshua are not bound by the same commandments. However, if you are a child of God and born again into His Kingdom, then His commandments are for you as every father has teachings and instructions for his children to obey. If you desire to understand how to love God and your neighbor more specifically, then the Torah is for you.

Yeshua said, *"If you love me, then you will obey my commandments"* (John 14:15). According to Yeshua himself, he and his Father are one, therefore his commandments will completely agree with his Father's commandments (John 10:30). Yeshua is the voice or Word of God in the flesh making him the mouthpiece of his Father (John 1:14). Everything Yeshua spoke to the people were the Words of his Father that he was commanded to say (John 12:49).

The Ten Commandments with the Aleph-Bet

When the Ten Commandments were given to Israel at Mount Sinai, they weren't written with Roman numerals or from left to right. They were written with Hebrew letters, right to left, and called the 'ten words'. A wonderful teaching tool for learning the Ten Commandments is to use the first ten letters of the Hebrew alphabet. Each of the letters are word pictures that actually reveal each commandment. The Ten Commandments listed below include new testament Scriptures showing that all the commandments were reiterated by Yeshua or the apostles in the New Testament.

Love God:
Number One: א Aleph - An Ox

The first commandment is represented by the the first letter of the Hebrew alphabet. The word picture for *aleph* is an Ox. The Ox is symbolic of strength, leader, first. We are to have no other gods except first and foremost, Yahweh, who delivers us from the bondage of slavery into freedom, from sin and death into fullness of life. It is only Yahweh who is able to destroy every power or 'other gods' as He did in Egypt.

"I am the LORD (Yahweh) your God, who brought you out of Egypt, out of the land of slavery, You shall have no other gods before me" (Exodus 20:2-3).

"Yeshua answered, 'It is written: 'Worship the LORD your God and serve him only'" (Luke 4:8).

Number Two: ב Bet - A House

The second commandment is represented by the second letter of the Hebrew alphabet. The word picture for *bet* is a Tent or House. This symbolizes a household, in, into and a family. In middle eastern culture, the gods were called 'household gods'. Rachel was guilty of sitting on her 'idol' when Laban came to Jacob (Genesis 31:19).

"You shall not make for yourself an idol in the form of anything in heaven above or on the earth beneath or in the waters below. You shall not bow down to them or worship them; for the LORD (Yahweh) your God, am a jealous God, punishing the children for the sin of the fathers to the third and fourth

generation of those who hate me, but showing love to a thousand generations of those who love me and keep my commandments" (Exodus 20:4-6).

"Dear children, keep yourselves from idols" (1 John 5:21).

Number Three: ג Gimel - A Camel

The third commandment is represented by the third letter of the Hebrew alphabet. The word picture for *gimel* is a Camel and is also the Hebrew word for 'camel'. The symbolic meaning is to lift up and pride. We, as believers in Yahweh are not to pridefully use His name. When we live lawlessly, against the commands, and call ourselves followers of the eternal God (saved by His Son) then we are misusing His name and profaning it among the world in which we live. This would be 'taking his name in vain.'

"You shall not misuse the name of the LORD (Yahweh) your God, for the LORD (Yahweh) will not hold anyone guiltless who misuses his name" (Exodus 20:7).

"Some of the traveling Jewish men who adjure evil spirits also undertook to call on the name of the Lord Yeshua over those who had evil spirits, saying, I solemnly implore and charge you by the Yeshua whom Paul preaches! Seven sons of a certain Jewish chief priest named Sceva were doing this. But one evil spirit retorted, Yeshua I know, and Paul I know about, but who are you? Then the man in whom the evil spirit dwelt leaped upon them, master two of them, and was so violent against them that they dashed out of that house in fear, stripped and naked and wounded" (Acts 19:13-16).

"As it is written: 'God's name is blasphemed among the nations because of you'" (Romans 2:24).

Dalet - A Door ד :Number Four ד

The fourth commandment is represented by the fourth letter of the Hebrew alphabet. The word picture for *dalet* is a Door and is also the Hebrew word for 'door.' The symbolic meaning is a pathway or a place to enter. Yeshua stands at the *dalet* and knocks. Anyone who opens the door to him, he 'enters' in and feasts with them (Revelation 3:20). The Sabbath is a 'door' we enter into so we can have a more intimate fellowship with the Father through Yeshua.

"Remember the Sabbath day by keeping it holy .... For in six days the LORD (Yahweh) made the heavens and the earth, the sea, and all that is in them, but he rested on the seventh day. Therefore the LORD (Yahweh) blessed the Sabbath day and made it holy" (Exodus 20:8).

"Then Yeshua said to them, 'The Son of Man is Lord of the Sabbath" (Luke 6:5).

"There remains, then, a Sabbath-rest for the people of God; for anyone who enters God's rest also rests from his own work (of creation), just as God did from his" (Hebrews 4:9,10).

The first three commandments explain how to love God; the following six explain how to love our neighbor. The Sabbath is the door or pathway that takes us from loving God to loving our neighbor.

"If anyone says, 'I love God,' yet hates his brother, he is a liar. For anyone who does not love his brother, whom he has seen, cannot love God, whom he has not seen" (1 John 4:20).

Love your Neighbor:
Number Five: ה Hey - A Window

The fifth commandment is represented by the fifth letter of the Hebrew alphabet. The word picture for *hey* is a Window and means to behold, observe or reveal. It is also 'the' like in 'Ha Shem' (The Name). When on the cross, Yeshua looks at John and says, *"John, BEHOLD your mother. Mother, BEHOLD your son"* (John 19:26). Even when Yeshua was dying, he honored his mother by giving her someone to care for her.

"Honor your father and your mother, so that you may live long in the land the LORD (Yahweh) your God is living you" (Exodus 20:12).

"Honor your father and mother - which is the first commandment with a a promise ..." (Ephesians 6:2).

Number Six: ו Vav - A Nail

The sixth commandment is represented by the sixth letter of the Hebrew alphabet. The word picture for *vav* is a Nail or Peg. It is symbolic of securing, binding, and is the conjunction 'and' as in *'chesed v'ahava'* (mercy and love). Yeshua was murdered, nailed, and secured to the cross.

"You shall not murder" (Exodus 20:13).

"Do not murder, and anyone who murders will be subject to judgment.' But I tell you that anyone who is angry with is brother will be subject to judgment" (Matthew 5:22).

Number Seven: ז Zayin - A Sword

The seventh commandment is represented by the seventh letter of the Hebrew alphabet. The word picture for *zayin* is a Weapon like an Axe. It is symbolic of cutting, separating or dividing. Adultery is like an axe that cuts and separates a married couple.

"You shall not commit adultery" (Exodus 20:14).

"Therefore what God has joined together, let man not separate" (Mark 10:9).

Number Eight: ח Chet - A Fence

The eighth commandment is represented by the eighth letter of the Hebrew alphabet. The word picture for *chet* is a Fence or Inner Room. The symbolic meaning is to separate as in to protect with a fence what is within its boundaries. A fence protects personal property from those who would steal. In Hebrew thought, the Torah is considered a 'fence'. For those who walk according to the teachings and instructions of Torah, their inner chamber of intimacy with the Father is protected.

"You shall not steal" (Exodus 20:15).

"You know the commandments: Do not commit adultery, do not murder, do not steal ... " (Luke 18:20).

"He who has been stealing must steal no longer, but must work, doing something useful with his own hands, that he may have something to share with those in need" (Ephesians 4:28).

Number Nine: ט Tet - A Snake

The ninth commandment is represented by the ninth letter of the Hebrew alphabet. The word picture for *tet* is a Snake. It is symbolic of twisting. It was the serpent who first twisted the truth and lied to Eve in the Garden.

"You shall not give false testimony (lie) against your neighbor" (Exodus 20:16).

"You know the commandments: 'Do not commit adultery, do not murder, do not steal, do not give false testimony...'"(Luke 18:20).

"You belong to your father, the devil, and you want to carry out your father's desire. He was a murderer from the beginning, not holding to the truth, for there is no truth in him. When he lies, he speaks his native language, for he is a liar and the father of lies" (John 8:44).

Number Ten: י Yod - A Closed Hand

The tenth commandment is represented by the tenth letter of the Hebrew alphabet. The word picture for *yod* is a Closed Hand. This is symbolic of a finished work or completed deed. When a person covets, their hand is not closed and content, but desiring more.

"You shall not covet your neighbor's house. You shall not covet your neighbor's wife, or his manservant or maidservant, his ox or donkey, or anything that belongs to your neighbor" (Exodus 20:17).

"Let your conduct be without covetousness; be content with such things as you have. For He has said, 'I will never leave you nor forsake you'" (Hebrews 13:5).

Thus saith the LORD (Yahweh) ...

"In the future, when your son asks you, 'What is the meaning of the stipulations, decrees and Torah the LORD our God has commanded you?'
Tell him: "We were slaves of Pharaoh in Egypt, but the LORD brought us out of Egypt with a mighty hand. Before our eyes the LORD sent miraculous signs and wonders - great and terrible - upon Egypt and Pharaoh and his whole household. But he brought us out from there to bring us in and give us the land that he promised on oath to our forefathers. The LORD commanded us to obey all these decrees and to fear the LORD our God, so that we might always prosper and be kept alive, as in the case today. And if we are careful to obey all this Torah before the LORD our God, as he has commanded us, that will be our righteousness" (Deuteronomy 6:20-25).

... His Word in the flesh, Yeshua

"I tell you the truth, until heaven and earth disappear, not the smallest letter, not the least stroke of a pen, will by any means disappear from the Torah until everything is accomplished. Anyone who breaks one of the least of these commandments and teaches others to do the same will be called least in the kingdom of heaven, but whoever practices and teaches these commands will be called great in the kingdom of heaven" (Matthew 5:18-19).

The Torah: A Foundation

"Many peoples will go and say, 'Come, let's go up to the mountain of Adonai, to the house of the God of Jacob! He will teach us about his ways, and we will walk in his paths.' For out of Zion will go forth Torah, the word of the LORD from Jerusalem" (Isaiah 2:2-4).

"Teach me, LORD, the way of your laws; keeping them will be its own reward for me. Give me understanding; then I will keep your Torah; I will observe it with all my heart. Guide me on the path of your commands, for I take pleasure in it" (Psalm 119:33-35).

Torah Defined

Using a *Vines Expository Dictionary of Biblical Words*, the Hebrew word *torah* is found under the heading, 'law'. The explanation given for *torah*: "law, direction, instruction. In the wisdom literature ... *Torah* signifies primarily direction, teaching, instruction: *"The law [Torah] of the wise is a foundation of life, to depart from the snares of death"* (Proverbs 13:14).

Three interesting concepts are learned from this definition of the Hebrew word *torah*. First, it is translated as 'law'. Second, its literal meaning is direction, instruction, and teaching. Third, it is used in the *wisdom* literature of Proverbs.

Vines expounds by stating that the instructions given by God to Moses and the Israelites became known as 'the law' or 'the direction'. *"Blessed are the undefiled in the way, who walk in the law [Torah] of the Lord'* (Psalm 11:1).

God communicated His 'law' that Israel might observe and live: *"And what nation is there so great, that hath statutes and judgments so righteous as all this law [Torah] which I set before you this day?"* (Deuteronomy 4:8).

The word *torah* has another meaning according to *Vines*. It comes from the Hebrew word *yarah* and means 'to cast, throw, or direct. *Torah* is that which God *cast or threw* to His people to direct them. If someone desires to go in the direction of God, *torah* will lead them in His ways. *"Show me your ways, LORD, teach me your paths"* (Psalm 25:4). In hundreds of verses in the Hebrew Scriptures, the word 'law' should have remained *torah* for wherever there is a teaching or instruction from Yahweh, it is *torah*.

According to 2 Timothy 3:16 *"All Scripture is inspired by God and profitable for teaching, for reproof for correction, for training in righteousness; so that the man of God may be adequate, equipped for every good work."*

At the time Paul wrote this letter to Timothy, all Scripture referred to what we call the Old Testament and that included what is known as *Torah* or the first five books of the Bible: Genesis, Exodus, Leviticus, Numbers and Deuteronomy. These writings teach the history of the world beginning with creation and man's fall into sin, the flood of Noah and life afterwards, the birth of the people of faith through Abraham, Isaac and Jacob, and the of the nation of Israel from the 12 sons of Jacob to slavery in Egypt, deliverance to Mount Sinai, and wandering in the wilderness until they entered the Promised Land.

God gave His *torah* or instructions to everyone from the beginning. Adam and Eve had instructions about food and eventually, blood sacrifice. Noah had instructions about clean and unclean animals, eating blood, murder and justice. The mixed multitude that left the land of Egypt were given further instructions for living as God's chosen people, a holy nation, and a kingdom of priests. They had instructions about what was considered food, guidelines for cleanliness in the camp, and rules for living morally as families in a community. There were regulations ordering the days, weeks and months that included requirements for the proper way to worship God through the the Tabernacle and a priesthood. There were commands for celebrating holy days that would honor God and bring glory to His name among the nations.

Hebrew Word Pictures

Torah - תורה

Tav ת - Crossed Sticks means 'sign or mark'

Vav ו - A Nail means 'tied together binding, and'

Resh ר - A Head means 'what is most important'

Hey ה - A Window means 'reveal or behold'

The Hebrew word picture for *torah*: *"The sign or mark of being bound to what is most important revealed."*

The Hebrew root word of torah is *or* or the word for light.

Light – *or* אור

Aleph א - An Ox means 'first or strength'

Vav ו - A Nail means 'tied together, binding, and'

Resh ר - A Head means 'what is most important'

The Hebrew word picture for *or*: *"The first and what is most important."*

The Torah for a Physical People

God gave His chosen nation ways to remember His *Torah*. He wanted His people to be different from the nations around them. By giving them outward physical symbols and signs, He expected His people would remember His teachings and instructions. He told them to write them on their doorposts, bind them to their heads, and wear tassels on the corners of their garments (Deuteronomy 6:8, 11:8).

"You will have these tassels (tzizit) to look and so you will remember all the commands of the LORD, that you may obey them and not prostitute yourselves by chasing after the lusts of your own hearts and eyes" (Numbers 15:39).

The teachings and instructions of God, however, were not meant to be not only outward and physical, they were to be embraced in the hearts of His people because He had delivered them from slavery in Egypt and its other gods. God desired them to show their love for Him through obedience.

"Love the LORD your God with all your heart and with all your soul and with all your strength. These commandments that I give you today are to be on your hearts. Impress them on your children. Talk about them when you sit at home and when you walk along the road, when you lie down and when you get up" (Deuteronomy 6:5-7).

Unfortunately, the people strayed away from God and worshipped idols. They did not obey God's teachings and instructions. There was not a problem with God's *Torah*. It was a people problem. Even after 40 years of wandering in the wilderness and a loss of a generation, God still found fault with the people. They still had hard stony hearts. Hard hearts could not obey God's *Torah* so He had to do something. He had to change them. They had to be circumcised.

Circumcision of the Heart

"The LORD your God will circumcise your hearts and the hearts of your descendants, so that you may love him with all your heart and soul, and live" (Deuteronomy 30:5-7).

Through Ezekiel, God expounds on the promise in Deuteronomy that one day He would turn their hearts from stone into flesh. He would put His Spirit within them so that they could keep his *Torah*.

"I will give them an undivided heart and put a new spirit in them. I will remove from them their heart of stone and give them a heart of flesh.

... I will give you a new heart and put a new spirit in you; I will remove from you your heart of stone and give you a heart of flesh. I will put my Spirit in you and move you to follow my decrees and be careful to keep my laws" (Ezekiel 11:19, 36:26-27).

The Hebrew word 'laws' in Ezekiel is *mishpat*. This word means judgments, regulations, and ordinances. *Torah* encompasses all of the *mishpatim* that God gave to Israel.

Jeremiah also prophesied about the day when God would not only give His people new hearts, but what He would do on those new hearts in the form of a 'new covenant.'

"But this is the new covenant which I will make with the house of Israel after those days," declares the LORD, 'I will put My law in their minds on their heart I will write it; and I will be their God, and they shall be My people. No longer will they teach their neighbor, or say to one another, 'Know the LORD,' because they will all know me, from the least of them to the greatest," declares the LORD... '" (Jeremiah 31:33-34).

The Hebrew word for 'law' in this passage is *Torah*. According to the terms of the new covenant, the *Torah*, God's teachings and instructions, would be written on the hearts and minds of His people. No longer would there be a need for 'teachers of *Torah*' that could distort the Word of Truth for everyone would know God personally.

Spiritual Torah vs. Carnal Man

"Is the law [Torah] sinful? Certainly not! Nevertheless, I would not have known what sin was had it not been for the law [Torah]. For I would not have known what coveting really was if the law [Torah] had not said, "You shall not covet" (Romans 7:7).

"The law [Torah] is spiritual, but I am unspiritual ... " (Romans 7:14).

The problem between *Torah* and man is that *Torah* is spiritual; man is not; he is carnal and lives by fleshly desires. Paul describes the carnal man as worldly, full of jealousy and strife and walking like a mere human being in the world. Every time an unspiritual, carnal man is confronted with the spiritual *Torah*, he hits a wall that he cannot penetrate. The man is reminded of his failures and inability to overcome them because of his carnality. Thus a battle ensues between the inner desire of man to obey the *Torah* and what actually happens - falling short and sinning. As Paul states, *"I found that the very commandment that was intended to bring life actually brought death.... So I find this law at work: Although I want to do good, evil is right there with me. For in my inner being I delight in God's law [Torah]; but I see another law at work in me, waging war against the law of my mind and making me a prisoner of the law of sin [and death] at work within me. What a wretched man I am!"* (Romans 7:10, 18-20).

Paul cries out in regards to this never-ending battle, *"who will rescue me from this body of death?* (Romans 7:24).

Yeshua, the Living Torah

"For what the Torah could not do by itself, because it lacked the power to make the old [carnal] nature cooperate, <u>God did by sending his own Son as a human being with a nature like our own sinful one</u> [but without sin]. God did this in order to deal with sin, and in so doing he executed the punishment against sin in human nature [death], so that the just requirement of the 'law of sin and death' might be fulfilled in us who do not run our lives according to what our old [carnal] nature wants but according to what the Spirit [of God] wants" (Romans 8:3-4).

Yeshua as the Son of God is the *Torah* (Word) in the flesh, the Living Torah. As the visible image of the invisible God, he desired the same devotion from his disciples as his Father wanted from the children of Israel. He wanted them to love him and obey the commandments (John 14:15). Yet he knew that the heart of man was the problem, not his Father's *Torah* and he established that fact in Matthew 5.

"Do not think that I came to abolish the Law or the Prophets; I did not come to abolish but to fulfill. "For truly I say to you, until heaven and earth pass away, not the smallest letter or stroke shall pass from the Law [Torah] until all is accomplished" (Matthew 5:17-18).

In *Vines*, the Greek word *kataluo* is translated 'abolish' and means 'to reduce to inactivity, overthrow, subvert, anul, destroy. ' Yeshua says TWICE that he did not come 'destroy or anul' the *Torah* and no one should even think that. The Greek word *genomai* is used in Matthew 5:18 and is translated 'fulfill'. It means 'to be performed and begin to be received' and is used in reference to the work Yeshua did on the cross. The Greek word *pleroo* is used in Matthew 5:17 and is also translated 'fulfill.' *Pleroo* means 'to abound, render perfect and to cause God's will (as made known in the *Torah*) to be obeyed as it should be, and God's promises (given through the prophets) to receive fulfillment.' Using these definitions of 'abolish and fulfill', Yeshua said in Matthew 5:17-18:

"I did not come to (kataluo) overthrow, render vain, subvert or anul the Torah, but to cause it to (pleroo) abound, be made perfect, and to cause God's will to be obeyed as it should be; and on the cross (ginomai) this will all come to pass, happen, be performed and begin to be received."

For a rabbi during this time, the words 'abolish' and 'fulfill' had even different meanings. *Abolish* meant to 'wrongly interpret' while *fulfill* meant to 'rightly interpret'. By using these words, Yeshua is is saying to Israel that he, as a Rabbi, has come to correctly interpret the *Torah* thus removing all manmade misinterpretations that caused the *Torah* to be burdensome. He confirms to the Jewish people listening that he really is the Messiah because the 'annointed One of God' would never transgress God's *Torah*.

Yeshua revealed the heart condition of men and their need for deliverance from the iniquity that caused them to sin. He taught that murder and adultery were not just sinful actions, but came from a hard heart of anger and lust. Yet, man could not change his hard heart; only God could do that.

Yeshua spoke of this spiritual change when he told Nicodemus that everyone who wants to enter the Kingdom of God must be born again. Though Nicodemus was a teacher in Israel, he didn't connect the dots that the good news of being born again of the Spirit would change his carnal nature into a spiritual one. He would no longer live his life according to his fleshly desires, but by the Spirit of God.

"Yeshua answered, "Yes, indeed, I tell you that unless a person is born from water and the Spirit, he cannot enter the Kingdom of God. What is born from the flesh is flesh, and what is born from the Spirit is spirit. Stop being amazed at my telling you that you must be born again from above! The wind blows where it wants to, and you hear its sound, but you don't know where it comes from or where it's going. That's how it is with everyone who has been born from the Spirit" (John 3:5-8)

Once the hearts of men were circumcised by the Spirit and they were born again, they would become a spiritual man. God's *Torah* would not just be used for pointing out their sin and making them feel like a failure every time they fell short, it would bring life. With the Spirit of God writing the *Torah* on their circumcised hearts, they would have the power to obey it with all their heart, mind and soul.

"But now, by dying to what once bound us, we have been released from the law [of sin and death] so that we serve in the new way of the Spirit, and not in the old way of the written code [legalistic observance of man's laws]" (Romans 7:6).

Spiritual Torah and Spiritual Man

"Because the Torah of the Spirit, which produces this life in union with Messiah Yeshua, has set me free from the law of sin and death" (Romans 8:2).

"But if a person looks closely into the perfect Torah, which gives freedom, and continues, becoming not a forgetful hearer but a doer of the work it requires, then he will be blessed in what he does" (James 1:25).

When the spiritual man looks into the spiritual *Torah*, there is no brick wall. He sees the *Torah* as giving him guidelines for life. It no longer produces condemnation, but brings life through the Spirit. The *Torah* becomes a covenant of love between the spiritual man and his heavenly Father.

"If you pay attention to these laws [of Torah] and are careful to follow them, then the LORD your God will keep his covenant of love with you" (Deuteronomy 7:12).

The *Torah* shows the spiritual man the ways to express his love to the One, who in His great mercy and grace, sent His Son to remove *the law of sin and death*. The power to overcome sin and obey comes from the Spirit of God living in the new heart. Obeying the Torah out of love for their Father was all that He ever wanted from His children.

"This is how we know that we love the children of God: by loving God and carrying out his commands. In fact, this is love for God: to keep his commands. And his commands are not burdensome, for everyone born of God overcomes the world. This is the victory that has overcome the world, even our faith" (1 John 5:2-4).

Love Psalms to the Torah

As King of Israel, David was filled with the Spirit of God suggesting he had a circumcised heart and was born again (Psalm 51). Not only did he have to write it out as king, the *Torah* was the only way he knew of guarding God's Word in his heart (Deuteronomy 17:18). David delighted in God's *Torah* and it had an important place in his life. The light that came from *Torah* became the 'sign that bound David to the headship' of God. Writing Psalm after Psalm about his love for God's *Torah* and his willingness to be corrected by its ordinances, statutes, and precepts were part of what made David a King given an eternal kingdom and a man after God's own heart.

"The law [Torah] of the LORD is perfect, reviving the soul. The statutes of the LORD are trustworthy, making wise the simple. The precepts of the LORD are right, giving joy to the heart. The commands of the LORD are radiant, giving light to the eyes. The fear of the LORD is pure, enduring forever. The ordinances of the LORD are sure and altogether righteous. They are more precious than gold, than much pure gold; they are sweeter than honey, than honey from the comb. By them is your servant warned; in keeping them there is great reward" (Psalm 19:7-11).

"How blessed is the man who does not walk in the counsel of the wicked, nor stand in the path of sinners, nor sit in the seat of scoffers! But his delight is in the Torah of the LORD, and in His Torah he meditates day and night. He will be like a tree firmly planted by streams of water which yields

its fruit in its season and its leaf does not wither; and in whatever he does, he prosper" (Psalm 1).

"Oh how I love your Torah! I meditate on it all day long. Your commands are always with me and make me wiser than my enemies. I have more insight than all my teachers, for I meditate on your statutes. I have more understanding than the elders, for I obey your precepts. I have kept my feet from every evil path so that I might obey your word. I have not departed from your Torah, for you yourself have taught me" (Psalm 119:97-102).

"For the commandment is a lamp, Torah is light, and reproofs that discipline are the way to life" (Proverbs 6:23).

"The mouth of the righteous articulates wisdom, his tongue speaks justice. The Torah of his God is in his heart; his footsteps do not falter" (Psalm 37:31-31).

Chapter Photo: Reading the Torah scroll at the Western Wall, Israel.

What's Wrong in Galatia?

"They stirred up the people, as well as the elders and the Torah-teachers; so they came and arrested him and led him before the Sanhedrin. There they set up false witnesses who said, "This man never stops speaking against this holy place and against the Torah..." (Acts 6:12-14).

Whenever our family tells a Christian that we keep the Biblical Sabbath, celebrate the Feasts of the Lord and we eat according to Leviticus, we are always referred to the book of Galatians and warned of legalism and Judaizing. What is it about Judaizing, legalsim and the so-called 'Galatian error' that incites people to react so defensively toward a non-Jew who wants to obey God's commands out of a heart of love, commitment and devotion?

The Word is "Compel"

"Those who want to make a good impression outwardly are trying to compel you to be circumcised. They only reason they do this is to avoid being persecuted for the cross of Messiah.... They want you to be circumcised that they may boast about your flesh" (Galatians 6:12-14).

According to this verse, new gentile believers were being *compelled* to undergo outward circumcision as a requirement to live out their faith in Yeshua of Nazareth. This happened because some Messianic Jews were fearful of being persecuted for their faith in Yeshua.

The Galatian error was not about faith obedience to the commands of God or Torah, it was not about the Sabbath, the Festivals or pork. The Galatian error was about a 'written code' that was inhibiting the non-Jew's freedom to live in obedience to God's commands and enjoy the blessings, promises and covenants that were now theirs through Messiah.

Circumcision

In order to understand Paul's teachings more fully, it is important to understand some of the terminology he used when referring to the Body of Messiah. So often circumcision verses are quoted out of context to defend an anti-circumcision (anti-semitic) doctrine and has come to mean 'forcing someone to obey God's commands.' This is not how Paul used the terms 'circumcision' and 'uncircumcision.'

One example is found in 1 Corinthians 7:19: *"Circumcision is nothing and uncircumcision is nothing. Keeping God's commands is what counts."*

This verse has nothing to do with the act of circumcision. It compares the flesh condition of two different groups of people: the Jews who were known as 'the circumcision' and the gentiles who were known as 'the uncircumcision.' Putting in the proper terminology, 1 Corinthians states that it doesn't matter if you are a Jew or a non-Jew, what matters is keeping God's commandments. From this verse it can be reasoned that Paul never taught a gospel that encouraged disobedience, but states that both Jew and gentile have a responsibility towards keeping God's commands which include Sabbath, festivals, and dietary laws.

Paul uses the same terminology in Galatians 6:16: *"Neither circumcision nor uncircumcision means anything; what counts is a new creation."*

Again, Paul is not speaking about the act of circumcision. He is saying "Neither Jew or non-Jew means anything; what counts is a new creation." He wants all the Galatians - and those who read Galatians - to understand that our flesh condition, our DNA, has nothing at all to do with our justification before God. We all, Jew and non-Jew, need to be born again into the Kingdom of God; we all , Jew and non-Jew, need to be new creations in Messiah.

Redemption from the Law

"But when the time had fully come, God sent his Son, born of a woman, born under the law, to redeem those under law, that we might receive full rights of sons" (Galatians 4:4).

Yeshua, who was fully God, humbled Himself and came down to earth as a human being. He was born into a world of sin and death just like every other human born of a woman. He lived under the laws of human nature with the temptation of sin, but he remained sinless because his Father was not Adam, but Yahweh. He never broke one of His Father's commands as written in Torah. He lived them and taught them correctly. Because he was completely righteous and without sin, his death was sufficient payment to free all mankind, Jew and non-Jew, from the law of sin and death and give them fullness of life now and forever as sons of God.

"You are all sons of God through faith in Messiah Yeshua, for all of you who were immersed into Messiah have clothed yourself with Messiah. There is neither Jew nor Greek, slave nor free, male nor female, for you are all one in Messiah Yeshua. If you belong to Messiah, then you are Abraham's seed and heirs according to the promise" (Galatians 5:26-29).

We all live under the law of sin and death until we are redeemed by the blood of the Lamb and become sons of God. No one in Galatia or anywhere else was ever justified by laws - man's or God's. As redeemed sons of God in Messiah, there is no spiritual differentiation between Jew and non-Jew, male or female, slave or free. When we come to faith in Messiah, we become Abraham's seed and evidence of the promise God made to Abraham that all nations would be blessed through him.

Zealous for 'the law'

"For you have heard of my previous way of life in Judaism, how intensely I persecuted the church of God and tried to destroy it. I was advancing Judaism beyond many Jews of my own age and was extremely zealous for the traditions of my fathers" (Galatians 1:13-14).

In his own words, Paul says that before he met Yeshua, he persecuted new Jewish believers regarding Judaism and the traditions of the fathers that he called 'the law'. If anyone went against the 'traditions of Judaism', they were persecuted and even put to death by him. Until his Road to Damascus experience, Paul was the greatest persecutor of Messianic Jewish followers of Yeshua who stopped adhering to traditional Judaism and the religious system that it included.

Conversion through Circumcision

Before Yeshua's death and resurrection, the only way for a gentile God-fearer to join in the 'commonwealth of Israel' was to convert to Judaism. This was done through the ritual of flesh circumcision. Though circumcision was initially given as a covenant sign of faith to Abraham, over the centuries circumcision had become an outward symbol of following Judaism which included adhering to all of the manmade traditions, yokes, burdens, and slavery that went with it.

In the Temple there was a 'wall of partition' that kept the people of Israel separate from the gentiles. Though a God-fearer from the nations could come to Solomon's Colonnade to pray, they could never enter the Temple unless they had legally converted to Judaism through ritual circumcision. It was this 'wall of partition' - the law to become legally Jewish so that a person could worship God with His people - that Yeshua destroyed in his flesh.

The problem in Galatia was not that Messianic gentiles were being forced to obey the commandments of God, but that non-Messianic Jews wanted gentile believers to convert to Judaism in order to obey the commandments of God. Paul made it very clear that faith in Messiah is not about circumcision of the flesh and gentile believers did not have to convert to Judaism to live out their faith in Yeshua.

In fact, Paul taught that all believers in Yeshua of Nazareth needed to remain in the flesh condition they were in when they were saved. If they were 'uncircumcised', they were to remain as gentiles. If they were circumcised, they were to remain as Jews. It is the witness of Jew and gentile worshipping the God of Abraham, Isaac, and Jacob together in a Biblical way that is the testimony of Messiah's Body.

"Circumcision has value if you observe the law [of Judaism], but if you break the law [of Judaism], you have become as though you had not been circumcised" (Romans 2:25).

Paul says that circumcision to become lawfully Jewish has no value because it is completely dependent on observing Judaism and its 'laws'. A legalistic circumcision has no foundation in faith, but in the traditions of the fathers; the traditions of men. These traditions or laws are easily broken and then it is as if the person was no longer circumcised (a Jew).

Paul understands this thought process more than anyone because he was a Judaizer himself. Moreover, he has learned through personal experience that being legally Jewish, of which he was as a descendant of Benjamin, is not as valuable as faith in Messiah Yeshua. It is faith in Yeshua that gives all believers - circumcised or uncircumcised - not only freedom from legalistic Judaism but the *law of sin that leads to death.*

Titus and Timothy

Enter Titus. Titus was a Greek believer (non-Jew). He did not feel compelled to be circumcised. He was quite content to remain in his non-Jewish condition, but it created some problems within the congregation that needed to be dealt with.

"This matter arose because some false brothers had infiltrated our ranks to spy on the freedom we have in Messiah Yeshua and to make us slaves" (Galatians 2:4).

Notice that Paul doesn't say Jewish believers are creating the problems, but rather 'false brothers' who had 'infiltrated' the body of believers in Jerusalem. In Jerusalem 'false brothers' would most likely be Jews who had rejected the Messiah and were Judaizing OR 'false brothers' could imply that they 'pretended, bore false witness' to the Messiah. The purpose of these 'false brothers' was to 'infiltrate' the Body of Messiah and compel the gentile believers to convert to Judaism through circumcision.

Titus was a test case. Though he personally did not feel the need to be circumcised, he was still being pressured to become legally Jewish. If Paul allowed him to be circumcised and become legally Jewish, then the whole message of salvation by faith for the nations would have been nullified. It would have changed justification by faith in Yeshua to works of the flesh - heritage or conversion. The gospel to the nations with which God entrusted Paul would have ended abruptly.

But what about Timothy? He was circumcised.

Timothy had a Greek father and a Jewish mother. His mother and grandmother raised him with the Hebrew Scriptures and he knew of his Jewish heritage. For him to be circumcised was not an issue of conversion from a gentile status to a legal Jewish one because he was already 'legally Jewish' through his birth mother. Furthermore, Paul was going to take Timothy with him on his missionary journeys to places where there were unbelieving Jews. Being an uncircumcised Jew would have been a huge a stumbling block for the Jewish people to hear and receive the message of salvation in their own Jewish Messiah.

Foolish and Bewitched

"You foolish Galatians! Who has bewitched you?" (Galatians 3:1). I cannot count how many times this verse has been quoted out of context to 'correct us' when we share with people that we are obeying God's commands. It is almost funny, if it wasn't so sad. We have met and known real people who sincerely believe that obedience to God's Torah is foolish and we are somehow being led astray by a 'bewitching spirit' and have 'fallen from grace'.

Justification for sin comes through Messiah Yeshua's atonement and by faith in Him alone. There is no argument there. To compel someone to become Jewish according to a written code involving circumcision of the flesh is most definitely a foolish error when it comes to the message of justification. However, when someone is sharing that they love the Lord God and desire to obey His commands out of that love, they are not bewitched or foolish and trying to compel their friends to legally convert to Judaism. In fact, it is quite the opposite when Yeshua Himself said, *"If you love me, you will obey my commands"* (John 14:15).

Zealousness and History

"Those people are zealous to win you over, but for no good. What they want is to alienate you from us, so that you may be zealous for them" (Galatians 5:17).

The unbelieving Jews only wanted gentile believers to 'mutilate their flesh' so they could boast about them. They liked the idea of multitudes following them and their rules. It boosted their egos and made them feel important and in control of this new movement of God. They wanted to be able to say, "Look how many gentiles are converting to Judaism!" Simply put, this was the Galatian error in Paul's day: forced gentile conversion to Judaism.

It is very possible the Messianic Jews didn't really know what to do with all the gentiles coming to faith in Yeshua. Though the Council in Jerusalem outlined the responsibility of a gentile turning to God, there was no guarantee that the ways of the nations wouldn't infiltrate and destroy the Messianic faith that was just out of the womb. The Messianic Jews were well aware that Yeshua didn't preach a kingdom of legal Judaism, but they also didn't want to lose their Jewish identity. In their defense after 2000 years of gentile 'infiltration', there was some merit to their worries and struggles.

In the beginning, there were more Jewish believers than gentile ones. Gentiles grafted into the 'commonwealth of Israel' and became part of the Olive Tree of Israel. They met in synagogues on the Sabbath and were taught the Torah (Acts 15:21). They took on a Biblically 'Jewish' identity while retaining their unique calling as gentiles. As they tried to live out their new faith in a Biblical way with Biblical truths, they felt the judgment of the Judaizers (non-believing Jews) who wanted adherence to the 'written code' that a non-Jew needed to convert to Judaism. Read in this context Colossians 2:16 takes on a whole new perspective and the freedom the gentile had received in the reality of Messiah:

"Therefore do not let anyone (Jew) judge you (gentiles) by what you eat or drink, or with regard to a religious festival, a New Moon celebration or a

Sabbath day. These are a shadow of the things that were to come; the reality, however, is found in Messiah."

When the Temple was destroyed in A.D. 70, the Jewish nation was scattered all over the world. Jerusalem was no longer central to the Jewish people and the Messianic faith. The Jewish congregation of believers led by James was no longer able to be an example of faith (1 Thessalonians 2:14).

As the centuries passed and the number of gentile believers increased, there was a loss of identity with Israel and Rome took its place. The Torah no longer came out of Zion nor the Word of the LORD from Jerusalem. Anti-semitism crept into the church and edicts from various church councils, including Nicea and Laodicea, made it illegal for believers in Yeshua to follow anything that looked Jewish including Sabbath, festivals, circumcision, dietary laws.

Unfortunately for the Body of Messiah, everything in the Bible looked 'Jewish' because God had entrusted His Torah to the Jewish people to guard and protect. Eventually the Rome took the place of Jerusalem, the Hebrew Scriptures turned Greek and Latin, and the Word of the LORD became the edicts of the Popes. Gentile believers easily fell into Roman catholicism against all warnings by Paul in his letter to the Romans, while Jewish believers either converted to Roman Christianity or died. Then, of course, came the Crusades, the Inquisitions and the Holocaust.

The Modern Error in Galatia

Judaizing is a non-issue in today's Christian church as Christians are no longer part of the Messianic Jewish community. They do not attend synagogues for their teaching and instruction as did the first century believers. They are not faced with 'false brothers' who *compel* them to convert to Judaism or be cast away from the God of Israel. The Christian church no longer teaches Torah as an outline for living a life of obedience. In fact, most if not all Biblical truths that were illuminated by Yeshua and lived out by the Apostles and first gentile believers (including some Jewish traditions that Paul commended the gentile believers for keeping) have been eliminated to the point that neither Paul, the Apostles or Yeshua would recognize the Body of Messiah today.

The modern Galatian error is a now a 'gentile code' that compels Jews to follow the ways of the nations imbedded in the Christian church. Jews who come to faith in Jesus Christ lose the vision of the eternal covenants and promises given to them. They 'legally convert' to Christianity through baptism into some denomination. Because of the twisting of a misunderstood, first-century problem, the Body of Christ prohibits anything Jewish and Jewish converts attend church services on Sunday and celebrate all manner of holidays that are foreign to them and prohibited by the God of Israel in the Scriptures. In these murky waters, they have lost their identity as Jews and their call to be a light to the gentiles.

Something has 'bewitched' the church and it's not a gentile desiring to obey God's commandments. It's a fear of distorted 'legalism' that paralyzes gentiles from understanding the promise to Abraham, the fullness of the new covenant, and walking in the commandments of God. Jew and gentile still remain separated and their testimony to the world of 'one new man' is impeded by a misrepresented error that no longer has its roots in Judaizing and compelling gentiles to become legally Jewish through ritual circumcision. The modern 'Galatian error' has become the anti-semitic catch phrase for arrogance and pride over the first century Messianic Jews who dared to allow gentiles to enter the commonwealth of Israel through faith in the Jewish Messiah.

Chapter Photo: The ruins of the synagogue in Capernaum by the Sea of Galilee where Yeshua taught.

The Flesh of Swine

"I made myself accessible to those who didn't ask for me, I let myself be found by ...a nation not called by my name. I spread out my hands all day long to a rebellious people... who follow their own inclinations; a people who provoke me to my face all the time...they eat pig meat and their pots hold soup made from disgusting things" (Isaiah 65:1-4).

It's not what goes into a man that makes him unclean, it's what comes out. Jesus made all foods clean in Mark 7. Read Acts chapter 10 if you don't believe me. Peter ate with gentiles so he had to have eaten pork. What about the Council of Jerusalem? There were only four requirements for gentiles. The broken record continues to skip, skip, skip.

Mark 7

"The Pharisees and some of the teachers of law Torah who had come from Jerusalem gathered around Yeshua and saw some of his disciples eating food with 'unclean' - that is, ceremonially unwashed- hands" (verse 1).

Notice two things. First, the disciples were eating food. The word 'food' in verse 1 is the Greek word *artos* and means 'bread.' The disciples were eating bread. Second, they had not washed their hands.

"The Pharisees and all the Jews do not eat unless they give their hands a ceremonial washing, holding to the tradition of the elders" (verse 2).

Verse 2 specifically states that hand washing was a prerequisite to eating food, in this case *bread*. Handwashing was a tradition and it even involved a certain way to wash the hands.

"When they come from the marketplace they do not eat unless they wash. And they observe many other traditions, such as the washing of cups, pitchers and kettles" (verse 3).

Verse 3 explains the tradition was not just about hand washing, but about everything they used. The traditions of the elders made cooking and eating a burden because of all the rules.

"So the Pharisees and teachers of the Torah asked Yeshua, 'Why don't your disciples live according to the tradition of the elders instead of eating their food with 'unclean' hands?" (verse 4).

The question asked in Verse 4 is not about what the disciples were eating, but why they were not following the tradition of the elders in regards to hand washing. The disciples were eating with 'unclean' or unwashed hands.

"Yeshua replied, 'Isaiah was right when he prophesied about you hypocrits; as it is written" 'These people honor me with their lips, but their hearts are far from me. They worship me in vain; their teachings are but rules taught by men. You have let go of the commands of God and are holding on to the traditions of men.' ...And he said to them, 'You have a fine way of setting aside the commands of God in order to observe your own traditions" (verses 6-8).

At this point, there is no further mention of food *artos* - clean or unclean. The issue being disputed is the traditions or manmade laws that nullify the commandments of God, specifically hand washing.

Yeshua continues to give other examples where the Pharisees and teachers of Torah *"nullify the word of God by your tradition that you have handed down"* (verse 13).

"Again Yeshua called the crowd to him and said, 'Listen to me, everyone, and understand this. Nothing outside a man can make him 'unclean' by

going into him. Rather, it is what comes out of a man that makes him 'unclean" (verse 14).

In Verse 14, Yeshua never mentions food (bread). He says that nothing outside a man can make him 'unclean' referring to something greater within the tradition of hand washing.

"After he had left the crowd and entered the house, the disciples asked him about this parable. 'Are you so dull?' he asked. 'Don't you see that nothing that enters a man from the outside can make him 'unclean'? For it doesn't go into his heart, but into his stomach, and then out of his body (into the latrine)" (verses 17-19).

Yeshua does not mention food at all when he explains the parable to his disciples. He says that 'no thing' that enters a man from outside can make him 'unclean'. Consider for a moment the issue being discussed: the ceremonial hand washing. Yeshua's disciples had come from the marketplace or a grain field or even the Sea of Galilee. Their hands were dirty and they were eating bread (*artos*). This offended those leaders who held to the tradition of the elders in regards to hand washing. According to the tradition, no one is supposed to eat food, in this case bread, with dirty hands. Yeshua tells his disciples that dirty hands don't make a man dirty or unclean in his heart. The dirt that may enter his mouth on the food (bread) and will go through his body and out into the toilet.

The next verse is the one that causes all the confusion. *"In saying this, Yeshua declared all foods clean"* (verse 19). In some versions of the Bible there is a footnote clarifying this parenthetical statement was added later by translators. This means that some translator was injecting their opinion rather than taking the Scriptural events at face value.

However, on some level what the translator wrote is true. Everything created by God for food is clean. However, the specific food spoken about his this passage, *artos* or bread, has always been, and always will be clean. Some Bible versions of Mark 7 have translated *artos* as 'meat' taking this discourse into a very different direction than what Yeshua meant and his disciples understood.

What God Considers Food

Leviticus 11:1-23 outlines what God considers food for those who put their faith in His Son Yeshua and enter into a new covenant relationship with Him inclusive of obeying the commandments.

"The LORD said to Moses and Aaron, "Say to the Israelites: 'Of all the animals that live on land, these are the ones you may eat: You may eat any animal that has a divided hoof and that chews the cud. "'There are some that only chew the cud or only have a divided hoof, but you must not eat them. The camel, though it chews the cud, does not have a divided hoof; it is ceremonially unclean for you. The hyrax, though it chews the cud, does not have a divided hoof; it is unclean for you. The rabbit, though it chews the cud, does not have a divided hoof; it is unclean for you. And the pig, though it has a divided hoof, does not chew the cud; it is unclean for you. You must not eat their meat or touch their carcasses; they are unclean for you.

"'Of all the creatures living in the water of the seas and the streams you may eat any that have fins and scales. But all creatures in the seas or streams that do not have fins and scales—whether among all the swarming things or among all the other living creatures in the water—you are to regard as unclean. And since you are to regard them as unclean, you must not eat their meat; you must regard their carcasses as unclean. Anything living in the water that does not have fins and scales is to be regarded as unclean by you.

"'These are the birds you are to regard as unclean and not eat because they are unclean: the eagle, the vulture, the black vulture, the red kite, any kind of black kite, any kind of raven, the horned owl, the screech owl, the gull, any kind of hawk, the little owl, the cormorant, the great owl, the white owl, the desert owl, the osprey, the stork, any kind of heron, the hoopoe and the bat.

"'All flying insects that walk on all fours are to be regarded as unclean by you. There are, however, some flying insects that walk on all fours that you may eat: those that have jointed legs for hopping on the ground. Of these you may eat any kind of locust, katydid, cricket or grasshopper. But all other flying insects that have four legs you are to regard as unclean.'"

It is interesting to note that there are more animals mentioned in Leviticus than just the pig. There is the rabbit, the camel, and the hyrax. There are creatures in the ocean without both fins and scales that are not considered food. Birds such as vultures, ravens, hawks and owls are not considered food. Insects that walk on all fours are also not considered food. Verse 11 clearly states that 'unclean' means 'not food': *"And since you are to regard them as unclean, you must not eat their meat."*

Noah Ate Everything, Right?

Noah lived before God gave dietary instructions to the Israelites. During his lifetime and before the flood, people ate only what they produced from the earth. According to the book of Enoch, the Nephilim ate everything: every animal, bird, creature, and they even drank the blood of men. They devoured the earth and defiled humanity. God not only saw the lawlessness of the Nephilim, but also every evil inclination in the heart of mankind. He decided to wipe the human race from the earth and with them, the animals, the birds and creatures that move along the ground (Genesis 6:5-7).

Noah built an ark. Noah was told to take with him into the ark *'seven pairs of every kind of clean animal, a male and its mate, and one pair of every kind of unclean animal, a male and its mate, and also seven pairs of every kind of bird, male and female, to keep their various kinds alive throughout the earth"* (Genesis 7:2-3).

"Pairs of clean and unclean animals, of birds and of all creatures that move along the ground, male and female, came to Noah and entered the ark, as God had commanded Noah" (Genesis 7:8).

Two times it is mentioned that Noah took 'clean and unclean animals' with him on the ark. Because Noah had never eaten the meat of animals, he probably did not know the difference between clean and unclean so God brought the animals to him. From what he was shown in pairs of two or seven pairs of two, he learned and understood the difference immediately.

After the flood Noah worshipped the Lord by offering a sacrifice.

"Then Noah built an altar to the LORD and, taking some of all the clean animals and clean birds, he sacrificed burnt offerings on it. The LORD smelled the pleasing aroma and said in his heart: "Never again will I curse the ground because of humans, even though every inclination of the human heart is evil from childhood. And never again will I destroy all living creatures, as I have done" (Genesis 8:19-21).

"Then God blessed Noah and his sons, saying to them, 'Be fruitful and increase in number and fill the earth. The fear and dread of you will fall on all the beasts of the earth, and on all the birds in the sky, on every creature that moves along the ground, and on all the fish in the sea; they are given into your hands. Everything that lives and moves about will be food for you. Just as I gave you green plants, I now give you everything" (Genesis 9:3).

It would seem that now Noah could eat of every animal that came with him on the ark because *'everything that lives and moves about will be food for you.'* However, if he ate one of the pigs or rabbits or hawks, they would have immediately become extinct since there were only one male and one female of every unclean animal.

Consider also that though Noah had eaten 'all green plants,' he probably didn't eat poisonous mushrooms or poison ivy or the green leaves of rhubarb. Just as some plants were not edible or created as food, some animals had purposes other than food. The camel is a beast of burden as is a horse. A hawk cleans up dead animals on the earth while shrimp and crabs clean up the dead, decaying creatures on the sea bottom. God saying that just as Noah had green plants so he has animals is not all inclusive given the information God had revealed to him regarding the number of animals brought onto the Ark and the command to multiply on the earth.

Part of the sacrificial/offering system that was eventually established by God had to do with feeding the Levitical priesthood. They had no land of their own, no livestock, no farms. They were fed from the sacrificed animals - all of which were clean animals or animals that God created for food. It is the same for Noah. He did not sacrifice and eat unclean animals; he sacrificed and ate the clean ones which had been given to him as food. From the animals that entered the Ark, he understood what God considered meat as food and what He did not.

Making all foods clean was not the purpose of Noah's deliverance from the polluted world of the Nephilim nor was it the message of the Prophets (Moses), the Gospel preached by Yeshua or the Apostles. It was not the purpose of Peter's vision nor the conclusion of the Council of Jerusalem.

What ABOUT Peter's vision?

"About noon the following day as they were on their journey and approaching the city, Peter went up on the roof to pray. He became hungry and wanted something to eat, and while the meal was being prepared, he fell into a trance. He saw heaven opened and something like a large sheet being let down to earth by its four corners. It contained all kinds of four-footed animals, as well as reptiles and birds. Then a voice told him, "Get up, Peter. Kill and eat."

"Surely not, Lord!" Peter replied. "I have never eaten anything impure or unclean."

The voice spoke to him a second time, "Do not call anything impure that God has made clean."

This happened three times, and immediately the sheet was taken back to heaven.

While Peter was wondering about the meaning of the vision, the men sent by Cornelius found out where Simon's house was and stopped at the gate. They called out, asking if Simon who was known as Peter was staying there.

While Peter was still thinking about the vision, the Spirit said to him, "Simon, three men are looking for you. So get up and go downstairs. Do not hesitate to go with them, for I have sent them."

Peter went down and said to the men, "I'm the one you're looking for. Why have you come?" (Acts 10:9-21).

This Biblical account is about a vision, a trance, not an actual event. Just as Joseph's dreams didn't literally come true, but had spiritual meaning, so does Peter's vision.

Peter went to the roof to pray. He was hungry and had a vision of a sheet filled with all kinds of unclean animals. (In the KJV, this sheet was bound at the four corners suggesting that it was a talit or prayer shawl which adds another dimension to the 'sheet'.)

When God tells Peter to *'get up, kill and eat'*, Peter's first response is, *"I have never eaten anything impure or unclean."*

Peter's first response is refusing to eat animals that are not considered food. This seems like a strange response from one of Yeshua's disciples. Peter would have been with Yeshua when he *'made all foods clean'* in Mark 7 if, in fact, that is what Yeshua actually did. Of course, after reading Mark 7, it is pretty clear that Yeshua was not talking about clean and unclean foods, but the tradition of ceremonial hand washing. If Yeshua had during his lifetime made all foods (meats, included) clean, Peter, of all his disciples, would have known and would have had a different reaction to the voice of God. If Yeshua had, after his resurrection, made all foods clean (and there are no Scriptures to support this idea), Peter, of all the Apostles, surely would have known and had a different first response.

God speaks to Peter a second time because Peter is not understanding the vision. Even after the second time, he doesn't understand and God speaks to him a third time. It is interesting that many well-meaning, but untaught Christians immediately conclude that this vision was about eating everything as food; however Peter, who experienced the vision, was still wondering about its meaning even after being told THREE TIMES! While Peter is still thinking about the vision, some men come to visit him.

A tradition at this time was that a Jewish person would not step foot in a gentile's home. This was an understood tradition and one that Yeshua himself honored. He never went into a gentile's home. NEVER. The Centurion in Matthew 8 understood this and told Yeshua he did not need to come to his home. He knew Yeshua was a man of authority and that whatever Yeshua said would be done. Yeshua commended him for having greater faith than those in Israel.

There was also the Canaanite woman in Matthew 15 who had a demon-possessed daughter. She asked Yeshua for help and was told it was not right to take food from children and give it to the dogs. Her response was that even the dogs eat the crumbs from under their owner's table. She, too, was commended for her great faith.

It isn't until the following day at the house of a gentile man, a Roman centurion named Cornelius, that Peter begins to understand the vision. Cornelius wasn't just any gentile. He was God-fearing and righteous. He was respected by all the Jewish people with whom he came in contact. Peter is finally able to interpret the vision. In the presence of Cornelius, he understands the message of Yeshua, the message of salvation was to go to the nations which were represented by the four-footed unclean animals.

"Then Peter began to speak: "I now realize how true it is that God does not show favoritism but accepts from every nation the one who fears him and does what is right" (Acts 10:34).

Notice what Peter states: God accepts people from every nation who not only FEAR Him, but DO what is right. What does this mean? To be a God-fearing gentile meant to 'obey God's commandments.' To be 'righteous' means to 'live rightly before God'.

Cornelius was a God-fearing and righteous gentile. From his interactions and relationships with the Jewish people around him, he already understood what was food and what was not food. Cornelius's eating habits were probably similar to those of the Jews who respected him and considered him righteous! No one in Cornelius' house ever mentioned food and eating pig or shrimp because food was never the purpose of Peter's vision. It was about going to the gentiles and entering their homes with the message of Yeshua. By putting their faith in the Jewish Messiah, Cornelius and his family became filled with the Holy Spirit and were immersed in water. Soon after this, the word spread throughout Judea that the gentiles were receiving the Word of God not having pork roasts.

Let's support for a minute that Cornelius did eat unclean foods as many Christians believe. Would not is new-found faith in the Messiah of Israel along with the righteous condition of his heart give him the desire to learn the Scriptures and obey God's commandments? Would not Peter have taught him God's ordinances or even more so, the Spirit of God by writing them on Cornelius' heart? Being a gentile was never an excuse for disobedience after receiving the Spirit of God and being immersed.

Peter went up to Jerusalem and was criticized for entering the homes of gentiles and eating with them. Again, it wasn't about WHAT Peter was eating, but WHO he was eating with. Table fellowship bound people together and the leaders in Jerusalem were worried that the Scriptures were going to become watered down if Peter fellowshipped with gentile believers. Peter had to explain that the gentiles were coming to faith in Messiah and living lives of repentance. Repentance means turning back to the ways of God which would include obeying the dietary commandments in the Scriptures.

"Starting from the beginning, Peter told them the whole story ..." (Acts 11:4). When they heard the conclusion that God had baptized the gentiles with the Holy Spirit, they had no further objections.

"When they heard this, they had no further objections and praised God saying, "So then, even to Gentiles God has granted repentance that leads to life" (Acts 11:18).

It is a serious distortion of Scripture to think that Peter, a faithful Messianic Jew, would suddenly eat animals that were not created to be food in order to win gentiles to faith in Messiah. In reality, it was the gentiles who were coming to faith in the Jewish Messiah that were challenged to leave behind their pagan, unBiblical practices and live according to the commandments of God. No one ever mentioned from the first moment of Peter's vision through its interpretation in Jerusalem that suddenly it was acceptable to eat all animals - clean or unclean. Instead, they were rejoicing that the gentles were being saved.

For the kingdom of God is not a matter of eating drinking, but of righteousness, peace and joy in the Holy Spirit" (Romans 14:17).

Council of Jerusalem

Some time after Paul began his ministry to gentiles, certain people came from Judea to Antioch and were teaching believers that unless they were circumcised they could not be saved. This caused dissension within the Body, and between Paul and Barnabas. They decided to go to Jerusalem to see the apostles and elders about the matter.

The apostles and elders considered the question and resolved that gentiles did not have to be circumcised in the flesh in order to be saved. (This means that gentiles did not have to convert to Judaism through a ritual conversion of circumcision, but could remain as gentiles.) Because the elders heard that God was purifying the gentiles' hearts and anointing them with the Holy Spirit, they concluded that justification is by faith in Messiah alone. They created a 'judicial statement' and decided they should not make it difficult for gentiles who are turning to God. They came up with four *beginning* requirements.

"Instead we should write to them, telling them to abstain from food polluted by idols, from sexual immorality, from the meat of strangled animals and from blood" (Acts 15:20).

These four requirements were given to gentiles coming from a pagan culture who were turning to God through repentance. Each of these requirements were part of pagan ritual worship and had to be removed from their lives in order not to pollute the growing Body of Messiah with the ways of the nations. This was to be the *beginning* of their turning to God NOT the ONLY things they ever had to do in their walk of faith. In fact, these four requirements encompass nearly all the Torah commands given to Israel: dietary laws, sacrificial laws, sexual morality/immorality laws, and idolatry.

The next verse is rarely quoted with the four requirements, but is just as important, if not crucial, to the growth of every new believer then, as well as now:

"For the Torah of Moses has been preached in every city from the earliest times and is read in the synagogues on every Sabbath" (Acts 15:21).

This final statement embodies the life of every believer whether Jew (circumcised) or non-Jew (uncircumcised). Born again non-Jews who were turning to God attended synagogues every Sabbath not churches. They were hearing the teachings and instructions given to Moses and were being convicted, challenged, and transformed through their new circumcised hearts. It was this joining of 'circumcised' and 'uncircumcised' believers in the synagogues that testified to the 'one new man' in Messiah.

Unlike today, for the first 30 years of the Messianic community, all gentile believers were being instructed in the first five books of the Bible. They did not have Acts chapter 10. They did not have a New Testament from which to learn about God. They only had the the Torah with which to learn the commandments. They only had the Prophets and Writings to understand their new covenant Messianic faith.

At the Council of Jerusalem, there was nothing mentioned about foods and dietary changes based on what was happening with the gentiles coming to faith. No one suggested or argued that eating pork, camel or dog was now acceptable because "Jesus had died on the cross." In fact, quite the opposite was true. Sacrificing and eating unclean animals along with idol worship was not to be among the gentiles who were turning to God through repentance. New believers from the nations obeyed these requirements because Yeshua's death and resurrection had brought them into the Kingdom of God and had given them a new life.

The Real Problem with 'Porky the Pig'

Did you know that Jewish people who were forced to convert to a new religion called Christianity (via Roman catholicism) were called *maranos*? This word in Spanish means 'damned, accursed, banned and HOG'. It was applied to Spanish/Portuguese Jews when they succumbed to eating the flesh of swine in order to save their lives.

Pig in the form of pork, sausage or bacon has been used throughout Christian history to force Jewish people to convert to Christianity on pain of death. Jewish people converted to this foreign religion with a trinity of gods to avoid cruel and inhumane persecutions based

117

solely on the fact that they obeyed Yahweh's commandments: did not eat pig, circumcised their sons, and kept the Sabbath along with the Feasts of the LORD. They were forced with threat of death to disobey commands in order to reside within the Christian community as a *marano* 'pig' convert.

The whole issue of eating pork, the flesh of swine, has been and continues to be used by the enemy to keep Jewish people from truly knowing the love of God through their own Messiah. It is used (and eaten) most explicitly by people who say they know and love Jesus Christ! This is unfortunate because Jewish people are looking for a Messiah who will teach the Torah in proper perspective as Yeshua did. They do not recognize a pork eating, Sabbath breaking Christian Jesus as their deliverer and they never will.

Millennial Kingdom

"Those who consecrate and purify themselves to go into the gardens behind one of their temples and eat the flesh of pigs, rats and other unclean things - they will meet their end together with the one they follow,' declares the LORD" (Isaiah 66:17).

This Scripture from Isaiah is about the time before the new heavens and earth during the Millennial Kingdom when Yeshua will judge the nations. One of the judgments is against those who eat the 'flesh of swine' behind their temples.

Pig roasts have become more and more prevalent in church celebrations today as Christians fight for and defend (almost to their own death) the eating of the flesh of swine. Bacon has become an almost revered food and flavor. If eating pig was no longer considered something 'unclean' in the eyes of God, then Isaiah would not have prophesied that those who eat this meat behind their 'temples' will meet their end with the one they follow.

Choose this Day Who You Serve

Yeshua did not make all bread clean for he did not have to. It was already a clean food and always will be. Noah understood the difference between which animals were considered food and which were not based on the number of pairs of animals God brought to the Ark. God's dietary outline for Israel had no mention of health or undercooked meats. The only requirement was their faith expressed through obedience. Peter's vision had nothing to do with removing unclean foods from a god-fearer's diet, but was revelation that the promise to Abraham was being fulfilled - the good news of salvation was going to the nations. The Council of Jerusalem laid the foundation for gentiles who were coming to faith in Yeshua which included obeying the Torah commands about idolatry, sexual immorality and food. Finally, Isaiah prophesied what will happen to those in the future who rebel against God and His commands by eating pig meat, the flesh of swine. They will meet their end with the one they follow who cannot be the Messiah of Israel.

As Joshua told the Israelites, *"Now fear the Lord and serve him with all faithfulness. Throw away the gods your ancestors worshiped beyond the Euphrates River and in Egypt, and serve the LORD. But if serving the LORD seems undesirable to you, then choose for yourselves this day whom you will serve, whether the gods your ancestors served beyond the Euphrates, or the gods of the Amorites, in whose land you are living. But as for me and my household, we will serve the LORD"* (Joshua 24:15).

Chapter Photo: Restaurant sign in Jerusalem with 'kosher' - כשר.

The Women's Covering of Authority

"I praise you for remembering me in everything and for holding to the traditions just as I passed them on to you. But I want you to realize that the head of every man is Christ, and the head of the woman is man, and the head of Christ is God. Every man who prays or prophesies with his head covered dishonors his head. But every woman who prays or prophesies with her head uncovered dishonors her head—it is the same as having her head shaved. For if a woman does not cover her head, she might as well have her hair cut off; but if it is a disgrace for a woman to have her hair cut off or her head shaved, then she should cover her head.

"A man ought not to cover his head, since he is the image and glory of God; but woman is the glory of man. For man did not come from woman, but woman from man; neither was man created for woman, but woman for man. It is for this reason that a woman ought to have authority over her own[c] head, because of the angels. Nevertheless, in the Lord woman is not independent of man, nor is man independent of woman. For as woman came from man, so also man is born of woman. But everything comes from God.

"Judge for yourselves: Is it proper for a woman to pray to God with her head uncovered? Does not the very nature of things teach you that if a man has long hair, it is a disgrace to him, but that if a woman has long hair, it is her glory? For long hair is given to her as a covering. If anyone wants to be contentious about this, we have no other practice—nor do the churches of God" (1 Corinthians 11:2-16).

I am often asked how I defend wearing my head covering when women respond with "That was a Jewish tradition", or "I've read that and the hair is a covering," or "I'm not good enough yet," or "My husband doesn't want me to wear one," or "It's not for today," or "My pastor doesn't teach this."

Wasn't this just a Jewish tradition?

"I praise you for remembering me in everything and for holding to the traditions just as I passed them on to you..." (Verse 2).

Yes, I believe veils were a Jewish tradition, but more so a Middle Eastern tradition. According to the first verse in the passage, Paul praises the Corinthians for *holding to the traditions* just as he taught them. Even Yeshua taught that all traditions weren't bad or sinful; only the ones that nullified a commandment (Mark 7:7). Being immersed in the Jewish culture, Paul would have understood the veil from a Jewish perspective especially within the context of betrothal and marriage. However, Paul's discourse about this tradition has deeper spiritual implications.

Covering of women is found in the Bible. Rebecca covers herself in Genesis 24:65 when she is about to meet her betrothed, Isaac. It is evident that Leah was covered when she married Jacob, and for this reason, Jacob didn't note the switch of women (Genesis 29). Tamar covers herself with a veil so that Judah doesn't recognize her as his widowed daughter-in-law (Genesis 38). In the Song of Songs Chapter 4, the Lover speaks of the beauty of his Beloved's eyes behind her veil.

As the apostle to the gentiles, Paul was speaking to a congregation in Corinth which was made up of non-Jewish men and women. Whether or not there were Jewish women present, didn't matter. He didn't need to teach them about the veil for they already understood its purpose. This was a Jewish tradition being explained to the non-Jewish women who were being grafted into the commonwealth of Israel. Apparently, it was also a tradition that some of the the women of Corinth were ignoring while the rest of the congregations practiced the tradition. These congregations would include the congregations in Jerusalem, Ephesus, Galatia, Philipi, and Collosae.

"However, if anyone wants to argue about it, the fact remains that we have no such custom [of unveiling] , nor do the Messianic communities of God" (Verse 16).

This verse is often used to *argue* that after Paul spends a lot of time writing about the deeply-rooted meaning and purpose for the veil, he negates the whole teaching by stating there is *no such custom*. What he means is that there is *no such custom* for a woman to remain unveiled and they as a congregation are to '*decide for yourselves: is it appropriate for a woman to pray to God when she is unveiled? Doesn't the nature of things itself teach you that a man who wears his hair long degrades himself? But a woman who wears her hair long enhances her appearance, because her hair has been given to her as a covering"* (Verses 13-15).

In the second letter to the Corinthians, it appears that Paul's correction about the traditional veil was heeded. Even more significant is that fact that now the veil was only covering the women's heads, not their faces. This allowed both men and women to reflect the glory of God. Second Corinthians 3:18 *"So all of us, with faces unveiled, see as in a mirror the glory of the LORD; and we are being changed into his very image, from one degree of glory to the next, by the LORD of the Spirit."*

It's not for today.

I believe first and foremost every believer, and in this case, women in the Body of Messiah must address the Scriptures prayerfully with a teachable heart and mind. Second Timothy 3:16, *"All Scripture is God-breathed and is useful for teaching, rebuking, correcting, and training in righteousness, so that the man of God may be thoroughly equipped for every good work."*

Do you honestly believe that all scripture is God-breathed or only some Scriptures? Which Scriptures do you think are not for today or were not given through the Holy Spirit? Is obedience to a command (your cross) more painful than Yeshua's death by the way of the cross? Do you desire to be trained in righteousness?

We must willingly lay down our lives every day so that we can be transformed into the image of Yeshua. The bottom line to any command in the Word of God begins in the heart of the believer. If you love God and believe in the inerrancy of His Word, then you should desire to show Him your love. Rooted in love for God, every command falls into place and becomes easy through the strengthening power of His Spirit. Justification for sin by faith in Yeshua is a free gift from God; sanctification, however, comes with a price.

As a parent who desires simple obedience to a command from my children, my loving Father expects nothing less. He has precious lessons to teach us, but he can only do that after we stop making rationalizations for disobedience. Yeshua says in John 14:15, *"If you love me you will obey my commands and I will ask the Father and He will send another counselor - the Spirit of Truth."*

With every command from the Father, you must become as a child. The *why* of the command isn't always understood until you obey and even then, the reason may not become apparent until you mature. The Spirit of Truth (understanding) follows our obedience.

My covering is my hair.

Using a Greek lexicon for the word 'cover' in 1 Corinthians 11, there are two different words used. Verses 6-7 use the Greek word *katakalupto* which means "to cover oneself". This is a verb which implies an action, something the woman has to do. In Verse 15, the Greek word *peribolaion* is used denoting "something thrown around." It is a noun, an object.

If Greek is Greek to you, then read the passage changing the word *covering* to *hair* beginning with Verse 4:

"Every man who prays or prophesies with 'hair on his head' dishonors his head. And every woman who prays or prophesies 'without hair' dishonors her head - it is just as though her head were shaved."

If hair were the covering or *katakalupto*, then every man should be *without hair* or bald while praying and prophesying. Concurrently, every woman who prays or prophesies *without hair* should shave her head. How can a woman shave her head if she is without hair?

Neither concept makes sense because the Greek word for 'covering' is not *hair*. It is an action taken, not a noun. In the American Standard Version Bible, Verse 6 uses the verb form of the Greek word correctly with the phrase *let her be veiled* as *let her have hair* makes no sense.

"For if a woman is not veiled, let her also be shorn: but if it is a shame to be a woman to be shorn or shaven, let her be veiled."

Let's do the same thing with Verse 15 and the noun *peribolaion:*

"... but that if a woman has long hair, it is her glory? For long hair is given to her as "hair".

In this verse when the noun is used, *hair* is given to a woman as *hair*. This makes sense. This latter Greek word denotes that the *noun* hair is given to a woman as "something thrown around" her literal head. There is nothing a woman has to do to let her hair grow. Hair is a natural occurrence.

Divine Order

"But I want you to realize that the head of every man is Messiah, and the head of the woman is man, and the head of Messiah is God. ... A man ought not to cover his head since he is the image and glory of God; but woman is the glory of man. For man did not come from woman, but woman from man; neither was man created for woman, but woman for man ..." (Verses 3, 7).

I put these verses together to show that God's divine order of God, Messiah, Man and Woman is found in the creational order. Man was created first in the image of God in order to glorify his Creator (Genesis 1:27). Because of this, he is not to cover his head. Then, woman was created from the flesh of man for the purpose of being the man's glory in Paradise.

Praying and Prophesying

"But every woman who prays or prophesies ..." (Verse 5).

Praying and prophesying are not cultural or traditions. They are spiritual actions done by believers in Messiah.

What specifically is praying and prophesying? I heard a pastor speak on this passage a long time ago and I thought he gave simple and logical definitions. I use them because I like them. Praying is talking to God and prophesying is talking about God. The Amplified Bible elaborates on what it is to prophesy in this verse: *"Any woman who (publicly) prays or prophesies (teaches, refutes, reproves, admonishes, or comforts) when she is bareheaded dishonors her head; it is the same as (if her head were) shaved."*

Before Yeshua came, Jewish men and women prayed and prophesied separately as is seen within the Temple design with a court specifically designed for women. It is the same today in an ultra-orthodox synagogue as well as at the Western Wall in Jerusalem. Men and women are separated and pray on different sides of a barrier fence. However, in Messiah, men and women are co-heirs through faith in Yeshua. There is no 'Jew or gentile, male nor female'. This is significant to the unity of worship of God through Messiah in the congregation that includes men and women, Jew and non-Jew praying and prophesying.

"As in all the congregations of the saints, women should remain silent in the churches. They are not allowed to speak ..." (1Corinthians 14:33-34).

Though this verse may sound harsh toward women, it is meant to avoid what is happening in the church today - *uncovered* women praying and prophesying aloud, giving testimonies, leading worship and teaching men. Many times the authority taken by women leads to complacent, unspiritual men. This is contrary to the *line of authority* established by God. Women, who want the authority to pray and prophesy publicly are to be covered or should remain silent. This allows for men to be the leaders they are supposed to be in the realm where they are supposed to lead. Whatever your personal conviction about these verses, if you are a woman in the Body of Messiah and desire greater spiritual leadership from your husband, I counsel you to seek the Lord seriously about remaining silent when in a congregational setting or covering your head.

If a woman is to remain silent in a public assembly, when does she teach, refute, reprove, admonish or comfort?

"Likewise, teach the older women to be reverent in the way they live, not to be slanderers.... then they can train the younger women to love their husbands and children, to be self-controlled and pure, to be busy at home, to be kind and to be subject to their husbands, so that no one will malign the word of God" (Titus 2:3-5).

A woman's place of authority is in the home where she is to be busy, teach and train her children, an be subject to her husband. While doing these profound spiritual works, she will be praying for her children and speaking the Scriptures to them. She will ultimately be blessing her husband as the helpmeet she was created to be and no one will malign the word of God. As she grows older, she has the opportunity to encourage the younger women God brings into her home.

What about women's conventions, rallies, and seminars? Many of these gatherings are not about encouraging women to be set apart for the Lord and strengthening them in the wisdom of Scripture. Most are emotional, feel-good milk toast formula messages interspersed with comedy and the mocking of the woman's soul, her home, her husband and her children. Take a closer look at the women who are leading these seminars and most of them are shorn, something that is called 'shameful' by God. When it comes to attending women's conferences, make sure the leaders are really *virtuous women* preaching and teaching the Word of God, encouraging you to become a Proverbs 31 woman warrior and not tickling your itching ears. Those who are leading, teaching, training, and rebuking should have their heads covered.

I'm not submissive enough to wear a covering.

I was told many years ago by a woman who didn't cover that *I* needed a covering because *I* wasn't submissive to my husband. At first I was hurt by her accusation because wives are to submit to their husbands as to the Lord and I didn't want to be falling short (Ephesians 5:22). However, if all women didn't have a problem with submitting to their husbands, God wouldn't have commanded us to do it. With that reasoning, the covering became a blessed reminder to honor my husband as I would the Lord. It wasn't long after our discussion that this woman began attending a church that taught the woman's covering. She had to choose whether or not to wear what she considered *a sign of submission.*

The Scripture doesn't give any prerequisite to wearing a covering. Nowhere does 1 Corinthians 11 even suggest that the woman's covering is a sign of submission to her husband or that she has to perfect *submission* before she wears it.

Sign of Authority

"It is for this reason [creational order] that a woman ought to have a sign of authority on her head ..." (verse 10).

This particular understanding of the veil was taught to me by the Spirit long after I put it on my head. As with many of God's commands, understanding doesn't come until there is obedience. At this point, let me say that wearing a head covering has nothing to do with salvation. This is an act of obedience after salvation, a step in sanctification that makes a woman more like Messiah. It becomes a blessing when a woman exercises her faith in God by covering.

When a woman covers her head, she acknowledges her submission to the divine order that God has established for her at Creation: God, Messiah, Man, Woman. If you follow this divine order to its literal conclusion, a woman should be taking her prayers to the man and the man to Messiah and Messiah to God.

In Messiah, however, a woman is a spiritual co-heir with man and can pray directly to God, the Father through Yeshua. She can prophesy about God to those He brings in her life just as a man does. She can make disciples from all nations and take authority over the enemy (Matthew 28:18-20, Luke 10:19). Because she has been given equal authority in the spiritual realm, a woman puts on a *sign of authority* so that it will be evident that such overwhelming power comes from God and not from herself (2 Corinthians 4:7).

In the practical realm of my life, as I teach my children at home, I wear the sign of authority so that my children know that God, Yeshua, and Daddy have put me in the position of teaching them and praying with them. It also shows them that I don't have to ask permission for every little thing that I plan to do. Authority has been given me by my head, my husband, and we're both under the authority of Messiah and God. There have been times that I have had to do spiritual battle with and for my children. As I wear the *sign of authority,* I am showing forth not only God's divine order, but the power He has given to me as a woman of faith.

Some versions of the Bible translate the veil to a *sign of power.* What kind of power does a woman, a prophetess have when wearing a veil? Though the power was misused, Ezekiel 13:20-22 gives a glimpse into the power behind the veil:

'Therefore this is what the Sovereign Lord says: I am against your magic charms with which you ensnare people like birds and I will tear them from your arms; I will set free the people that you ensnare like birds. **I will tear off your veils and save my people from your hands, and they will no longer fall prey to your power.** *Then you will know that I am the Lord.* **Because you disheartened the righteous with your lies,** *when I had brought them no grief, and* **because you encouraged the wicked not to turn from their evil ways and so save their lives ...."**

God says that he will tear off the veils of false prophetesses in order to save His people from their power. The fact that the veil is a *sign of power* over people becomes clear. Even more telling is that when women falsely prophesy (tell lies) and encourage wickedness (lawlessness), their veils are removed. Up until the 1960s women wore hats in church. Then came the women's liberation movement that infiltrated not only society, but the church. Could the fact that the head covering is missing from American Christian women today suggest that it was God Himself who removed the *sign of power* from women because they forsook His ways? God won't tolerate false prophetesses in His Kingdom any more than He tolerated false prophets in Israel.

Because of the Angels

"For this reason and because of the angels, the woman ought to have a sign of authority on her head" (Verse 10).

For this reason follows the outline of creational order already discussed. *And* adds another dimension to the reason for a woman's covering - *because of the angels.*

What are some things we know about angels. They are created beings (Colossians 1:16). They ascend and descend from heaven (Genesis 28:12). They stand in the presence of God (Job 1:6). They obey God's will (Psalm 103:20). They minister to those who inherit salvation (Hebrews 1:14). They will separate the wicked from the righteous (Matthew 13:49). They never die (Luke 20:36). They are in submission to Yeshua who is at the Right Hand of God (1 Peter 3:22). They long to know the gospel as it has been given to mankind (1 Peter 1:12). They guard the congregations of Messiah (Revelation 1:20). They will be judged by men (1 Corinthians 6:3). They give signs and need signs (Luke 2:12, 1 Corinthians 11:10).

Though Paul is not specific about the reason the *sign of authority* is needed *because of the angels,* they obviously need one. Angels, unlike God, cannot see or know what is in our hearts and minds. Perhaps the angels need the *sign of authority* so they can recognize a woman who has placed herself willingly within God's divine order. What if when it comes to separating the wicked from the righteous, the woman's head covering sets her apart from the unrighteous? What if the angels in the spiritual realm are put into a state of confusion when an uncovered woman prays or prophesies and they can't battle for her in the heavenly realm? Psalm 91 says *"He will command his angels concerning you to guard you in all your ways...."* How do angels know the women to guard, the women who have inherited salvation?

There is another group of angels that Paul may be referring to as well. The fallen ones.

Jude Verse 6 (Amplified Bible): *"And the angels who did not keep (care for, guard, and hold to) their positions of authority (own first place of power) but abandoned their own home (proper dwellings) - these he has kept in darkness, bound with everlasting chains for judgment on the great Day."*

Notice that some angels did not keep their first place of authority, but abandoned their proper dwelling place and went somewhere else. They didn't value their *first place of power* and *abandoned their own home.* Because of this, they are being *kept in darkness, bound with everlasting chains* waiting for judgment. Could *because of the angels* have something to do with these angels?

Jude actually quotes these verses from the Book of Enoch as there was no 'canon of Scripture' when he was writing.

"Go and make known to the Watchers of heaven who have abandoned the high heaven, the holy eternal place, and have defiled themselves with women" (1 Enoch 12:4).

"For what reason have you abandoned the high, holy, and eternal heaven; and slept with women and defiled yourselves with the daughters of the people....I did not make wives for you for the proper dwelling place of spiritual beings of heaven is heaven" (1 Enoch 15:3, 7).

"Bind Azazel hand and foot and throw him into the darkness....He covered his face in order that he may not see light; and in order that he may be sent into the fire on the great day of judgment" (1 Enoch 10:4-6).

"Bind Semjaza and the others who are with him, who fornicated with the women, that they will die together with them in all their defilement...Bind them for seventy generations underneath the rocks of the ground until the day of their judgment and of their consummation, until the eternal judgment is concluded" (1 Enoch 10:11-12:).

From the verses in Enoch, the fallen angels are most likely those spoken of in Genesis before the flood. These are the angels who left their place of authority in the heavenly realm and came to earth. They had sexual relations with the daughters of men and gave birth to giants. There are some allusions in the Book of Enoch that these angels were attracted to women's beautiful long hair. Could the woman's head covering be a *sign* to the angels that this woman is 'off limits' to their seductive powers? Could the covering of her hair be a woman's protection as the world enter the 'days of Noah' again? Could the covering actually be a protection *for the angels* that have not fallen, but may be tempted?

In this modern feminist era, women need to understand what abandoning their their husbands, children, and homes means in the eyes of God. He uses the angels as an example to those who refuse to accept their first position of authority. Believing they have been liberated from the bondage of God's divine order, women leave their homes for church leadership and worldly careers. They pass the fruit of this disobedience onto their children. They lack discernment and live in darkness, bound by spiritual chains that may eventually cost them and their children (daughters) protection. *Because of the angels* gives the woman's head covering definitive spiritual significance.

The Glory of God, Man and Woman

"A man ought not to cover his head, since he is the image and glory of God; but woman is the glory of man. ... that if a woman has long hair, it is her glory?" (Verses 7,15).

The Hebrew word for 'glory' is *kavod* and brings with it the idea of 'something heavy' or 'falling down upon.' In Greek, the word 'glory' is *doxa* and means 'great honor, praise and splendor' specifically in reference to people. It also carries with it the idea of delight. Combining the Hebrew and Greek definitions, glory is the honor, praise and splendor falling down upon the people of God bringing Him delight.

Using this terminology, man is the delight and splendor of God, woman is the delight and splendor of man, and hair is the splendor of woman. In the natural realm, God gives women hair in which to delight. How many women spend unending hours and wads of money fixing their hair for church? What are the motives behind beautiful hair during worship? Make other women jealous? Entice men?

However, when a woman covers herself, she chooses to cover her own glory and protect men. God wants men made in His image to pray and prophesy without distraction. Hair is very seductive to men, and we have seen even seductive to angels. Women with uncovered long hair are mostly likely leading some man into lust of the flesh or testing the ministering angels. Is that what a Godly woman wants to be doing in a church setting? Is it worth stumbling a brother because of your hair?

Many years ago, I had a man in church ask me why I covered my head when I had such beautiful hair. I responded with, "Why are you looking at my hair when you should be worshiping the Lord?" He was embarrassed and remained silent, and my hair was covered! How many men are distracted in church because of the woman's unwillingness to follow a simple ordinance?

I once met an elderly Jewish woman who was the wife of a rabbi. She was not saved, but she was blessed by my covering. She was awed that I, a gentile woman, would cover myself in the presence of a holy God. It actually brought tears to her eyes. I had never really been enlightened to that aspect of the covering. For me, it suddenly becamse symbolic of Moses taking off his shoes because he was standing on holy ground or wearing a veil because the glory of God was so powerful that no one could look at him. My covering touched her heart enough to open the door for me to share Yeshua, the Jewish Messiah and salvation, with her.

God doesn't want our glory, our delight to be shining in the sanctuary. He wants His, and man is His glory. There is something magnificent about acknowledging God's holiness by covering our hair and allowing His glory to fall powerfully and without distraction.

The Age of Accountability

I have had some women question the age or marital status when a covering should be worn. I looked up *woman* in my Greek lexicon, but the word *woman* in I Corinthians 11 wasn't listed. So, I am depending on the Spirit of God to show me the answer to this question. Logically, I would think it should include all women, not just married women. I say this because divine order shouldn't just apply to married women. Divine order is a command for all women who are part of God's Kingdom. If the passage were only for married women, single women would be free to live out of God's divine order. This is foolishness because a woman should always be (or at least used to always be) under the authority of a man, whether it's her husband, father, or brother. The *sign* that a single woman knows and accepts the order of headship is just as important as a married woman accepting that order.

At what age should a single woman wear a veil if the ordinance is for all women? I would think when she enters womanhood. In the Old Testament, a boy became a man at 12. I would assume that a girl became a woman around 12, too. At this time, I would present the Scripture to a young woman and then let the Lord do His work in her heart regarding the veil. She needs to hear and be informed of the passage from an early age so that she has time to be challenged by God and changed by His Holy Spirit. If we force or require a young woman to wear a veil, then her heart is not at the bottom of the issue.

My husband doesn't want me to wear a covering.

Most women have read the passage, but want to continue in their rebellion. They love their hair and don't want to cover it. They may have tried to wear one, but it slips off. Maybe they are praying for the 'right time' that never comes. Many times women use their husbands as an excuse for not wearing the head covering.

Of course your husband doesn't want you covered. You are his glory, his delight. He loves your long hair. It is attractive to him. This is good and right. However, when it comes to the glory of God that should be honored, it is his own flesh desires that keep him from allowing you to obey. This is sin.

From what I read in 1 Corinthians 11, wearing a covering is not up for discussion between husbands and wives, men and women. God desires obedience in all areas of our lives and this one area is no exception. Though we are commanded to submit to our husbands, should our husbands encourage us to dishonor this tradition if we are truly being led by the Spirit?

If this is your case and you truly desire to cover, I would suggest you be in earnest prayer for your husband's eyes to be opened to the deeper meaning of the Scripture. Pray for his heart to be changed regarding this unique tradition given to women. Pray for him have the glory of God fall on him.

I was blessed that my husband bought me my first covering. This is not always the case. Most husbands shy away from the woman's covering for the reasons already mentioned and others, too.

Several years ago my husband has asked if I would remove my covering when we're just hanging out at home. He does enjoy my hair and as his wife, I submitted to that request. However, whenever we have guests or I leave my home, I am covered because I have no idea if God is going to call on me to pray or prophesy and I want to have His *sign of authority.*

My pastor doesn't teach this.

Why isn't the woman's head covering taught in most American churches today? Simply put, feminism in the Body of Messiah. Feminism is as old as Eve picking the fruit, taking it to Adam, pressuring him to do what she wants and he submits. They both die in disobedience.

It's in a woman's sin nature not to be submissive and it is fed by a culture of women's equal rights. Pastors know this and fear it because feminism is Satan's stronghold in America. How many pastors want to lose their jobs over a woman's head covering? These male leadership insecurities cause women in the Body to miss an incredible blessing and cause unnecessary confusion in the divine order.

Romans 13:2 states *"He who rebels against the authority is rebelling against what God has instituted, and those who do so will bring judgment on themselves."* This verse is talking about governing authorities that have been established by God. First Corinthians 11 outlines one such governing authority and the sign that shows it is being heeded.

Personal Battles and Some Thank Yous

This has not been an easy walk for me. I have been attacked by women, men and especially pastors. I have been called names and been told I was a heretic. I have had my moments of rebellion and disobedience. There were times I'm sure I had an attitude of self-righteousness and coercion because I was weary of standing alone. Sometimes the Lord gently reminded me of my falling away and brought me back; other times He had to jolt me with guilt and sorrow for my disobedience to the truths He has so generously taught me through the head covering.

I know wearing a veil has brought attention to me, but that is part of my witness to what God has done in my heart and life. People should know and see I am a follower of Messiah and not of the world. I am not to make my sisters stumble into sin, but I am to challenge them into good works. If I have stumbled anyone into sin through my covering, I ask forgiveness. My prayer has always been that women of God would be convicted by the Holy Spirit and desire a deeper understanding of being Messiah's pure and holy bride.

Judy and Shelley, you blessed me on that Tabernacles day. Mr. African pastor, (God knows your name), you blessed and encouraged me, too. I learned that at least in the greater Body of Messiah around the world, I have covered sisters. Carol, you encouraged me in ways that you will never completely understand. Thank you. Divine intervention happens when we submit to the Living Word. That sword surely is two-edged. Pam, it was a joy to meet someone through the internet (in the early years) who willingly wore a veil in a church that taught the covering without coercion. The heart of your daughter was a blessing to me. Kathy, thank you for receiving my Passover gift and wearing it expectantly. Kay, thank you for the beautiful silk head covering that came from your heart. Lucette, thank you for telling me to "stand firm". I know there will continue to be times ahead where I am persecuted, challenged and even discouraged by believers because of my head covering. Theresa, thank you for asking so many questions and being the watering can. Renee, what can I say but praise God for your conviction that took me deeper into this walk. Calling me a faithful sister in your book was quite an honor. Teresa, it was worth the wait for a like-minded sister. Pastors Dave, Doug and Greg, thank you for all the persecution. Your words and actions only helped to challenge me to pray and ask my heavenly Father why the head covering incites judgment, mockery and disrespect among male leaders. I bless you with revelation, understanding, wisdom, and true discipleship in the Word of God.

Finally, thank you Yeshua for giving me such an incredible walk and testimony. I have an answer now for anyone who asks why I wear the head covering. Simply, I obey the Word of God.

Chapter Photo: Wearing one of my many assortment of head coverings in Mitchell, Nebraska during the Feast of Tabernacles.

Tithe to Who?

"Then Melchizedek king of Salem brought out bread and wine. He was priest of God Most High, and he blessed Abram, saying, 'Blessed be Abram by God Most High, Creator of heaven and earth, and praise be to God Most High, who delivered your enemies into your hand'. Then Abram gave him a tenth of everything" (Genesis 14:18-20).

Abram heard that five kings had taken his nephew captive along with all the possessions and food of Sodom and Gomorrah. He gathered 318 of his trained men and went in pursuit of them. They attacked and routed them. They recovered everything and retrieved Lot and his possessions. In the Valley of Shaveh, the King's Valley, the King of Sodom met him and asked him to return the people and keep the goods for himself. Abram, on oath to God, refused to give the King of Sodom anything.

The King of Salem, Melchizedek, also also met him. Melchizedek, whose name in Hebrew means 'King of Righteousness', brought out bread and wine - a shadow of the promised covenant that would come through Abram's seed. Together Abram and this priest of the 'most high God' fellowshipped. Melchizedek blessed Abram by the Creator of heaven and earth who delivered his enemies into his hand. In response, Abram gave this king a *tenth of everything* as dividing the spoils of war with rulers and religious leaders was commonplace.

The voluntarily giving of one-tenth of a part of something to another is called a *tithe*. The custom is as ancient as this exchange between

Abram and Melchizedek. It is also a custom that became part of the Torah given to Israel. *"The Torah requires the descendants of Levi who become priests to collect a tenth from the people - that is their fellow Israelites - even though they also are descended from Abraham. This man (Melchizedek), however, did not trace his descent from Levi, yet he collected a tenth from Abram and blessed him who had the promises"* (Hebrews 7:4-6).

Levitical Priesthood

From Abraham came Isaac and Jacob. Levi was the third son of Jacob from Leah. From Levi came the Tribe of the Levites who eventually became the priesthood of God because of their faithfulness in the wilderness. The Levites were given duties within the Tent of Meeting along with the responsibilities surrounding offerings and sacrifices. Their duties continued throughout their generations whenever there was a Temple where all Israel gathered together.

The Levites, unlike the other tribes, were not given a land inheritance and were dispersed throughout the land of Israel. Because they owned no land, they had no way of growing their own food or raising their own livestock. God commanded the *tithe* be given to them as their inheritance payment for doing His work among the people of Israel. *Tithes* of grain and oil became their sustenance along with the meat of a firstborn offspring of a cow, sheep, or a goat.

"I give to the Levites all the tithes in Israel as their inheritance in return for the work they do while serving at the tent of meeting. ...They will receive no inheritance among the Israelites. Instead, I give to the Levites as their inheritance the tithes that the Israelites present as an offering to the LORD. That is why I said concerning them: 'They will have no inheritance among the Israelites'" (Numbers 18:21, 23-24).

In turn, the Levitical priests gave a *tithe* to the LORD. From everything they received from the Israelites, they were to present the best portion to God. In order that Aaron and his sons would have sustenance, God gave His portion to Aaron. They were to consider it holy and all Aaron's sons and daughters were to eat it as their share of the inheritance.

"The LORD said to Moses, "Speak to the Levites and say to them: 'When you receive from the Israelites the tithe I give you as your inheritance, you must present a tenth of that tithe as the LORD's offering. ...From these tithes you must give the LORD's portion to Aaron the priest. You must present as the LORD's portion the best and holiest part of everything given to you" (Numbers 18:25-29).

Tithes went to the Levitical priests because they were the overseers of God's holy system. There were different divisions with different responsibilities. Some ministered at the Altar of Sacrifice with burnt offerings, fellowship offerings, sin offerings, guilt offerings and drink offerings while others led worship, supervised weights and scales, witnessed legal agreements, and made judicial decisions. The greatest responsibility was reading the commands of God to Israel in such a way that the people understood it and could obey it.

"The Levites - Yeshua, Bani, Sherebiah, Yamin, Akkub, Shabbethai, Hodiah Maaseiah, Kelita, Azariah, Yozabad, Hanan and Pelaiah - instructed the people in the Torah while the people were standing there. They read from the Book of Torah of God, making it clear and giving the meaning so that the people understood what was being read" (Nehemiah 8:7-8).

"In keeping with the ordinance of his father, David, he appointed the divisions of the priests for their duties, and the Levites to lead the praise ..." (2 Chronicles 8:14).

"In Jerusalem also, Jehosaphat appointed some of the Levites, priests and heads of Israelite families to administer the Torah of the LORD and to settle disputes" (2 Chronicles 19:8).

"Hezekiah assigned the priests and Levites to divisions - each of them according to their duties as priests ... to give thanks and to sing praises at the gates of the LORD's dwelling" (2 Chronicles 31:2).

Unfortunately, the priests did not always do what they were called to do. They began to steal from the people and did violence to God's Torah and profaned His holy things.
"They do not distinguish between the holy and the common; they teach there is no difference between the unclean and clean; and they shut their

eyes to the keeping of my Sabbaths, so that I am profaned among them" (Ezekiel 22:25-26).

Since A.D. 70 and the Roman invasion of Jerusalem, there has been no Temple. Only the walls and over tuned stones where it once stood remain. There is no altar of sacrifice or a Holy Place that requires a Levitical priesthood. The priests have been scattered throughout the world waiting for the day when there is another Temple and God's promise of the eternal priesthood to Aaron is restored (Numbers 18:8).

Because of the destruction of the Temple along with the misunderstanding that God is through with the Levitical priesthood, many Christian leaders wrongly teach that one priesthood has been eternally replaced with another, that some old divine order of worship has been replaced with a newer one.   They use the reasoning that all of God's instructions were too difficult to keep and an unnecessary bondage that Jesus had to come to remove everything found in Torah … well, almost everything.   They still teach the *tithe*.

The Priesthood of Melchizedek

"But you are a chosen people, a royal priesthood, a holy nation, a people belonging to God, that you may declare the praises of him who called you out of darkness into his wonderful light" (2 Peter 2:9).

As believers, we are called the royal priesthood. We get our royal status from Yeshua whose Kingly lineage comes through Judah and King David. We get our priestly status from Yeshua as High Priest in the order of Melchizedek (Psalm 110:4, Hebrews 5:6,10; 6:20). This is the same "King of Righteousness" to whom Abram tithed in Salem (Jerusalem) before Levi, his great-grandson, was born. Because the *tithe* existed long before the Levitical priesthood, the idea of the *tithe* still has value, but only in the realm of it's ordained purpose for priests of the Most High God.

According to God's command, *tithes* were given to priests who ministered in the Temple, offered praises to God and taught His Torah. *Tithes* were given to those who taught the difference between the unclean and the clean, who distinguished between the holy and the profane and who did not shut their eyes to God's Sabbaths and other 'appointed times.'

In steps the royal priesthood redeemed and sanctified not by the blood of animals, but by the blood of Yeshua of Nazareth, the Son of God. The royal priesthood under the authority of Yeshua, the High Priest, is commanded to equip the man of God through teaching, rebuking, correcting and training in righteousness with the God-breathed Scriptures, the Torah, Prophets and Writings (2 Timothy 2:16).

It would follow that the modern-day *tithe* should be given to those who teach the Torah, to those who correctly handle the word of Truth, dividing it correctly. However, it is very difficult to find such leaders in a walk of faith as expected by the royal priesthood, a much higher calling than the Levitical priesthood. Most church leaders do not use the full counsel of God's Word from Genesis through Revelation. They do not teach righteous living through obedience to God's commandments.

If they do, they pick and choose which commandments work for them and promote their personal and financial agenda. They keep their followers walking in darkness by not lighting the lamp of the Word for their paths (Psalm 119:105). Worse yet, modern-day pastors do severe violence to God's Torah by teaching lawlessness (1 Peter 4:17). Consequently, God's name is not only profaned throughout the world, but within the hearts and minds of the Temples of His Holy Spirit. Should such leaders, pastors and teachers receive God's *tithes*? Was the command for the *tithe* to be given to them?

Gifts and Offerings

Our family has struggled with the *tithe* for years especially when it comes to giving it to church institutions and pastors who have judged our walk of faith. How can we give teachers who say the 'law is done away with' the *tithes* that are commanded in the Torah? How can we financially support leaders who do not distinguish between the holy and the profane, teach there is no difference between the unclean and clean, and shut their eyes to the keeping of God's holy days? It was through prayer and the guidance of the Spirit that we searched the Scriptures and found Biblical alternatives for *tithing* the non-existent priesthood.

"Religion that God our Father accepts as pure and faultless is this: to look after orphans and widows in their distress ... " (James 1:27).

James says that believers should look after widows and the fatherless. In an agricultural society, the corners of fields were left for the widow, the fatherless and the foreigner (Deuteronomy 24:19). Though we may not have a field with corners that we can designate for the poor, we do have the means to help them in the time of their distress. We can watch children, help with housework, buy food, pay a bill, take them to the doctor, or just be a comfort in the days of their sorrow. We have a huge responsibility to look after these unique people because we do not live in a culture that encourages supporting the widow and orphan; we leave it to the government. We should never be found on the wrong side of the One who *"defends the cause of he fatherless and the widow, and loves the foreigner residing among you giving them food and clothing..."* (Deuteronomy 10:18).

There is nothing wrong with giving to ministries that take care of orphans. However, we have a personal standard that it must not only teach the children about Yeshua and salvation, it must also teach them about God's commandments. We do not support any humanistic, philanthropic outreach. Though they are noble, they are not bringing glory to the Creator of the Universe. Christian ministry outreaches like World Vision and Compassion International are wonderful as they reach children with the message of salvation. Unfortunately, they don't meet the standards our family has maintained for support as they refrain from teaching the commands of God and take some unBiblical doctrines of the American church to these children. Whatever you choose to do, do it for God's glory and be convinced in your own mind.

"Share with the Lord's people who are in need. Practice hospitality" (Romans 12:12-14).

"Do not forget to show hospitality to strangers, for by so doing, people have shown hospitality to angels without knowing it" (Hebrews 13:2).

These are two other ways to give to the Lord as part of the royal priesthood. Sharing our material goods with those who are in need and practicing hospitality to strangers shows that we live the truth in our lives as we help and encourage people who are homeless, jobless, and penniless (3 John 1:8).

Hospitality is a lost art in today's culture of busy-ness. We have found that by guarding the Biblical Sabbath, we always have an evening/day available to invite people into our home for a meal. Sharing our material goods can be very challenging because there is no guarantee that it will be appreciated (even if it's only a meal). We have experienced criticism numerous times when we have been hospitable and treated others generously; however, because we know that God works everything for His glory, we continue to step out and bless, encourage and offering hospitality.

Paul suggests another way of *tithing* citing examples of what the gentile congregations in Asia Minor and Galatia did. They gave their *tithes* to the believers in Jerusalem. Originally, a *tithe* per year was to go to Jerusalem so Paul recommends that the gentiles who have come to faith in Messiah set aside money on the first day of the week (never collected on Sabbath) and give their collections to Messianic Jews in Jerusalem. He reasons *"the Gentiles have shared in the Jews' spiritual blessings, they owe it to the Jews to share with them their material blessings"* (Romans 15:27).

"Now about the collection for the Lord's people: Do what I told the Galatian churches to do. On the first day of every week, each one of you should set aside a sum of money in keeping with your income, saving it up, so that when I come no collections will have to be made. Then, when I arrive, I will give letters of introduction to the men you approve and send them with your gift to Jerusalem" (1 Corinthians 16:1-3).

"For Macedonia and Achaia were pleased to make a contribution for the poor among the Lord's people in Jerusalem. They were pleased to do it, and indeed they owe it to them. For if the Gentiles have shared in the Jews' spiritual blessings, they owe it to the Jews to share with them their material

blessings. So after I have completed this task and have made sure that they have received this contribution..." (Romans 15:26-28).

"And in these days prophets came from Jerusalem to Antioch. Then one of them, named Agabus, stood up and showed by the Spirit that there was going to be a great famine throughout all the world .... Then the disciples, each according to his ability, determined to send relief to the brethren dwelling in Judea" (Acts 11:27-29).

Giving to ministries in Jerusalem is one that modern-day believers can actually do with the restoration of the state of Israel. There are many ministries not just in Jerusalem, but in the Land that need support, especially those who are Messianic Jews trying to bring the message of Yeshua to their own people. Poverty abounds in Israel especially with immigrants. Some of the ministries in Israel that we have supported over the years include Dugit Messianic Outreach Center in Tel Aviv, Shiloh Israel Children's Fund for child victims of war and terrorism, the IDF soldiers, the Magen David Adom or the Israeli Red Cross, Vision for Israel run by Messianic Jews Barry and Batya Segal, Heart of G-d, a family of musicians who encourage Jewish people around the world to make 'aliyah', and Israel Vision - Jerusalem Vistas a media ministry who sent us a prayer map with a street in the Old City of Jerusalem for which we prayed.

Abram, our father shared a tenth of his goods with the King of Salem, Melchizedek, the priest of God who was eternal (Hebrews 7:3). Like our father Abraham, we should *tithe* to those who are 'kings of righteousness' within the Kingdom of God who teach the Torah. Or, as Paul suggests, we should give to our Messianic Jewish brothers and sisters in Jerusalem because they have preserved and guarded the ways of God allowing us to know the riches of His inheritance.

Chapter Photo: Western Wall at night, Jerusalem, Israel.

Ways of the Nations

"This is what the LORD says: 'Do not learn the ways of the nations ..." (Jeremiah 10:2).

When Israel finally entered the Promised Land, God instructed them not to learn the 'abominable practices of the nations.' The word 'nations' in this verse means non-Hebrew people. Non-Hebrew people were called *goy* or gentiles. The word *goy* also carried with it the idea of pagans and pagan practices. The pagan practices of the nations were called abominations and God hated them; the practices disgusted Him.

As a gentile or one of the nations called into a relationship with the God of Israel, it is difficult to see and accept that Christian holidays have spiritually pagan roots. We have been taught that what we think in our heart matters more than what we actually do and participate in forgetting that our hearts are deceitful and wicked (Jeremiah 17:9). We are taught that freedom includes that personal interpretation for practices is the standard for what is right and wrong rather than the Word of God. This mindset could be compared to the days in Israel when everyone did what was right in their own eyes. That time period was called Judges! According to Romans 11:16, if a root of something is holy then so are the branches that come from it, but that also suggests the converse is true: if the roots are pagan and unholy, then what grows as a beautiful tree from those roots is also pagan and unholy.

This chapter of the 'inherited lies' is going to bring out the worthless idols and false gods still embraced by the nations today and defended by the largely gentile Christian church under the pretext of 'that's not what it means to me' rather than looking at 'what it means to God'.

Even more indefensible is telling Jews who come to know the Messiah of Israel that they should also embrace these practices. Writing as a gentile who has left these pagan practices behind through many challenges and spiritual battles, it breaks my heart to hear Messianic Jewish ministries in America suggest to new Jewish followers of Yeshua that they should mix the holy and the profane as part of some restoration between Jews and gentile. This is just not Biblically sound and God's chosen people should not combine their rich spiritual heritage with the ways of the nations around them.

If you are not interested in learning about the unholy roots of your cherished holidays, then this chapter is not for you. If you are ready to come face to face with the other gods and idols rooted in Christian history, then proceed.

All Hallows Eve

This time of year brings cooler weather, autumn leaves and the harvest of corn. Fall is such a special season. In the midst of the pumpkins and puffy clouds, there is an air of excitement that arises from the celebration of Halloween. Every year that excitement is intertwined with the fear and anxiety of child abductions, poisoned candy, and destruction of public property. Every year this celebration of darkness continues to grow in grandeur with more and more super Halloween venues - stores and haunted houses - while people nationwide shake their heads and wonder what is happening to our world.

The celebration of *All Hallows Eve* is not mentioned in the Bible because the Word of God is explicit about things done in darkness. Halloween celebrations take place mostly at night and center on spiritually dark things. Decorations glorify death and fear: spiders, witches, skeletons, and black cats. Children dress up in costumes that honor death and horror: ghosts, witches, devils, skeletons, vampires and zombies. Of course there are other costumes to soften or mask the dark side: Cinderella, Little Bo Peep, Spiderman, Jack Sparrow and whatever is popular with Disney and the media. Teenagers, bored with masquerading, show their real character as mobsters by destroying public and private property.

The Bible states in Genesis 1:1-2, *"In the beginning, God said, 'Let there be light' and there was light."* Before the light, there was darkness and empty space. When God spoke, light came into this world and the Light of the World was there with God.

"In the beginning was the Word, and the Word was with God, and the Word was God. ...In him was life, and that life was the light of men. The light shines in the darkness, but the darkness has not understood it.... "This is the verdict: Light has come into the world, but people loved darkness instead of light because their deeds were evil" (John 1:15, 3:19).

"When Jesus spoke again to the people, he said, 'I AM the light of the world. Whoever follows me will never walk in darkness, but will have the light of life.... "While I am in the world, I AM the light of the world.... "I have come into the world as a light, so that no one who believes in me should stay in darkness" (John 8:12, 9:5, 12:46).

Jesus calls himself the Light of the World and there is no darkness in him. He came into the world to destroy the work of darkness and the spiritual powers and principalities associated with it. Because people love the darkness more than the light, they do not understand the light nor do they come near the light. Unfortunately, the world has contaminated the minds and hearts of many believers accordingly. Rather than being transformed by the renewing of their minds, they play with the fruitless deeds in the darkness rather than expose it for what it is. Our praise should be about being called out of darkness into God's glorious light not paying tribute to the darkness (1 Peter 2:9, 2 Corinthians 6:17-7:1).

"And having disarmed the powers and authorities, he made a public spectacle of them, triumphing over them by the cross" (Colossians 2:15).

There has been such a diluting of Christ's victory over death with an infatuation of death that Christians can't see the difference between their gift of eternal life and the celebration of death. They have traded their precious redemption through the blood of the Son of God for things that bring no profit to their present life or future rewards (Romans 6:4, Colossians 2:8-12).

"Let no one be found among you who sacrifices their son or daughter in the fire, who practices divination or sorcery, interprets omens, engages in witchcraft, or casts spells, or who is a medium or spiritist or who consults the dead. Anyone who does these things is detestable to the LORD; because of these same detestable practices the LORD your God will drive out those nations before you. You must be blameless before the LORD your God" (Deuteronomy 10:10-14).

Scripture never indicates that Jesus celebrated any holiday with pagan foundations because he obeyed the commands of his Father. Jesus didn't go out in the spiritual darkness of *Samhain* to shine or be a light. He didn't hand out gospel tracts or tell his disciples to do that. His life of obedience to his Father was his testimony; ours must be too.

As the Son of God he did not imitate evil nor should we. He didn't pretend or masquerade to be something that he wasn't. That is Satan's method of operation and should not be ours.

"For such people are false apostles, deceitful workers, masquerading as apostles of Christ. And no wonder, for Satan himself masquerades as an angel of light. It is not surprising, then, if his servants also masquerade as servants of righteousness. Their end will be what their actions deserve" (2 Corinthians 11:12-15).

Christians have become so lukewarm, mixing the holy and the profane that they no longer have the maturity to discern good from evil. They do not see that witchcraft with all of its gnarly fingers has grasped hold of children and young adults in their homes, schools and towns. They are blind to demons and evil spirits presented in television programs and movies. Just consider that zombies are walking dead people who are glorified by those who have eternal life.

"Be alert and of sober mind. Your enemy the devil prowls around like a roaring lion looking for someone to devour. Resist him, standing firm in the faith because you know that the family of believers throughout the world is undergoing the same kind of sufferings (having to separate themselves?)" (1 Peter 5:7-9).

A popular saying in Christendom has been "What Would Jesus Do?" This is a powerful question to be asked regarding any unBiblical holiday, but especially Halloween. What WOULD Jesus Do? Would he try to redeem something rooted in the ways of the nations back to God or would he call it for what it is and not participate in pagan ways. The Christian church has been more than willing to say that everything Jewish is 'evil' or 'wrong', but legitimate evil practices at Halloween are not. They create 'Christian' alternatives so that they can disguise their disobedience and continue to keep one foot in the world and one foot ... in the world.

"Dear friend, do not imitate what is evil but what is good. Anyone who does what is good is from God. Anyone who does what is evil has not seen God" (3 John 1:11).

The god of this world has blinded the minds of unbelievers and will continue to do so until Christ's return. He is also being allowed to deceive and blind believers who want to do what is 'right in their own eyes' and live a lawless unaccountable life. There is a great deception happening to believers in Jesus. Those who claim to have the Light still desire to embrace the darkness in ways that they see as fun or harmless. Where in Scripture is anything surrounded by darkness harmless?

"The god of this age has blinded the minds of unbelievers, so that they cannot see the light of the gospel that displays the glory of Christ, who is the image of God" (2 Corinthians 4:4).

For those who truly have asked Jesus to be their Savior, it's important to allow Him to be Lord of your life. Though it may be a challenge and even difficult to step out and stay out of the darkness, you have a responsibility to yourself, your children and your testimony to the world around you about Jesus' salvation and redemption from death and darkness. You have a responsibility to God.

"Do not be yoked together with unbelievers. For what do righteousness and wickedness have in common? Or what fellowship can light have with darkness?" (2 Corinthians 6:14).

There will always be those who scoff at the idea of not taking part in Halloween festivities. The Bible mentions them, too. For doubters, research *All Hallows Eve* and *Samhain* using an encyclopedia or browse the internet. Talk to a law enforcement official in your local town and find out about witchcraft activity during Halloween. Read the newspaper and note all the crime and death that takes place during Halloween. Just recently near Denver, Colorado a shed was found with bones of many human remains along with articles of witchcraft. This is the information age. If you want information, it's readily available on the internet.

"You adulterous people, don't you know that friendship with the world means enmity against God? Therefore, anyone who chooses to be a friend of the world becomes an enemy of God" (James 4:4).

If you call on the Light of the World for your salvation and have repented from a sin-filled life, then you have to choose between being a friend of God or a friend of the world. When you choose to be God's friend, you will receive your spiritual sight and be set free from the human traditions and the elemental spiritual forces of this world. Both are incorporated into the celebration Halloween. No longer will you shake your head in wonderment at the growing evil in the world, but you will know the truth and you will be set free to understand whose holiday this really is. You will begin to walk in the wisdom of God's Word and you will not only know what Jesus did, but more importantly you will know what Jesus did NOT do. He did not celebrate any pagan holidays including Halloween!

"See to it that no one takes you captive through hollow and deceptive philosophy, which depends on human tradition and the elemental spiritual forces of this world rather than on Christ. For in Christ all the fullness of

the Deity lives in bodily form, and in Christ you have been brought to fullness. He is head over every power and authority" (Colossians 2: 8-10).

The victory over death, spiritual powers and authorities in high places cost Jesus his life. That's what Jesus did. "What will you do?

The Spirit of Christmas

"Dear friends, do not believe every spirit, but test the spirits to see whether they are from God, because many false prophets have gone out into the world" "This is how you can recognize the Spirit of God: Every spirit that acknowledges that Messiah Yeshua has come in the flesh is from God, but every spirit that does not acknowledge Yeshua is not from God. This is the spirit of the antichrist, which you have heard is coming and even now is already in the world" (1 John 4:1-3).

"What is the 'spirit of Christmas"? Many will respond with 'warm fuzzies,' family and a sense of emotional well-being. However, it is during the Christmas season that people incur huge debt and the rate of suicide escalates. How can a 'spirit of emotional well-being' breed debt and death?

The spirit behind Christmas has actually deceived the masses while perpetuating a false god worship that began in Mesopotamia with the god, Marduk. It progressed through early Europe and the Celts with the Yuletide and Scandinavians and "the Prodigal Sun". As time passed Persians celebrated it centered on the god Mithra, and eventually in Rome, it was commemorated as Saturn's day or the Saturnalia.

"For how many years shall this festival abide! Never shall age destroy so holy a day! While the hills of Latium remain and father Tiber, while thy Rome stands and the Capitol thou has restored to the world, it [Saturnalia] shall continue."

Originally, Saturnalia was celebrated for one day on December 17, but then grew into a week-long spectacle of pleasures culminating on December 24. Rome borrowed most of its cultural celebrations from primarily the Greeks. However, the Saturnalia has its roots in Egyptian culture with Osiris and Isis, two gods that were judged when Israel was delivered from Egypt.

The Saturnalia began by dedicating the temple to Saturn through human sacrifices, especially children. Saturn was connected with the Greek Kronos, also known as Father Time, who looks a lot like Santa Claus, and ate small children. Could this be why small children fear Santa? Could this be why so many people take their lives at this time? Could it be they are the human sacrifices that the 'spirit of Saturnalia' requires?

After the human sacrifices were completed, celebrants would shout *"Io, Saturnalia!"* and the week-long festivities would begin. Huge public banquets were prepared. Cookies were made with simple face shapes. People would eat, drink, and be merry. It was a time for friends and relatives to exchange gifts especially wax candles and little dolls. Slaves would be set free and wore peaked woolen caps that symbolized their freedom.

Many of the Saturnalia decorations involved greenery, swathes, garlands and wreaths, being hung over doorways and windows. *Sigillaria* or figurines made out of clay were hung on pine trees. A Saturnalia tree was common in Egypt and Rome long before Christianity incorporated it into Christmas observance. In Egypt it was a palm tree to honor Baal-Tamuz (Ezekiel 8:14). In Rome, the fir was used to honor the same god, but then called Baal-Berith. It was from a branch of these trees that the Yule Log evolved. Trees in these cultures were not cut down and brought inside, but remained outside where they were decorated with sunbursts, stars and faces of the God Janus.

The Sol Invictus, the god of the sun, was the main god of the Roman Empire. The Roman emperor Aurelian made Sol Invictus the official religion of the empire combined with their other gods: Jupiter (supreme diety), Apollo (destroyer), Sylvanus (guardian of the flocks, shepherd). The image of the Sol Invictus appeared on coins minted by Constantine in spite of his supposed conversion to Christianity. After the weeklong celebration of Saturnalia and the end of the solstice, December 25 became known as the "Birthday of the Sun."

In the fourth century, the Roman church united all religions and their gods under a catholic vision. Religious observances were given new names and the Saturnalia was transformed into the Christ Mass. The word 'mass' comes from the Latin word *missa* and means a 'death sacrifice.' How ironic that the date for the birth of Jesus Christ which has been believed and accepted for many centuries as December 25, is actually the death sacrifice part of the Saturnalia.

Throughout the centuries these catholic holidays and their traditions became deeply rooted into the church and church doctrines. Even the Protestant Reformation through Martin Luther did nothing to remove itself from the pagan practices in which it was steeped. Today all Christian churches no matter what denomination embrace the roots of the Saturnalia as Christmas. Remember, if the root is unholy, so are the branches.

Unfortunately most Christians celebrate this holiday while claiming to be anything but catholic. Many honor the Reformation and the breaking away from the Roman Catholic Church, but continue to celebrate many traditions that have their roots in unholy catholic practices. Yeshua warns in Mark 7 that if a tradition nullifies a command of God, it should not be adhered to. There is one Christmas tradition specifically mentioned in Jeremiah that needs to be addressed.

"Hear what the LORD says to you, people of Israel. This is what the LORD says: 'Do not learn the ways of the nations ... for the practices of the peoples are worthless. They cut a tree out of the forest, and a craftsman shapes it with his chisel. They adorn it with silver and gold; they fasten it with hammer and nails so it will not totter" (Jeremiah 10:1-4).

Many people read these verses in Jeremiah and say that cutting down a tree and decorating it has nothing to do with a Christmas tree. They argue that they don't shape it into an idol, however, let's look at the verses in context. Cutting down a tree is a way of the nations, a way of the gentiles, that Israel was not to imitate. When gentiles enter a covenant relationship with the God of Israel, they are to leave their pagan ways behind so they do not mix the holy things of God with the idolatries of the nations.

Most people would agree that we don't craft the tree into a literal idol, but that's because we're either too busy or too lazy. Then there are fake or artificial trees. These are poles with branches fashioned by the hands of man to represent something on earth that God created. This is called idolatry in Exodus 20:4.

The tree, whether cut down from the forest or not, is central to a holiday from the nations that was never meant to honor God or His Son. It cannot stand on its own; it needs some sort of tree stand. Both inside and outside trees are adorned with gold ornaments and silver icicles. They are lit up with strings of lights. On top of it is the face of an angel or a star. Beneath it is the visual sacrifice of finances through extensive gift giving. The decorated tree becomes the holy place in a home, central to the celebration of Christmas and adored by those who erect it and those who visit the home .

The most common argument for having a Christmas tree is that we can transform something pagan into something holy because we have sanctified it and given it to the LORD. With this rationalization, the Christmas tree sounds like a modern-day golden calf.

The Golden Calf

"When the people saw that Moses was so long in coming down from the mountain, they gathered around Aaron and said, 'Come, make us a god who will go before us....

"Aaron answered them, 'Take off the gold earrings that your wives, your sons and your daughters are wearing, and bring them to me.' So all the people took off their earrings and brought them to Aaron. He took what they handed him and made it into an idol cast in the shape of a calf, fashioning it with a tool. Then they said, "Here is your god, Israel, who brought you up out of Egypt.'

"When Aaron saw this, he built an altar in front of the calf and announced, 'Tomorrow there will be a festival to the LORD'" (Exodus 32:1-4).

This passage is about the infamous golden calf. It is important to recognize several things. First, Aaron who was chosen as one of the leaders of Israel guides the people into the worship of a false god. They had no excuse for listening to Aaron. They had just been miraculously set free from slavery in Egypt. They had witnessed the destruction of Egypt's gods by the power of *Yod Hey Vav Hey*. Yet, with their new-found freedom, they did not listen to the Words of the LORD.

We must always be like the Bereans in Acts 17:11 and make sure that what our leaders have been taught and are telling us to do lines up with God's Word. The Israelites had already had their encounter with God at the foot of Mt. Sinai. They had experienced His presence and heard His Words from the first of the Ten Commandments.

"I AM the LORD your God, who brought you out of Egypt, out of the land of slavery. You shall have no other gods before me" (Exodus 20:1-2).

Second, Aaron created an idol; he cast in an image. The image was of a calf and something worshipped in Egypt. Having been enslaved for 400 years, the Israelites had lost their understanding of the God of Abraham, Isaac, and Jacob and had absorbed the concepts and ideas of worshipping other gods. They knew they had been brought to the mountain to worship their God, *Yod Hey Vav Hey*, but they had no idea how to do that. While Moses was getting the details from God on the mountain, they became impatient. They made their own way according to what they had learned in slavery. There was immoral revelry, dancing and celebration around the golden calf. So much so that Moses had to ask Aaron, *"What did these people do to you, that you led them into such great sin?"* (Exodus 32:21).

Third, Aaron built an altar and dedicated the golden calf to the God of Israel. He took a pagan symbol and sanctified it to God. The result of this was that God struck the people with a plague and many died (Exodus 32:35). What had they done? They had worshipped and reveled around an idol and claimed they did it for the One True Living God. They mixed the holy and the profane, the hot and the cold and became lukewarm.

Moses took the calf the people had made and burned it the fire. He scattered its powder on their water. He made the Israelites drink the contaminated water? Is this the same water you are drinking, water polluted with the remains of pagan gods?

"If it seems bad to you to serve the LORD, then choose today whom you are going to serve! Will it be the gods your ancestors served beyond the River? or the gods of the Emori, in whose land you are living? As for me and my household, we will serve the LORD!" (Joshua 24:15).

Today many Christians want to put Christ back in Christmas. Their voices in the ears of God sound much like that of Aaron and the Israelites. The salvation of the world was never in Christmas. It is a great deception led by a false priesthood that has turned true believers in the Messiah away from the worship of the God of Israel in the ways He outlined. Generations have accepted this unholy rooted festival because the Word of God was not available to them. Today, however, there is no excuse. Everyone has access to the Word of God, and to whom much is given, much is expected.

Several years ago I came across a poem about Saturnalia. Even though our family had stopped celebrating Christmas for many years, the shock of the words in the poem brought the whole deception to a brighter light. There are those who are alive and well on planet earth today who worship Saturn and celebrate Saturnalia. The poem thanked Christianity for keeping their pagan holiday alive for millennia. The unholy roots of the holiday became even more clear when that particular year we received a "Happy Saturnalia" card from friends.

The Easter Women

When my children were growing up, I had a little book I read to them every Easter about the women going to the tomb and seeing the empty grave. It wasn't until I understood who the Easter women really are that I stopped reading the book. I realized that combining the holy with the profane does not bring glory to the plan of salvation through the God of Israel, but keeps alive the worship of foreign goddesses that I couldn't have in my life or the lives of my children if I wanted to love the God of Israel with all of my heart.

"So Samuel said to all the Israelites, "If you are returning to the LORD with all your hearts, then rid yourselves of the foreign gods and the Ashtoreths and commit yourselves to the LORD and serve him only, and he will deliver you out of the hand of the Philistines'" (1 Samuel 7:3).

Nimrod, from Genesis 10, had wife whose name was Semiramis. She was an adulteress and an idolator. When her husband died, she gave birth to an illegitimate son claiming that he was supernaturally conceived in order to hide her own immoralities. She even said that he was the promised seed so there would be no judgment against her behavior. When he was born, she named her son Tammuz and declared that he was Nimrod reborn. This allowed her to have an immoral mother son relationship. Not only was Tammuz worshipped, but so was his mother, Ishtar, from whom we derive the English Easter and the Hebrew Ashtoreth.

Tammuz was a shepherd and one day while herding his flocks, he was killed by a wild boar. Ishtar, his mother turned lover mourned for him and descended into the underworld to deliver him from death. She weeped for him 40 days which eventually made the god of water and wisdom send a heavenly messenger to the underworld to rescue her and her son. The mourning for Tammuz was known as "The Lament of the Flutes for Tammuz" and was celebrated in Babylonia by women on the second day of the fourth month known as Tammuz (our April).

"Then he brought me to the entrance to the north gate of the house of the LORD, and I saw women sitting there, mourning for Tammuz. He said to me, "Do you see this, son of man? You will see things that are even more detestable than this" (Ezekiel 8:14)

After the 40 days ended, there was a great festival for Ishtar full of sexual immorality and dancing around Asherah poles on the 'high places'. The worship of Ashtoreth and Asherah overlapped and together were known in ancient Israel as the Queen of Heaven.

"Judah's sin is engraved with an iron tool, inscribed with a flint point, on the tablets of their heart and on the horns of their altars. Even their children remember their altars and Asherah poles beside the spreading trees and on the high hills" (Jeremiah 17:1-2).

As with Christmas, the catholic church embraced the pagan trinitarian worship of Nimrod, the Queen of Heaven and Tammuz. For forty days before Easter, there is a 40 day period of time known as Lent. On the days before Lent begins, there is great feasting and immoral parties. Remnants of these pagan traditions are embedded in Carnival of Brazil and Mardi Gras in New Orleans. When the first day of Lent arrives, known as Ash Wednesday, those same immoral crowds (along with Protestants and Evangelicals) flock to churches to receive ashes on their forehead. Ashes are symbolic of the mourning and sorrow for the dead and the soulful 40 day preparation for holy week culminating in a great celebration called Easter - the memorial of Tammuz, the son of the Queen of Heaven, coming back from the dead.

"The children gather the wood, the fathers light the fire, and the women knead the dough to make cakes for the queen of heaven; and, just to provoke me, they pour out drink offerings to other gods!" (Jeremiah 7:18).

Though this all appears Biblical, the God of Israel warned his people about the worship of Tammuz through mourning and honoring the Queen of Heaven with cakes (hot cross buns). Dancing around a 'May Pole' is nothing more than honoring the the pagan goddess Asherah with a sexual symbol made from a tree. Even colored eggs have been embraced by the church through unholy catholic unions. During the season of Lent, all eggs are removed from the home for forty days and then they are colored red like blood as a sacrifice for Ashtoreth and Asherah. The God of Israel gave His people ways to memorialize the death and resurrection of Yeshua and it didn't include 40 days of mourning, blood red eggs and consuming the flesh of the wild boar .

Jeremiah's warning is not heeded by the men or women in Israel. They didn't care that they worshipped other gods contrary to what God commanded. Instead they remained rebellious in their stony hearts and fervently declared they weren't going to change their wicked ways. They believed that their prosperity came from the Queen of Heaven and not from the God of their father Abraham so they continued in their abominations until judgment came.

We are to learn from Israel's mistakes and not have hardness of heart when we hear His voice. When we of the nations join with Israel by faith, it is up to us to repent from these disgusting practices and return to a pure worship of the God of Israel. We should not invent cutesy little stories as ways to justify traditions that are abominable to God who redeemed us with the blood of His Son and not the immoral god murdered by a wild pig.

"Then all the men who knew that their wives were offering incense to other gods, along with all the women standing by, a huge crowd, all the people living in Patros in the land of Egypt, answered Jeremiah: "As for the word you have just spoken to us in the name of the LORD, we will not listen to you. Instead, we will certainly continue to fulfill every word our mouths have spoken: we will offer incense to the queen of heaven and pour out drink offerings to her, as we have done, we and our ancestors, our kings and our leaders, in the cities of Judah and the streets of Jerusalem. For then we had plenty of food; everything was fine, we didn't experience anything unpleasant. But since we stopped offering to the queen of heaven and pouring out drink offerings to her, we have lacked everything, and we have been destroyed by sword and famine" (Jeremiah 44:15-18).

Venerable Day of the Sun

Sunday church was part of my life growing up. I attended weekly services as a child and sang in the choirs as a teenager. I never questioned Sunday worship because it was just what everyone I knew did. We went to church on Sunday. Period. As an adult, I continued to attend Sunday church services until the Lord showed me His better way of the Sabbath.

Many years ago our family had some visitors from New Zealand. After spending several days with us and learning about our Messianic walk of faith, they asked if they could stay for Sabbath. While reading some Scriptures, the husband interrupted and asked why the church doesn't keep the Sabbath any more. Before anyone in our family could answer his question, his wife responded, "The catholic church changed it."

"...Instead of the seventh day, and other festivals appointed by the old law, the church has prescribed the Sundays and holy days to be set apart for God's worship; and these we are now obliged to keep in consequence of God's commandment, instead of the ancient Sabbath" (The Catholic Christian Instructed in the Sacraments, Sacrifices, Ceremonies, and Observances of the Church By Way of Question and Answer, RT Rev. Dr. Challoner, p. 204.)

As with Christmas and Easter, Sunday worship has its roots not in the Scriptures, but in the history of the world and ultimately the church fathers who created the idea that Sunday was the memorial day for Jesus' resurrection. Sunday is named for the 'venerable day of the sun' and probably came from Egyptian astrology.   It is also the first day of the week according to all calendars, historic and modern-day.

In 321 C.E., Constantine decreed that Sunday would be observed as the Roman day of rest: *"On the venerable Day of the Sun let the magistrates and people residing in cities rest, and let all workshops be closed. In the country, however, persons engaged in agriculture may freely and lawfully continue their pursuits; because it often happens that another day is not so suitable for grain-sowing or vine-planting; lest by neglecting the proper moment for such operations the bounty of heaven should be lost"* (Philip Schaff, History of the Christian Church: Vol. II: From Constantine the Great to Gregory the Great A.D. 311–600 (New York: Charles Scribner, 1867) page 380 note 1.)

This doctrine was codified at the Council of Nicea in 325 C.E. with its many other anti-semitic regulations further separating the Jewish

Sabbath from the Christian Sunday. In 363 C.E. the Council of Laodicea prohibited Christians from observing the Biblical Sabbath and encouraged them to work on Saturday and rest on the Sunday. The fact that this edict was issued indicates that Sunday worship was still not totally accepted by Christians.

Yeshua sent an angel to the church in Laodicea warning them about mixing the holy and the profane, the hot and the cold. It makes him vomit! He tells this lukewarm congregation that he stands at the door and knocks and if anyone hears his voice and opens the door, he will eat with them (Revelation 3:14-20). This is a reference to the Sabbath day, the fourth *dalet* commandment along with the words, *the ruler of God's creation.* It would seem that Yeshua already knew that Laodicea would fall away from the truth and mix it with lies. Only those with 'ears to hear' would be victorious and sit on thrones to rule and reign with Him.

Contrary to God's command for the Sabbath day, Sunday worship was mandated by the Roman catholic church as the sabbath of Christian worship. The outline of God's week of working for six days and resting on the seventh was transformed into a Sunday sabbath having people rest on the first day of the week and then working. I remember when an elder in a church I attended brought that little fact to my attention. Though we worshipped on Sunday, he commented, "I wonder how God will deal with the church for turning His order around - resting then working rather than working and resting."

Of course, we can worship God any day of the week we desire. In fact, we should worship Him every day as Creator of the Universe and for all the blessings and promises fulfilled in our lives. However, that doesn't mean His holy day of Sabbath should have become a day disdained by Christianity and Scriptures misinterpreted that undeniably suggest that early Jews and gentiles worshipped on Sabbath in synagogues. Acts 20:7 is one example.

"On the first day of the week we came together to break bread. Paul spoke to the people and, because he intended to leave the next day, kept on talking until midnight."

Without even suggesting that days were rendered evening to evening, is it really possible that Paul began to speak during a Sunday morning worship service until midnight on the first day of the week and then left the next day? Would people really sit for 15-20 hours and listen to him proclaim the Word of God when today an hour is too long?

Verse 8 continues *"There were many lamps in the upstairs room where we were meeting."* Biblical days are from sunset to sunset. This means that when Paul started speaking on the first day of the week, it was probably after sunset or Saturday evening. He talked for four or five hours, Eutychus goes to sleep, falls out the window and dies. After Eutychus is resurrected from the dead, Paul leaves in the morning which would be Sunday morning.

"On the first day of every week, each one of you should set aside a sum of money in keeping with your income, saving it up, so that when I come no collections will have to be made" (1 Corinthians 16:2).

This verse is used to support collecting tithes and offerings at Sunday morning church services. Does this verse really suggest passing the offering plates on Sunday morning?

"And let us ... not give up meeting together, as some are in the habit of doing, but encouraging one another—and all the more as you see the Day approaching" (Hebrews 10:25).

There is nothing in this verse to suggest that *meeting together* was to happen on the first day of the week or forsaking the fellowship meant not going to church on Sunday.

Sunday is often called 'The LORD's Day' as if the Yeshua actually honored it as such. In Matthew 12:8 and Mark 2:28, Yeshua said *"So the Son of Man is Lord even of the Sabbath."* At the time he made this statements, the Sabbath was still the seventh day, therefore the 'Day of the LORD' should be the Sabbath. Since the word Sabbath has its Hebrew root in *sheva* or 'seven', it would always have to be the seventh day, not the first, third or any day that man desires.

"On the Lord's Day I was in the Spirit, and I heard behind me a loud voice like a trumpet, which said: "Write on a scroll what you see and send it to the seven churches: to Ephesus, Smyrna, Pergamum, Thyatira, Sardis, Philadelphia and Laodicea" (Revelation 1:10).

Many interpret this Scripture to mean that on a Sunday morning, the apostle John was in the Spirit and given revelation. However, the passage doesn't say it was on a Sunday. This inference comes from centuries of Christian theology that moved the Sabbath to the first day of the week and then called it The LORD's Day.

John was a Jew and well-versed in the Hebrew language of the Hebrew Scriptures. To him the phrase en *teé juriake heem'ra* (The LORD's Day) would imply what is called by the prophets Isaiah, Joel and Amos as "The Day of the LORD" or the time of the coming destruction that brings forth the Messianic age.

There are other clues in the passage to the timing of The LORD's Day and neither have anything to do with Sunday. John heard a loud voice that sounded like a trumpet. Since the book of Revelation is about prophecy, to use the sound of the trumpet as a prophetic voice is appropriate. Also, the Feast of Trumpets is believed to be the time for preparing for God's judgment of earth and its people.

The trumpet voice tells John to send seven messages to the seven churches in East Asia. These messages contain warnings for 'The Day of the LORD' so those in the congregations who have 'ears to hear' will recognize the times and be prepared.

Still, some Christians perpetuate Sunday as The LORD's Day, but this is really the result of ignorance. When they wish someone a 'Happy Lord's Day' they are really wishing them a 'Happy Judgment Day' quite different from saying Shabbat Shalom or Sabbath Peace on the Sabbath. The real blessing of the 'The LORD's Day' is not about wishing someone a great worship time on Sunday, but in reading book of Revelation and the prophecy it contains (Revelation 1:1-3).

The change from the Sabbath command to a first day of the week memorial to the god of the sun was not begun by Yeshua or the Apostles, but by the Roman church that didn't heed Paul's warnings about arrogance. This catholic mandate brings misunderstanding to the prophetic revelation given to John regarding the events of the 'Day of the LORD' and the return of the Messiah of Israel to earth.

"He then brought me into the inner court of the house of the Lord, and there at the entrance to the temple, between the portico and the altar, were about twenty-five men. With their backs toward the temple of the Lord and their faces toward the east, they were bowing down to the sun in the east" (Ezekiel 8:16).

Ezekiel had vision of the Temple in Jerusalem before the glory of the LORD departs through the Eastern Gate of Jerusalem and stops over the Mount of Olives. Digging through a hole at the entrance to the court, Ezekiel witnesses seventy elders of Israel offering incense to foreign gods. Twenty-five men are in the inner courts near the altar. They face east with their backs toward the Temple and bow to the sun. These detestable things, the worship of the sun in the east, force God to remove His glory from the Temple. His glory will not return until Yeshua sets his feet on the Mount of Olives and removes all the detestable practices of the nations from his Kingdom.

Learning about some of the the roots of Halloween, Christmas, Easter and Sunday, perhaps Galatians 4:8-11 can be read and understood in the context in which it was written to gentiles:

"Formerly, when you did not know God, you were slaves to those who by nature are not gods. But now that you know God—or rather are known by God—how is it that you are turning back to those weak and miserable forces? Do you wish to be enslaved by them all over again? You are observing special days and months and seasons and years! I fear for you, that somehow I have wasted my efforts on you" (Galatians 4:8-11).

Part Two
The Ancient Paths

"Here is what Adonai says:
"Stand at the crossroads and look;
ask about the ancient paths,
'Which one is the good way?'
Take it, and you will find rest for your souls"
(Jeremiah 6:16).

The Feasts of the LORD

"What will you do on the day of your appointed festivals, on the feast days of the LORD?" (Isaiah 9:5).

"Here, I'm standing at the door, knocking. If someone hears my voice and opens the door, I will come in to him and eat with him, and he will eat with me" (Revelation 3:20).

There are many different calendars in the world today. There is the Gregorian/Julian calendar which is internationally accepted as the civil calendar. This calendar begins in January and ends in December and includes American holidays like New Year's Day, the Fourth of July, Labor Day, and Thanksgiving.

There is the liturgical calendar that was generated by the Roman catholic church with the holidays that have been universally embraced by the Christian church worldwide. On this calendar is the weekly Sunday and yearly dates for Advent, Christmas, Lent, and Easter.

There is also the Biblical calendar established by God with Israel at Mount Sinai. This calendar focuses on the weekly and annual festival days called *The Feasts of the LORD*. These are the times that God has set to meet with His people in prophetic ways.

The *Mo'edim* or Appointed Times

The Hebrew word for 'feasts or festivals' is *mo'edim* and means 'set or appointed times.' Within the meaning of *mo'ed* is the idea of a 'meeting of two or more at a certain place and time.' "*Mo'edim* is the word used in Genesis 1:14 for the word 'seasons' when God created the sun, moon and stars. *The Feasts of the LORD* are seasons determined by the sun, moon and stars. From that account, days are rendered sunset to sunset as 'there was evening and morning,'for each day. Months are approximately 28 days based on the lunar cycle. Years are determined by the constellations that move across the heavens. Outlined in Leviticus 23 are the *Mo'edim of the Yahweh* or the 'set meeting times' of the LORD.

"The LORD said to Moses, 'Speak to the Israelites and say to them: 'These are my appointed festivals, the appointed festivals of the LORD, which you are to proclaim as sacred assemblies" (Leviticus 23:1).

The 'appointed times' given by God were called sacred assemblies or holy convocations. In Hebrew, the word for 'assembly' or 'convocation' is *mikrah*. This word has its root in *qara* and means to 'call out loudly' or be 'invited.' *Mikrah* has the added nuance of 'rehearsal' associated the 'appointed times' of God with being *invited to a rehearsal dinner.*

These 'appointed times' were not given just to the Tribes of Israel, but also Egyptians who had heeded Moses' command to put lamb's blood on their doorposts. This mixed multitude of men, women and children left Egypt and became one community known as Israelites.

The 'appointed times' of the LORD had agricultural foundations with festivals for firstfruits and harvests giving each festival a spiritual significance to the complete redemptive plan of God. Each festival was a shadow of the Messiah who was, is, and will be. Yeshua became the reality of the spring 'appointed times'; he will become the reality of the fall festivals at their 'appointed times.'

"Therefore do not let anyone judge you by what you eat or drink, or with regard to a religious festival, a New Moon celebration or a Sabbath day.

These are a shadow of the things that are coming; the reality, however, is found in Messiah" (Colossians 2:16-17).

This verse in Colossians has been used for a proof-text that gentiles or non-Jewish believers don't need to celebrate the Biblically appointed times because they have Jesus in their lives. Instead of understanding the Scripture in the context that judgment should not come from Jews when gentiles join together with them in celebrating their holy days, they rid themselves from what is found in *the reality of Messiah*.

Shadows and realities go together. Shadows imply that there is some substance causing it while something of substance causes a shadow. If we are *in Messiah* and he *in us*, then we have the the light that brings the reality out of the shadows. The shadows spoken of in these verses to the Colossians are in the progressive present tense, *that are coming*, meaning that they are still in process in the present and have yet to all be fulfilled.

This inherited lie has kept the believing gentile separated from their full inheritance in the Messiah of Israel.   Instead of accepting the spiritual blessings that come from celebrating the Sabbath and the New Moon, they reject the very substance of Yeshua's life in their own.

Weekly Appointed Time

Sabbath is the first appointed time given by the LORD.

"There are six days when you may work, but the seventh day is a day of sabbath rest, a day of sacred assembly.   You are not to do any work; wherever you live, it is a sabbath to the LORD" (Leviticus 23:3).

Present Shadow and Reality

The seventh day Sabbath is a memorial to Creation 'in the beginning.' It is so important that God put it in the 10 Commandments as well as listed it the first of the *mo'edim*. Yeshua taught that God made the Sabbath for mankind and he is the Lord of the Sabbath (Matthew 8:12, Mark 2:27).

First of Months and the Spring Feasts

These *mo'edim* of the LORD have been fulfilled by Yeshua on their appointed day and time. The first three represent the past work of Yeshua justifying the individual before God and bringing the hope of redemption to the world.

Passover is the second appointed time given by the LORD.

"These are the LORD's appointed festivals, the sacred assemblies you are to proclaim at their appointed times: The LORD's Passover begins at twilight on the fourteenth day of the first month" (Leviticus 23:4-5).

Shadow

The Passover festival is a memorial to the deliverance of the people of God from Egypt through the blood of the lamb. They were taken from a life of slavery to a life of freedom. They were taken from the darkness of a pagan world into the light of the God's Kingdom.

Fulfilled Reality:

Yeshua is our Passover lamb. Through his sacrificial death, we are taken from a life of slavery in sin to a life of freedom in righteousness. We are taken from the darkness of the sinful world to the light of the Kingdom of God.

Feast of Unleavened Bread is the third appointed time given by the LORD.

Shadow:

This festival is in memorial to the haste in which the Israelites left Egypt. They had no time to let their bread dough rise.

Fulfilled Reality:

Yeshua was the sinless, unleavened bread of life. He was hastily taken off the cross and buried before the Feast of Unleavened Bread would begin. He was wrapped in cloths and put in a tomb.

The Feast of Firstfruits is the fourth appointed time given by the LORD.

Shadow:

This festival is a memorial to the firstfruits of the harvest. It is celebrated on the first day of the week after the weekly Sabbath following Passover.

Fulfilled Reality:

Yeshua rose from the dead and ascended to his Father and offered himself as the first sheaf of grain from the harvest.

The Feast of Weeks is the fifth appointed time given by The LORD. This festival represents the present work of Yeshua sanctifying the individual through the Holy Spirit and preparing him for the world to come.

Shadow:

There are 50 days between the Feast of Firstfruits and the Feast of Weeks called Counting the Omer. For 40 of these days Yeshua walked on the earth, met and ate with his disciples. Then, he ascended into heaven.

Fulfilled Reality:

The Spirit of God came mightily upon the Jewish believers in Messiah as part of the promised new covenant. Tongues of fire reseted on them and filled them with power to speak in other languages and take the gospel to the nations.

Fall Appointed Times

"For the revelation awaits an appointed time; it speaks of the end and will not prove false. Though it linger, wait for it; it will certainly come and will not delay" (Habbakuk 2:3).

These *mo'edim* of the LORD have not yet been fulfilled by Yeshua. This is the future work of Yeshua restoring the glory of God to Israel and the nations. These 'appointed times' are a vision of hope.

The Feast of Trumpets is the sixth appointed time given by the LORD.

Shadow

The Feast of Trumpets is a memorial to something that has not yet happened.

Reality is yet to come

At the trumpet call of God, the dead will be raised and changed from mortal to immortality.

The Day of Atonement is the seventh appointed time given by the LORD.

Shadow

On this day, the high priest went into the Holy of Holies in the Temple and made atonement for himself and the nation of Israel.

Reality is yet to come

On this day, all Israel will be saved.

The Feast of Tabernacles is the eighth appointed time given by the LORD.

Shadow

The Feast of Tabernacles is a memorial to the Tabernacle in the wilderness when the LORD lived among His people.

Reality is yet to come

When Yeshua returns, he will Tabernacle with the nation of Israel and rule the nations from Jerusalem.

The Eternal Sabbath

<u>Shadow</u>

We are living in the shadow of the eternal Sabbath with the vision of a remaining Sabbath rest (Hebrews 4:8).

<u>Reality is yet to come</u>
The restoration of the Kingdom of God and the New Jerusalem.

The weekly and annual cycle of *The Feasts of the LORD* give us the complete picture of God's plan of salvation. Yeshua was, is and will be the reality in each and every *mo'edim*.

"Blessed (happy, fortunate, to be envied) are the people who know the joyful sound (who understand and appreciate the spiritual blessings symbolized by the feasts); they walk, O Lord, in the light and favor of Your countenance" (Psalm 89:15 The Amplified Bible).

Chapter Photo: Festival banner hanging in our home.

The Prophetic Feasts Chart

The Sabbath: *"The Sabbath was made for man not man for the Sabbath"* (Mark 2:27). *"By the seventh day God has finished the work he had been doing; so on the seventh day, He rested from all His work"* (Genesis 2:2). *"Remember the Sabbath Day by keeping it holy"* (Exodus 20:8). *"Keep my Sabbaths holy, that they may be a sign between us. Then you will know that I am the LORD your God"* (Ezekiel 20:20). *"There remains then a Sabbath-rest for the people of God…"* (Hebrews 4:9).

The Way - Justification, the Messiah			The Truth - Sanctification, The Torah	The Life - Glorification, the Father		
"To declare innocent, to make righteous" Past Life, Saving Grace, Water Baptism Repentance of Sin, enter into death and Yeshua's resurrection			*"To be set apart, sanctified through holy conduct"* Present Life, Enabling Grace, Spirit Baptism Walking in faith and the power of God's Spirit	*"To dignify, honor and magnify"* Future Life, Eternal Grace, Baptism in Fire Gathering of Saints, Yeshua returns, Millennial Kingdom		
The LORD's Passover	**Unleavened Bread**	**Feast of Firstfruits**	**Feast of Weeks**	**Feast of Trumpets**	**Day of Atonement**	**Feast of Tabernacles**
Shadow Leviticus 23:5 14th day of first month at twilight	**Shadow** Leviticus 23:6-8 15th day for seven days	**Shadow** Leviticus 23:9-11 Day after the weekly Sabbath	**Shadow** Leviticus 23:15-16 50 days after Firstfruits Counting the Omer	**Shadow** Leviticus 23:23-24 1st day of seventh month on the new moon	**Shadow** Leviticus 23:26-32 10th day afflict your souls	**Shadow** Leviticus 23:23-39 15th day for seven days 8th day is a holy convocation
Fulfilled Yeshua's Death	**Fulfilled Yeshua's Burial**	**Fulfilled Yeshua's Resurrection**	*"From the day you brought the wave offering, seven Sabbaths shall be completed. Count 50 days to the day after the seventh sabbath …"*	**Next to be Fulfilled Yeshua Raises the Saints from the Dead**	**Unfulfilled Yeshua Returns with Armies**	**Unfulfilled Yeshua Reigns From Jerusalem**
"For Messiah, our PASSOVER was sacrificed for us." (1 Corinthians 5:7).	*"I am the Living Bread, I give I give my 'flesh'"* (John 6:51).	*"But now Messiah is risen from the dead and has become the FIRSTFRUITS…"* (1 Corinthians 15:20)	**Present Reality The Spirit of God Writes the Torah on the Heart** (Jeremiah 31:33) *"Now when Shavuot had fully come, they were all filled with the Holy Spirit…"* (Acts 2:1-4) The Spirit of God will empower, convict the world of guilt in regard to sin, righteousness and judgement and will guide into all Truth. (Acts 1:8, John 16:8,13).	*"For the Lord himself shall descend from heaven with the TRUMPET of God…"* (1 Thessalonians 4:16)	*"At that time the sign of the Son of Man will appear in the sky and all the nations of the earth will MOURN…"* (Matthew 24:30)	*"The kingdom of the world has become the KINGDOM of our God and of his MESSIAH and he will reign forever and ever"* (Revelation 11:15).

The Sabbath: *"The new heavens and the new earth that I make will endure … one Sabbath to another all mankind will bow down before me…"* (Isaiah 66:22-23).

"Behold I am coming … My REWARD (Linen Garment, Crowns, Robes) is with me and I will give to everyone according to what he has done. Blessed are those who wash their robes, that they may have the right to the Tree of Life and may go through the gates into the city, the New Jerusalem" (Revelation 22:12-14).

"Then I saw a new heaven and a new earth… I saw the Holy City, the New Jerusalem coming down out of heaven, prepared as a bride beautifully dressed for her husband" (Revelation 21:1-2).

"Blessed, happy (to be envied, fortunate are the people who know the joyful sound (who understand and appreciate the spiritual blessings symbolized by the Feasts); they walk, O LORD, in the light and favor of your countenance!" (Psalm 89:15-16, The Amplified Bible).

The Biblical Sabbath

"On six days work will get done; but the seventh day is Shabbat, for complete rest, set apart for the LORD.... The people of Israel are to keep the Shabbat, to observe Shabbat through all their generations as a perpetual covenant."
(Exodus 31:15-16)

There is a lot of confusion today about the Sabbath. Some people believe that it was done away with when Yeshua died on the cross. Other people believe that the day was changed from the seventh day to the first. Still others say that all but the fourth commandment are in force because it was not reiterated in the New Testament. Some even go further and say there are no longer any real commandments we have to obey because we've been 'set free from the law'.

In the Beginning

The first mention of Sabbath is Genesis 2:1-2: *"Thus the heavens and the earth were completed in all their vast array. By the seventh day God had finished the work he had been doing; so on the seventh day he rested from all his work. And God blessed the seventh day and made it holy, because on it he rested from all the work of creating that he had done."*

In the beginning, God created a day to honor 'ceasing from his creative work.' He made it holy or set it apart from the rest of the week. This is the foundation for the seventh-day rest known as the Sabbath.

In Hebrew the word for Sabbath is *Shabbat* and its root is the word *sheva* meaning 'seven'. This gives witness to the Sabbath day being the seventh day of the week.

The letters in the Hebrew alphabet or aleph-bet have word pictures. When the individual letter pictures are joined together, a word picture develops that gives insight into the word. Below are the Hebrew letter pictures for the Sabbath:

Shabbat שבת

Shin ש - A Tooth means 'consumed or Shekinah, 'the Divine Presence of God'

Bet ב - A House means 'home, family'

Tau ת - A Sign means 'covenant'

The Hebrew word picture for *shabbat*:
The covenant sign of God's divine presence in the home or family.

Sabbath Instructions

The next time Sabbath is mentioned is in the wilderness after Israel had spent 400 years in slavery never getting a day of rest. God gave the Sabbath rest to this mixed multitude of people with specific guidelines about gathering manna:

"I will rain down bread from heaven for you. The people are to go out each day and gather enough for that day. In this way I will test them and see whether they will follow my instructions. On the sixth day they are to prepare what they bring in, and that is to be twice as much as they gather on the other days. ...Keep in mind that the LORD has given you the Sabbath; that is why on the sixth day he gives you bread for two days. Everyone is to stay where he is on the seventh day; no one is to go out. So the people rested on the seventh day" (Exodus 16:4-5,29).

Sabbath was a test of faith. God wanted to see if His newly formed nation would simply follow His instructions. It was no different than Adam and Eve in the Garden. If they would just simply obey

His Word and prepare for the Sabbath by gathering enough manna on the sixth day, they could stay in their tents and rest on the Sabbath. Some, however, did not listen to God's Word and their disobedience brought maggots and stench to the community!

"... Some of them paid no attention to Moses; they kept part of it [the mann] until morning, but it was full of maggots and began to smell" (Exodus 16:20).

The Ten Commandments

God includes the Sabbath in the Ten Commandments, part of His instructions to the holy nation of Israel.

"Remember the Sabbath day by keeping it holy. Six days you shall labor and do all your work, but the seventh day is a Sabbath to the LORD your God. On it you shall not do any work, neither you, nor your son or daughter, nor your manservant or maidservant, nor your animals, nor the alien within your gates. For in six days the LORD made the heaven and the earth, the sea, and all that is in them, but he rested on the seventh day. Therefore the LORD blessed the Sabbath day and made it holy" (Exodus 20:8).

The commandment about Sabbath begins with the word *remember*. 'Remember' that only a couple of chapters earlier the Israelites were tested regarding to the Sabbath day and *some of them paid no attention.* To begin this commandment with *remember* suggests it will be the one most likely forgotten. The Sabbath was not only to be a weekly reminder that God was the Provider for Israel's sustenance and life, but that He was the Creator.

To ignore the Sabbath is to lose the picture of God's cycle of working for six days and resting on the seventh. The modern-day result of forgetting the Sabbath, along with work-aholism, is the acceptance of evolution within the Body of Messiah. Some pastors teach there is evolutionary creation with each day being 1000 or even 1 million years. Such thinking negates the sign of Jonah that Yeshua gave for his time in the grave: three days and three nights as the Hebrew word, *yom*, is used for each day of creation as well as the three days Yeshua was in the grave. Each *yom* of creation was identified numerically from one to seven, 'evening to morning' defining a 24-hour day within a 7-day weekly cycle culminating with the Sabbath.

Appointed Time

Sabbath is also given to God's people as the first of the 'appointed times'.

"There are six days when you may work, but the seventh day is a Sabbath of rest, a day of sacred assembly. You are not to do any work; wherever you live, it is a Sabbath to the LORD" (Leviticus 23:3).

From previous instructions given by God for the Sabbath along with this one, families were to assemble in their tents in a sacred manner to remember their Creator and rest from their labors. It was to be remembered whether they lived in the wilderness, the Promised Land, or the dispersion.

Sabbath Regulations

God gives more regulations to His people regarding the Sabbath in the Torah and through the Prophets. These guidelines defined what He considered work so that Israel would rest and remember Him and not fall back into a lifestyle of bondage.

"Six days you shall labor, but on the seventh day you shall rest; even during the plowing season and harvest you must rest" (Exodus 34:21).

"Do not light a fire in any of your dwellings on the Sabbath day" (Exodus 35:3, Leviticus 26:2, and Deuteronomy 5:12).

"While the Israelites were in the desert, a man was found gathering wood on the Sabbath day. ...Then YHVH said to Moses, the man must die" (Numbers 15:32).

"When the neighboring peoples bring merchandise or grain to sell on the Sabbath, we will not buy from them on the Sabbath or on any holy day" (Nehemiah 10:31).

"When evening shadows fell on the gates of Jerusalem before the Sabbath, I ordered the doors to be shut and not opened until the Sabbath was over. I stationed some of my own men at the gates so that no load could be brought in on the Sabbath day" (Nehemiah 13:19).

From these Scriptures came the following Sabbath instructions: Do not kindle a fire, do not gather wood, do not buy or sell, do not carry a load, rest in season and out, and a Sabbath's day 'walk'. None of the regulations resulted in harsh punishment except once because God never killed anyone for random disobedience. After watching His people live in slavery for 400 years, He had to show them that He was serious about ceasing from work. He knew that one rebellious person would cause everyone else to be disobedient.

Yeshua

"In the beginning was the Word, and the Word was with God, and the Word was God. He was with God in the beginning. Through him all things were made; without him nothing was made that had been made" (John 1:1-3).

In these two verses, Yeshua refers to the beginning when Sabbath was created. He was there in the beginning with his Father when He spoke the seventh-day into existence. As the spoken word of God, Yeshua was an integral part of creating the Sabbath.

Yeshua did give one ordinance for the Sabbath when he was accused of disobeying man's traditions. He made it *lawful to do good*. He demonstrated what was good by healing the sick and feeding his disciples. He wanted to show the people that that they were to live by the Torah and not die by it.

"How much more valuable is a man than a sheep! Therefore it is lawful to do good on the Sabbath" (Matthew 12:12).

"Now if a child can be circumcised on the Sabbath so that the law of Moses may not be broken, why are you angry with me for healing the whole man on the Sabbath" (John 7:23).

"One Sabbath Yeshua was going going through the grain fields, and his disciples began to pick some heads of grain, rub them in their hands and eat the kernels. Some of the Pharisees asked, 'Why are you doing what is unlawful on the Sabbath?' Yeshua answered them, 'Have you never read what David did when he and his companions were hungry? He entered the house of God, and taking the consecrated bread, he ate what is lawful only

for priests to eat. And he also gave some to his companions.' Then Yeshua said to them, 'The Son of Man is Lord of the Sabbath'" (Luke 6:1-5).

On the Sabbath, Yeshua went into the synagogue and taught his brothers and sisters, the lost sheep of the House of Israel. He read Scriptures according to the Sabbath custom, he he healed people and he cast out evil spirits. Not only were the Jewish people amazed, they believed in him.

"When the Sabbath came, he began to teach in the synagogue, and many who heard him were amazed" (Mark 6:2).

"Even as he spoke, many [Jews] believed in him" (John 8:30).

Throughout the centuries rabbis and other leaders compiled their own interpretations to the instructions given through the prophets which added great burdens on the people. This was not God's purpose for the Sabbath so Yeshua untwisted men's interpretations showing that the Sabbath was made for mankind and not men's rules.

"Then he said to them, 'The Sabbath was made for man, not man for the Sabbath. So the Son of Man is Lord even of the Sabbath" (Mark 2:27-28).

As the Son of God, Yeshua has authority over Sabbath. Though man can enjoy the day, determine how he will spend the day in rest, he has no authority to change it, remove it, add to it or take anything away from it. No man, except Yeshua, would have had this authority and he never took it.

Only for the Jews

Many people still believe, in spite of all the Biblical evidence, that the seventh-day Sabbath is only for the Jewish people. When Yeshua stated that Sabbath was created for man, he spoke in a broader sense than just Jewish or even Israelite men and women. After all, Sabbath was created 'in the beginning' before there was ever a Noah, Shem, Abraham, Isaac, Jacob and Tribe of Judah. There was only Adam and Eve in the Garden of Eden and Sabbath was created for them to fellowship with their Creator.

Though Yeshua never spoke Greek, it is important to note that the Greek word *anthropos* translated "man" in Mark 2:27 literally means "man-faced". According to *Vine's Expository Dictionary of Hebrew and Greek Words*, the primary definition of *anthropos* is, "a human being, whether male or female, without reference to sex or nationality, to include all human beings." This means that Yeshua knew and understood that Sabbath was created for all human beings, not just his Jewish brothers and sisters.

Yeshua never taught that the Sabbath was abolished or would ever be. In fact, he taught just the opposite when he says that nothing will disappear from the Torah until heaven and earth pass away. Just because he angered the leaders didn't mean he was in any way breaking the Sabbath as God intended; he was challenging their manmade rules that had become so steeped in tradition that they were blinded to the commands of God (Mark 7:8).

These Scriptures in the Gospels, spoken and lived out by Yeshua, confirm that Sabbath was re-iterated in the New Testament. Yeshua, the one who was with the Father at the creation of the Sabbath day, kept the day holy as it was meant to be and called himself the Lord of the Sabbath for all men everywhere who would come to him and put their faith in God.

After the Resurrection

"Then they returned to Jerusalem from the hill called the Mount of Olives, a Sabbath day's walk (or 3/4 miles) from the city" (Acts 1:12).

The Apostles and the early church remained faithful to the Sabbath. This short walk shows that the disciples didn't break the Sabbath. Even with the resurrected Messiah, they still respected the allowable travel distance given to Israel.
Paul reasoned in the synagogues and spoke the gospel on the Sabbath.

"On the next Sabbath almost the whole city gathered to hear the word of the LORD ..." (Acts 13:44).

"Saul [Paul] spent several days with the disciples in Damascus. At once he began to preach in the synagogues that Yeshua is the Son of God" (Acts 9:20).

"On the Sabbath they [Paul and his companions] entered the synagogue and sat down. After the reading from the Law [Torah] and the Prophets, the leaders of the synagogue sent word to them, saying, "Brothers, if you have a word of exhortation for the people, please speak" (Acts 13:15-19).

"As Paul and Barnabas were leaving the synagogue, the people invited them to speak further about these things on the next Sabbath" (Acts 13:32).

"Instead we should write to them [the gentiles], telling them to abstain from food polluted by idols, from sexual immorality, from the meat of strangled animals and from blood. For the Torah of Moses has been preached in every city from the earliest times and is read in the synagogues on every Sabbath" (Acts 15:20-21).

Nothing changed regarding the seventh-day Sabbath after Yeshua's resurrection. Jews and gentiles who wanted to know God and hear the Word of the Lord gathered in the synagogues on the Sabbath.

Prophetic Signs and Promises

"I am the LORD your God; follow my decrees and be careful to keep my Torah. Keep my Sabbaths holy, that they may be a sign between us. Then you will know that I AM the LORD your God" (Ezekiel 20:19-20).

The prophet Ezekiel reminds the Israelites of the continued importance of Sabbath as a sign between God and His people. No matter where they lived, Sabbath was the sign they were in covenant relationship with Yahweh, the King of the Universe. By keeping the Sabbath, they remained in the center of God's promises and divine will.

"Say to the Israelites, 'You must observe my Sabbaths. This will be a sign between me and you for the generations to come, so you may know that I am the LORD who makes you holy" (Exodus 31:13).

The Nations and the Sabbath

Isaiah prophesied blessings for those from the nations who keep the Sabbath. Foreigners or gentiles who are joined to God (through faith in Yeshua), who serve Him, love His Name and worship Him, may enjoy all the Sabbath blessings included in the covenant and promises He made with Israel. They are no longer excluded and strangers. They can worship God together with Israel on His holy hill and receive joy in His house of prayer.

"Let no foreigner who has joined himself to the LORD say, the LORD will surely exclude me from His people.' And foreigners who bind themselves to the LORD, to serve Him, to love the name of the LORD and to worship Him, all who keep the Sabbath without desecrating it and who hold fast to my covenant - these will I bring to my holy mountain and give them joy in my house of prayer" (Isaiah 56:7).

"If you keep your feet from breaking the Sabbath and from doing as you please on my holy day, if you call the Sabbath a delight and the LORD's holy day honorable, and if you honor it by not going your own way and not doing as you please or speaking idle words, then you will find your joy in the LORD and I will cause you to ride on the heights of the land and to feast on the inheritance of your father Jacob" (Isaiah 58:13-14).

Just like the Jewish people, the nations are to enter into the Sabbath and focus on the God of Israel. They are to take delight in the Sabbath and honor it by staying home and resting, not doing their own thing. Their blessing is finding joy in the LORD and feasting on the inheritance given to Jacob.

Eternal Sabbath

"As the new heavens and the new earth that I make will endure before me,' declares the LORD, 'so will your name and descendants endure. From one New Moon to another and from one Sabbath to another, all mankind will come and bow down before me,' says the LORD. And they will go out and look upon the dead bodies of those who rebelled against me; their worm will not die, nor will their fire be quenched, and they will be loathsome to all mankind'" (Isaiah 66:22-24).

These words of Isaiah prophesy of the time after Yeshua's Millennial Kingdom, the time of the new heavens and earth. They also speak of mankind.   The word *mankind* means everyone regardless of nationality, gender, religious affiliation or doctrinal views of the Sabbath. There will be *mankind* who will obey and worship Yahweh and there will also be *mankind* who do not.   Just like in the wilderness, the consequence for disobedience is that their worm will not die (maggots) and they will be loathsome.

When God created the Sabbath, He never said, *"There was evening and morning, the seventh day."* Sabbath was supposed to be eternal fellowship between God and his glorious creation: *mankind.* Adam and Eve and all of their descendants were to live in the Garden of Eden forever, but sin ended that eternal fellowship. In order that *mankind* would not forget God's promise of redemption, He commanded remembering the weekly Sabbath as a memorial to the Garden of Eden and a foretaste of the future.   As it was 'in the beginning' so it will be again when there is a new heavens and a new earth.   The New Jerusalem will down out of heaven and Yahweh will once again make His dwelling with mankind (Revelation 21, 22). It is with this vision and hope of the eternal Sabbath and everlasting fellowship with our Father that we should remember the weekly Sabbath 'appointed time' with joy and delight.

Chapter Photo: The menorah burns at sunset during Sukkot in Sterling, Colorado.

The Sabbath Rest Remains
A Look at Hebrews 4:1-13

"Therefore, since the promise of entering his rest still stands, let us be careful that none of you be found to have fallen short of it" (verse 1).

There is a promise for entering God's rest and it still stands even within the context of the new covenant. The Sabbath rest has not been done away with or changed for it is an eternal reminder of the Creator's rest. We must be careful that we do not fall short of entering His rest. 'Falling short' is the Hebrew idiom for sin, and like in archery, we must not 'fall short' and *miss the mark*.

"For we also have had the gospel preached to us, just as they did; but the message they heard was of no value to them, because those who heard did not combine it with faith" (verse 2).

Sometimes it is surprising to hear that the Israelites had the gospel preached to them. This is because we think of the gospel as being the new testament only with John 3:16 as its foundation. However, the Israelites received the promise of salvation through a coming deliverer who they were to listen to (Deuteronomy 18:15). It was a veiled gospel; of good things to come.

Their obedience to God's commandments would be the evidence of their faith and would set them apart from the rest of the world. If they followed His ways, they would be a light to the nations from which salvation for the world would come.

They chose, however, to listen to Moses rather than have God speak to them directly (Ex. 20:19). Moses became the mediator between God and the people because they did not want to hear to God's voice themselves. They had more fear than faith in God's loving-kindness so His words were of no value to them and they didn't mix them with faith and. Without faith it is impossible to please God (Hebrews 11:6).

How often do we accept and believe the word of men over faith in the Word of God because we fear having to change, suffer or be alone? We must not be hearers of the Word only; we must be doers of the Word (James 1:22). We must believe and obey the commands of God by faith and put aside the teachings of men and centuries of watered-down inaccurate doctrines. According to Hebrews, faith and obedience go hand-in-hand. You can't have one without the other.

"Now we who have believed enter that rest, just as God has said, 'So I declared on oath in my anger, 'They shall never enter my rest...'" (verse 3).

We who put our faith in God and the truth of His Word enter God's rest. However, if we anger God by a lack of action-based faith, we will be no different than the Israelites in the wilderness who did not enter His rest (Psalm 95:11). *"And to whom was it that he swore that they would not enter his rest? Those who were disobedient. So we see that they were unable to enter because of lack of faith."* Hebrews 3:18-19 states the reason the Israelites missed the mark was a lack of faith.

"And yet his works have been finished since the creation of the world. For somewhere he has spoken about the seventh day (Sabbath) in these words: 'And on the seventh day God rested from all his work" (verse 4).

This verse is a direct reference to the seven-day creation account. God rested from all his creative work on the seventh day. His example set the cycle for our weekly lives by showing us that we are to work and be creative for six days and then rest on the seventh. The seventh day is not just any day that we choose, it is the day that our Creator chose. *"He also blessed the seventh-day and made it holy"* (Genesis 2:3).

"It still remains that some will enter that rest, and those who formerly had the gospel preached to them did not go in because of their disobedience" (verse 6).

The seventh-day Sabbath rest still remains; some will enter into it through obedience, some will not. In the wilderness, some of the children of Israel collected the right amount of manna on the sixth day so they would have enough on the seventh. Others collected too much or not enough and suffered the consequences. The disobedient children of Israel did not enter into God's Sabbath rest. Their persistent disobedience caused an entire generation of Israelites to die in the wilderness. According to Corinthians, we are to learn from the Israelites' mistakes and not fall into their same faithless disobedience (1 Corinthians 10:11).

"Therefore God again set a certain day, calling it Today, when a long time later he spoke through David, as was said before: 'Today if you hear his voice, do not harden your hearts'" (verse 7).

God set aside a certain day. He called it *Today*. He didn't bless *Today* like He did the Sabbath. He gave *Today* another purpose.

'Today' is *ha yom* in Hebrew and means 'the day'. *Today* is not about the Sabbath. *Today* is not about you setting aside whatever day works for you to rest or pick a new day to call the Sabbath. *Today* is THE day, if you have ears to hear His voice, that you are to commit your heart to Him. *Today* is THE day you make a choice. *Today* is THE day of God's favor (2 Corinthians 6:2). *Today* may fall the seventh-day Sabbath or *Today* may just be the day that the Creator chooses to write His Sabbath on your heart so that you can enter into His rest. *Today*, when He speaks, you are to obey His words.

"For if Joshua had given them rest, God would not have spoken later about another day" (verse 8).

Though Joshua led the people from the wilderness into the Promised Land, he did not give them rest. In fact, it was through Joshua that the Israelites slowly claimed their Land through battles and wars with kings and pagan nations. It wasn't until King Solomon that Israel had 'rest' and peace with the nations around them.

"There remains then, a Sabbath-rest for the people of God; for anyone who enters God's rest also rests from his own work, just as God did from his" (verse 9).

Some like to spiritualize the above verse. To do this brings confusion to the fourth commandment of remembering the Sabbath day. Read the verse again slowly. What do you see? *God rested from His creative physical work.* Those of us who desire to enter His rest must imitate Him and rest from our own creative works, our daily jobs just as He did.

There is no suggestion in this verse that 'resting from works' means resting from meaningless Jewish manmade traditions, denominational doctrines, or works of the law for salvation. These were not the works God rested from in the beginning. He did not need to rest from traditions or doctrines nor did He need salvation from sin.

There are some who believe that the Sabbath is a representation of the Messiah himself. They believe that when we accept Yeshua's work on the cross for our salvation that we somehow enter a personified Sabbath rest. Though we may liken our spiritual rest in Messiah to a type of 'sabbath', he is not the seventh-day weekly Sabbath rest that we are commanded to remember. When we observe the seventh-day Sabbath, God pours His light onto one of the shadows of His 'appointed times'. Then, we begin to see and understand the reality of the Sabbath and the Messiah who called himself "Lord of the Sabbath."

"Let us, therefore, make every effort to enter that rest, so that no one will fall by following their (Israelites) example of disobedience" (verse 11).

Entering God's rest takes effort because the world never rests; even most church goers never rest. There will always be activities and opportunities for breaking the Sabbath command. Entering into the Sabbath takes serious action on the part of the believer. This is not works-based action in order to be saved; it is faith expressing itself through love for our Father and his commandments (Galatians 5:6).

Though we are to make an effort to enter God's rest, to believe that keeping the Sabbath is a burden is a twisting of Scripture (1 John 5:3). Sabbath is one of the Ten Commandments. It is one of the guidelines in how we are to love God; our response to His incredible love, grace, and mercy to us. He wants us to rest from our creatives works whether it's seedtime or harvest and not be a slave to the world which is really where the burdens really lie.

Not entering God's rest is considered 'falling short'. This is the second time this is mentioned in the passage meaning that it is something important to remember. Falling is sin and sin is willful disobedience and not learning from Israel's example.

"For the word of God is living and active. Sharper than any double-edged sword, it penetrates even to dividing soul and spirit, joints and marrow; it judges the thoughts and attitudes of the heart" (verse 12).

The Word of God, the commands of God, the Torah, and the law are all the same expression for God's sword that penetrates our soul and spirit. God is able to judge the thoughts and attitudes of our minds because His Word is living and active. It is meant to 'cut us' so we look within ourselves and turn from disobedience and live by faith.

When it comes to the seventh-day Sabbath, there are many anti-semitic attitudes that need to be 'cut out' of our hearts. The sword of God's Word needs to penetrate our souls and spirits to remove anti-law doctrines and renew our minds.

"Nothing in all creation is hidden from God's sight. Everything is uncovered and laid bare before the eyes of him to whom we must give account" (verse 13).

Nothing in creation is hidden from God, especially the hearts of His people. He knows the iniquity in our hearts; he sees every sin we commit and every justification we create. Our actions of faith or faithlessness in this life will be uncovered and laid bare before our Father's eyes just like it was with the Israelites. We will all stand before the Judge of the Universe and give an account for the actions in our lives and He will use His commandments as the standard for righteousness.

The Sabbath was created in the beginning by God as part of His eternal redemption plan. It was given to Israel and how they lived it out is our example. This same Sabbath still remains and we have the same decision to make: enter into God's rest by faith or disobey.

God's command to rest from our creative work still stands because we are imitating Him. By making every effort to enter the weekly Sabbath and ceasing from our own creative works, we show the world that we have put our faith in the Creator of the Universe and trust His provision for our lives. When we mix our faith with action, we live out the fullness of the gospel and show that we believe in the coming Kingdom of God and an eternal Sabbath rest.

Faith in Yeshua does not nullify the Sabbath rest because he is Lord of the Sabbath. As the Son of God, he continued to guard the 'appointed time' obeying his Father's command. If Yeshua is Lord of our lives and he is Lord of the Sabbath, then Sabbath that remains until the end of time should be part of his Lordship in our lives.

Chapter Photo: Our Sabbath table in Jerusalem, Israel.

The New Moon - Rosh Chodesh

"So David said, "Look, tomorrow is the New Moon feast, and I am supposed to dine with the king.... Then Jonathan said to David, "Tomorrow is the New Moon feast. You will be missed, because your seat will be empty" (1 Samuel 20:5, 18).

New Moon celebrations are mentioned throughout the Scriptures. In Hebrew, the New Moon is called the *Rosh Chodesh*. According to *Vine's Dictionary of Biblical Terms*, the Hebrew word *rosh* means 'head'; *chadash* means to 'renew' in the sense of 'refresh'. The noun form of *chodesh* means 'moon' and so the *Rosh Chodesh* is literally the 'renewing of the moon' at the beginning of each month.

Using the calendar God gave to the Israelites, there are 12 months of 28 days. Each month is based on the lunar cycle and begins with the new moon; 14 days after the new moon, there is a full moon.

Sighting the New Moon

According to Rabbinical tradition during the Temple period, the *Rosh Chodesh* was determined by people in Jerusalem who separately witnessed the 'horns of the new moon'. Fires were lit and then two witnesses from the Sanhedrin who had seen the fires went to the high priest. With the agreement of the arrival of the new moon, the shofar would blow and the New Moon festival would begin. Up until that moment, no one knew when the 'appointed time' began.

There is no command in the Scriptures for 'sighting of the new moon' whether it's a conjunction, sliver or crescent. There is no command that a 'sighting' must come from Jerusalem, South Africa or Antarctica. There is no Biblical provision that any one person, rabbi, prophet high priest, king or best friend of any of those people, has the authority to determine the sighting of new moon for anyone else in any other part of the world.

Because of traditions created by men, there are many interpretations about when the New Moon celebration actually begins. With these misunderstandings comes division within the Body of Messiah to the point where people condemn others because they are celebrating holy days on the 'wrong day'.   To be sure, there is a right interpretation and we are to use the Scriptures and the Spirit's wisdom to discern the truth.   Believers are to be in unity because God is not the author of this confusion.

According to the command given in Leviticus 23, the 'appointed times' of Passover and Sukkot must begin on the full moon as they begin on the 15th day of the month.   With this knowlege, 14 days earlier has to be a new moon. Using astronomical calculations, this would make the new moon a conjunction.   Had the Israelites counted from a sliver or crescent moon, they would not have put the blood on their doorposts on the night that God passed over Egypt. Yeshua was crucified at Passover on the 14th day of the month. Counting 14 days from a crescent moon would have placed his crucifixion several days after God's 'appointed time'.

The Crescent Moon

The crescent moon has roots in pagan cultures and cannot be the new moon. Crescents were hanging on the camels' necks of the two Arab men that Gideon killed. Jeremiah warned about worshipping The Queen of Heaven who is depicted with a crescent moon. Paul talks about Artemis (aka Diana) in Athens, Greece. She is also depicted with a crescent moon. Islam derives its ideology from the moon-god, Allah, and a crescent moon sits on top of every mosque. Isaiah 3:18 issues a warning for those who attach themselves to the crescent moon, *"In that day the LORD will snatch away their finery: the bangles, the headbands and their crescent necklaces."*

David and Jonathan

"So David said, "Look, tomorrow is the New Moon festival, and I am supposed to dine with the king; but let me go and hide in the field until the evening of the day after tomorrow" (1 Samuel 20:5).

How did David know that the next day was the new moon? Did he see a sliver and know? Did he mention a crescent? Did he say anything about the blowing of the shofar from Jerusalem? No, to all of the above. He and Jonathan were at Ramah which is a short distance from Jerusalem. If there had been a shofar blast, he could have heard it if that is what he was listening for, but there was no Temple at this time. It was his son Solomon who was going to build the first Temple. So, how did he know that the next day was the new moon?

David would probably have done one of two things. Either he counted 14 days from the previous, obvious full moon or he understood looking at the final sliver of the old waning moon that the 'concealed' dark moon to follow was the new moon. The later can been seen in David's own writings.

Psalm 81 written by King David

"Sound the ram's horn at the New Moon, and when the moon is full on the day of our feast." This verse is taken from the NIV. It would seem from this version that the shofar is to be blown at the New Moon and the full moon.

"Blow up the trumpet in the new moon, in the time appointed, on our solemn feast day." This is from the KJV. This version doesn't mention the full moon, but says 'appointed time'.

Now to read the verse from the Psalm 81 in Hebrew. Note that it only has six words:

תקעו בחדש שופר בכסה ליום חגנו

The words are *taqa* (blow) *b'chodesh* (in the moon) *shofar* (trumpet) *b'kese* (in appointed) *yom* (day) *hachag* (the festival).

This is pretty straightforward except that *kese* doesn't mean 'appointed' as translated in the KJV or 'full moon' as translated in the NIV. The root word for *kese* is *kacah*. *Kacah* means 'to cover, to conceal, to hide, to clothe.' This means that *kese* cannot mean 'full moon' as a full moon isn't hiding nor is it concealed. *Kese* must then refer to when the moon cannot be seen at all or the dark moon.

A more proper translation from the original Hebrew would be: *"Blow the shofar on the concealed, hidden moon on the festival day."*

Feast of Trumpets is the only Feast of the LORD that occurs on a New Moon. It is also known as *Yom HaKeseh* or 'the day of our concealment.' Feast of Trumpets begins the 10 days of awe leading up to Yom Kippur and the Day of Judgment that has been kept 'hidden' from the enemy'. (It is an interesting type and shadow that David hid from his enemy, King Saul, on a concealed new moon.)

"But about that day or hour no one knows, not even the angels in heaven, nor the Son, but only the Father" (Matthew 24:36).

There are two interesting Hebrew idioms for the New Moon festival. The first is 'the day or the hour is not known'. This is has special significance for the Feast of Trumpets because it does fall on a new moon when 'no one ever knew the day or the hour' that the festival began until the moon was sighted. This is still true today and will continue to be true until Yeshua returns.

"Twinkling of an eye' also finds its roots in the conjunction of the moon. It is an ancient reference to when the sun, moon and Earth are aligned for a 'twinkling of an eye'. It is at this moment, on a New Moon celebration that transformation of the saints from mortal to immortality will occur.

"In a flash, in the twinkling of an eye, at the last trumpet. For the trumpet will sound, the dead will be raised imperishable, and we will be changed" (1 Corinthians 15:52).

An Amazing Water Coincidence

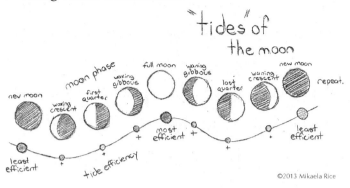

©2013 Mikaela Rice

Tides are created because the Earth and the moon are attracted to each other. The moon tries to pull at anything on the Earth to bring it closer. The Earth's gravity is able to hold tightly onto everything except water. Since water isn't solid, the moon is able to pull and move large bodies of water. This periodic rise and fall of the oceans is is known as the tides.

There are two high tides and two low tides during a 24 hour period. When the sun and moon are aligned, there are strong gravitational forces causing very high and very low tides. These are called spring tides. When the sun and moon are not aligned, the gravitational forces cancel each other out and the tides are not as dramatically high and low. These are called neap tides.

Spring tides, which have nothing to do with the season, occur during the full moon and the new moon. What is interesting from tide charts is how the spring tide of the new moon falls on a concealed moon. Also, the actual spring tide, in the springtime of the year at the concealed new moon, when the months of God's year begin, is stronger than any other tide of the year.

We should not take it upon ourselves to determine the new moon apart from the information given in Scripture. The Creator of the Universe gave us everything we need to correctly establish His appointed times and either we use them or wait until Messiah returns and there will be no question.

The LORD's Passover

"This is a day you are to commemorate; for the generations to come you shall celebrate it as a festival to the LORD—a lasting ordinance" (Exodus 12:14).

The LORD's Passover is the first annual Feast of the LORD. It is the memorial to the extraordinary account of God's judgment on Egypt's gods and Israel's miraculous deliverance from a life of slavery. The Passover, or *Pesach* in Hebrew, began Israel's physical redemption as God's holy nation and they were to remember their salvation from death to life in the 'appointed time' called Passover.

Hebrew Word Pictures

Passover - *Pesach* פסח

Peh פ - A Mouth means 'to speak'

Samech ס - A Prop means 'to support and protect'

Chet ח - A Fence means 'inner chamber'

The Hebrew word picture for *pesach*: *"To speak support and protection in the inner chamber."*

For hundreds of years the descendants of Jacob were enslaved in Egypt building Pharaoh great cities. They were oppressed with hard labor from digging clay to making bricks to all kinds of field work. They were shown no mercy by their overseers. In spite of this oppression, their population increased. Pharaoh asked that the midwives kill all baby boys as they were born, but because they feared God, they let the boys live. Pharaoh then ordered that all baby boys be thrown into the Nile River.

One baby boy from a Levite family was placed in a papyrus basket and floated in the river. He was found by Pharaoh's daughter who named him Moses or Moshe which means *'pulled out of the water.'* She located his mother and paid her to nurse him. When he was old enough, he left his mother and went to live in Pharaoh's house as a prince of Egypt.

As an adult Moshe struggled with what he saw happening to his people, the Hebrew people. In a moment of anger, he killed a man. When word of it spread to Pharaoh, he feared for his life and ran to the land of Midian on the northwest of the Arabian peninsula. He became a shepherd and married Tzipporah, the daughter of a Midian priest. They had a son named Gershom.

God heard the cries of the children of Israel. He saw their bondage and their misery. Through a burning bush, He called Moshe to become their deliverer. He told Moshe to go to Pharaoh and tell him to let His people go. Even so, God warned Moshe that He would harden Pharaoh's heart until he understood through the death of his firstborn son that Israel is the firstborn son of God. Armed with a staff in his hand and the name of God - the *Yod Hey Vav Hey*, the I Am that I Am - Moses started out for Egypt. During his journey, Moshe met Aaron and they returned to confront Pharaoh together.

Egypt was culture of death. Their gods and goddesses glorified death. Their Pharaohs were immortalized in grand pyramid tombs filled with symbols of death. Their book for immortalizing those who passed on was called the "Book of Death". So God gave them what they worshipped and honored the most - death.

Through Moshe, God judged each of the gods of Egypt with plagues: water to blood, frogs, gnats or lice, flies, cattle disease, boils, hailstones, locusts, darkness, The people of Egypt suffered. The land of Egypt suffered. Even with the loss of livestock and crops, Pharaoh would not relent and set his slaves free. Then, God's 'appointed time' of deliverance arrived.

"Moshe said [to Pharaoh], "Here is what the LORD says: 'About midnight I will go out into Egypt, and all the firstborn in the land of Egypt will die, from the firstborn of Pharaoh sitting on his throne to the firstborn of the slave-girl at the handmill, and all the firstborn of the livestock. There will be a horrendous wailing throughout all the land of Egypt — there has never been another like it, and there never will be again. But not even a dog's growl will be heard against any of the people of Israel, neither against people nor against animals. In this way you will realize that the LORD distinguishes between Egyptians and Israel. All your servants will come down to me, prostrate themselves before me and say, "Get out! — you and all the people who follow you!" and after that, I will go out!' " And he went out from Pharaoh in the heat of anger" (Exodus 11:4-8).

Preparations Begin

"The LORD said to Moses and Aaron in Egypt, "This month is to be for you the first month, the first month of your year. Tell the whole community of Israel that on the tenth day of this month each man is to take a lamb for his family, one for each household" (Exodus 12:1-3).

Though the children of Israel experienced the first three plagues against Egypt, God guarded them from the rest. In order to protect His people from the death of the firstborn, He had them bring a lamb or goat into their home for four days. It had to be an animal without defect, a first-year male, and enough to feed each household.

"Take care of them [the goat or lamb] until the fourteenth day of the month, when all the members of the community of Israel must slaughter them at twilight. Then they are to take some of the blood and put it on the sides and tops of the door frames of the houses where they eat the lambs"
(Exodus 12:-6-7).

After caring for their animals for four days, the Israelites were to slaughter them at twilight, after sunset, when the sun is below the horizon and a soft glowing light emanates from the sky. They were to put some of the animal's blood on the sides and tops of the door frames where they were going to eat the meal.

In the Hebrew alphabet, the eighth letter is *chet* ח and represents the number 8 and 'new beginnings.' The word 'life' or *chaim* also comes from *chet* and means 'life'. The manner in which the blood was placed around the door sides and top formed the the letter *chet* - a new beginning of life.

"On that same night I will pass through Egypt and strike down every firstborn of both people and animals, and I will bring judgment on all the gods of Egypt. I am the Lord. The blood will be a sign for you on the houses where you are, and when I see the blood, I will pass over you. No destructive plague will touch you when I strike Egypt" (Exodus 12:12-13).

As the Israelites remained in their homes, the blood on their doorposts was a sign for God, the Destroyer. When He saw the sign of the blood, He would 'pass over' the firstborn sons who were in the home protected by blood while allowing the firstborn of Egypt to die.

"This is how you are to eat it [the meal]: with your cloak tucked into your belt, your sandals on your feet and your staff in your hand. Eat it in haste; it is the LORD's Passover" (Exodus 12:11).

The Passover meal consisted of roasted lamb, bread without leaven, and bitter herbs. The Israelites were not to break the bones of the lamb or take any of the meal outside of their homes. They were to eat it in haste.

"At midnight the LORD struck down all the firstborn in Egypt, from the firstborn of Pharaoh, who sat on the throne, to the firstborn of the prisoner, who was in the dungeon, and the firstborn of all the livestock as well. Pharaoh and all his officials and all the Egyptians got up during the night, and there was loud wailing in Egypt, for there was not a house without someone dead" (Exodus 12:29-30).

Lasting Ordinance

"And when your children ask you, 'What does this ceremony mean to you?' then tell them, 'It is the Passover sacrifice to the Lord, who passed

over the houses of the Israelites in Egypt and spared our homes when he struck down the Egyptians" (Exodus 12:27).

Passover was to be celebrated throughout all the generations of the Israelites no matter where they lived. There were also specific regulations regarding the Passover. No foreigner, slave or traveler was to eat the meal unless they were circumcised. Once circumcised they would be considered a citizen of the Land and could take part in the meal. The meal was always to be eaten in the house and no meat was to be taken outside. The bones of the Passover lamb were never to be broken.

In Joshua chapter 5, there is the account of the Israelites celebrating Passover in Gilgal after taking flint knives and circumcising all the men who had come out of the wilderness. In 2 Kings 23, Josiah destroys all the high places and idols from Israel and the the nation celebrates Passover in Jerusalem for the first time since the days of the Judges. In Ezra chapter 6, when the Israelites returned from captivity, all who renounced the pagan practices of the nations celebrated the Passover. Ezekiel 45 speaks about Passover being celebrated in the Millennial Kingdom by putting blood on the door-frames of the house [Temple], on the four corners of the Altar's ledge and on the supports of the gate of the Inner Courtyard.

The 'Appointed Time' of Messiah

"He [Yeshua] replied, "Go into the city to a certain man and tell him, 'The Teacher says: My appointed time is near. I am going to celebrate the Passover with my disciples at your house'" (Matthew 26:18).

The 'appointed time' of Passover was celebrated by Yeshua with his disciples. Using two cups of wine and unleavened bread handed down in the traditional Passover memorial called a seder, he began to renew the marriage covenant given to Israel at Mount Sinai (Luke 22). However, in order to institute the new covenant, there had to be the shedding of blood. His blood.

Another cup of wine, a third cup, was also poured at a traditional seder to remember the plague judgments on Egypt with the final one being the death of the firstborn. Yeshua didn't mention this cup of wine at his seder probably because he knew the plague of death was coming for him as the Lamb of God. Even though he prayed earnestly for his Father to allow the cup of death to 'pass over' him, he knew he had to go forth with the plan. There would be no lamb's blood on the doorposts of any house to protect his life. His blood was going to be poured out.

"They are the Israelites who are to be given wholly to me. I have taken them as my own in place of the firstborn ..." (Numbers 8:16).

Isaac, the beloved firstborn son of Abraham, had experienced the pass-over when the blood of a ram saved him from death. This 'binding of Isaac' became the vision of redemption for God's people. When God allowed the firstborn the sons of Israel to live through the plague of death with the substitute sacrifice, He again revealed His plan of salvation through a lamb. When Yeshua hung on the cross, he cried out, "It is finished." With those words he died. The beginning of the salvation of Israel and the world began with the substitute sacrifice of the Lamb of God.

"For Messiah, our Passover lamb, has been sacrificed. Therefore let us keep the Festival ..." (1 Corinthians 5:7).

Chapter Photo: Our family's Passover table ready for guests.

A Betrothal Ceremony

"And he [Yeshua] said to them, "I have eagerly desired to eat this Passover with you before I suffer. For I tell you, I will not eat it again until it finds fulfillment in the kingdom of God" (Luke 22:15).

Yeshua longed to celebrate his final Passover with his disciples. He knew his time was short and he wanted to explain God's plan of reconciliation at its 'appointed time.' As the the Lamb of God, he offered salvation to his brothers and sisters who were enslaved by sin and the consequences of their rebelliousness. As the Son of God, he would transform the Passover seder's traditional elements into a betrothal ceremony with a groom, a bride, a cup of wine, the bride's father, the bride price, wedding preparations, and wedding guests. With this Passover seder, Yeshua would institute the renewed covenant of marriage that would restore Israel to her Husband.

The Groom

"He had no beauty or majesty to attract us to him, nothing in his appearance that we should desire him. He was despised and rejected by men, a man of sorrows, and familiar with suffering. Like one from whom men hide their faces he was despised, and we esteemed him not. Surely he took up our infirmities and carried our sorrows, yet we considered him stricken by Yahweh, smitten by him, and afflicted" (Isaiah 53:2-5).

The groom is Yeshua himself. Scripture describes him as having no beauty or majesty. He was not handsome like King David; he had no desirable outward appearance. He was so unattractive that men hid their faces from him, yet he desired a Bride.

The Bride

In a Jewish betrothal ceremony, the hopeful groom would offer the potential bride a cup of wine as his proposal for marriage. He would drink from the cup first and then offer it to her. If she accepted the proposal, the woman would drink from the cup of wine. By sharing the cup with the man, she agreed to be 'set apart' as his bride. She would remain faithful to him until the day of their wedding when their marriage would be consummated. A week-long wedding feast would follow with friends and family.

"After taking the cup [of Sanctification], he gave thanks and said, 'Take this and divide it among you. For I tell you I will not drink again of the fruit of the vine until the kingdom of God comes'" (Luke 22:14-16).

In the Passover seder, the first cup of wine is called the "Cup of Sanctification." After blessing the cup, Yeshua offered the cup of wine to his disciples. As each one drank from the cup, they acknowledged they were accepting Yeshua's marriage proposal. It became their individual testimony they were going to become Yeshua's sanctified, holy, and set apart Bride.

Once the Cup of Sanctification had been shared, the bridegroom would not drink the fruit of the vine until the wedding feast. The bride, however, was to remember her betrothed and the marriage covenant she entered every time she drank from the cup.

"For whenever you eat this bread and drink this cup, you proclaim the Lord's death until he comes" (1 Corinthians 11:26).

The Bride's Father

"If God were your Father, you would love me, for I [Yeshua] came from God and now am here. Why is my language not clear to you? Because you are

unable to hear what I say. You belong to your father, the devil, and you want to carry out your father's desire. He was a murderer from the beginning..." (John 8:44-6).

After the bride accepts the groom's proposal, the bride's father sets the bride price. Generally it was something of value because the father was losing a daughter. In Israel's case (and ours), our father is the devil and murder is his speciality. He would rather have Israel destroyed than to have her redeemed. He would rather see us die in our sins than be restored to eternal life. The Adversary required the highest price that could be paid to take us from him. He required that our Betrothed die for us. He required that he be beaten, bruised and killed. He required that he shed his blood.

The Bride Price

"And he took bread, gave thanks and broke it, and gave it to them, saying, 'This is my body given for you; do this in remembrance of me.' In the same way, after the supper he took the cup (of Redemption), saying, "This cup is the new covenant in my blood, which is poured out for you" (Luke 22:19).

Then Yeshua poured a second cup of wine. In the Passover seder, this cup is called the "Cup of Redemption". Along with some unleavened bread, he held up the cup and made a powerful declaration. For us, his Beloved, he would pay the required bride price.

"... He humbled himself and became obedient to death - even death on a cross!" (Philippians 3:10).

Another cup of wine, a third cup called 'The Cup of Plagues" was poured to remember the judgments on Egypt with the final one being the death of the firstborn. Because God allowed the firstborn of Israel to live, they had to redeem or 'buy back' their firstborn sons with the sacrifice of a lamb. Now, the Lamb of God was going to 'buy back' God's firstborn son, Israel (Exodus 4:22). Yeshua did pour this cup with his disciples in the upper room, instead he wrestled with it as he prayed to his Father on the Mount of Olives and sweat great drops of blood.

"Father, if you are willing, take this cup from me; yet not my will, but yours be done." An angel from heaven appeared to him and strengthened him. And being in anguish, he prayed more earnestly, and his sweat was like drops of blood falling to the ground" (Luke 22:42-44).

A fourth cup of wine called "The Cup of Completion" was not consumed during the Passover in Yeshua's time. Instead, it was consumed the next day to complete the Passover memorial. Yeshua drank this now soured cup of wine while he was hanging on the cross. With the words, *"It is finished,"* he completed the Passover memorial, gave up his spirit, and died. The bride price had been paid.

"Knowing that everything had now been finished, and so that Scripture would be fulfilled, Yeshua said, "I am thirsty." A jar of wine vinegar was there, so they soaked a sponge in it, put the sponge on a stalk of the hyssop plant, and lifted it to Yeshua's lips. When he had received the drink, Yeshua said, "It is finished." With that, he bowed his head and gave up his spirit" (John 18:28-30).

The Groom's Preparation

"In my Father's house are many rooms; if it were not so, I would have told you. I am going there to prepare a place for you. And if I go and prepare a place for you, I will come back and take you to be with me that you also may be where I am" (John 14:2,3).

After sealing the marriage covenant, the bridegroom would leave for a time to prepare a home for his bride. In Middle Eastern culture, he would add a room onto his father's house. The addition could take anywhere from two days to two years. Before Yeshua dies, resurrects and ascends to his Father, he tells his newly Betrothed, that he was going to prepare a place in his Father's house (which is the Temple in Jerusalem). He promised to return for them so that they could be where he would be.

The Bride's Preparation

"Since we have these promises, dear friends, let us purify ourselves from everything that contaminates body and spirit, perfecting holiness or sanctification out of reverence for the Lord" (2 Corinthians 7:1).

The bride, now bought with a price, would spend her time preparing herself for her wedding day (1 Corinthians 6:20). It would arrive at an unknown day and hour so she always had to be ready. Waiting as a wise virgin, she would light an oil lamp in her window just in case her bridegroom arrived during the night. She had known of other brides being swept away sometime near midnight and she wanted to be ready when she heard, *'Here's the bridegroom! Come out to meet him'!' ... The virgins who are ready went in with him to the wedding banquet. And the door was shut"* (Matthew 25:6,10).

In Greek sanctification is *hagiasmos* and means 'to be set apart for a holy purpose'. Sanctification is the process by which a person is incorporated more fully into the physical and spiritual reality of Messiah being made more like him and doing the will of his Father. Being 'set apart for a holy purpose' is more than just drinking a small glass of wine and eating a dissolving wafer or piece of bread every other week. Sanctification is the course of life consistent with those who are separated out of the world as the Bride of Messiah.

Sanctification comes through Yeshua: *"For them I sanctify myself, that they too may be truly sanctified"* (John 17:19). Sanctification comes through studying the Scriptures: *"Sanctify them by the truth; your word is truth"* (John 17:17) . Sanctification comes through the power of the Holy Spirit: *"... Who have been chosen according to the foreknowledge of God the Father, through the sanctifying work of the Spirit ..."* (1 Peter 1:2).

Sanctification must be pursued by the Bride earnestly and unswervingly. The Bride will make every effort to be holy for without holiness no one will see Yeshua (Hebrews 12:14). The Bride of Messiah will *"make every effort to be found spotless, blameless and at peace with him"* when Yeshua comes (2 Peter 3:1-4).

The sanctified, holy character of the Bride is not transferred from one person to another. This is the meaning of Yeshua's Parable of the 10

Virgins.   Those Virgins who had oil in their lamps could not give it away.   Oil is bought at the cost of *"keeping oneself from being polluted by the world"* (James 1:27).   The Bride of Messiah will be ready with oil and her lamp lit when her Bridegroom arrives at an unknown hour (Matthew 25).

The Father of the Groom

"For the Lord himself will come down from heaven, with a loud command, with the voice of the archangel and with the trumpet call of God…" (1 Thessalonians 4:16).

The father of the groom determined the time that his son would return for his bride.   The groom could only return for his bride when the addition to the house was complete.   This was so that the groom wouldn't rush, but properly prepare a home for the arrival is his bride.

Neither the groom nor the bride knew the exact day or the hour of their wedding, but it would arrive with the fanfare of the groom's best friends and the excited wedding party. There would be lots of noise and shouting.   The excited bridegroom would then enter the bride's home and 'snatch her away'.   Together they would return to his father's house and enter the wedding chamber where they would consummate their marriage.   A week later they would reappear and the wedding feast would begin.

On a day and hour unknown, at the 'appointed time' of his Father, Yeshua will be coming back for his Bride.   He will arrive with a great shout, a trumpet blast and his Bride will rise to meet him in the air. They will go to the bridal chamber where they will consummate their marriage and then live in his Father's house.

The Wedding Guests

"Then the angel said to me, "Write this: Blessed are those who are invited to the wedding banquet of the Lamb!" And he added, "These are the true words of God" (Revelation 19:9).

Only a select few consisting of bridesmaids, groomsmen along with parents and immediate family members attend a wedding rehearsal dinner with the bride and groom. The friends and relatives of the bride and groom make up the enormous guest list.

Yeshua is speaking about the wedding feast when he says it will occur in the Kingdom of heaven (Matthew 8:10-12, Luke 13:28-30). The Kingdom of heaven is not some remote corner of the sky hidden above the clouds. The Kingdom of heaven, according to Yeshua, is here on earth and will be here on earth. He will return here for his Bride, have the ultimate wedding feast [Passover] and then take his Bride to his Father's house [the Temple] and within its many rooms they will live.

Yeshua describes the guests that will be at wedding feast of the Lamb in different parables. He says that many will come from the east and west and take their places at the feast with Abraham, Isaac, and Jacob.

"After this I looked, and there before me was a great multitude that no one could count, from every nation, tribe, people and language, standing before the throne and before the Lamb. They were wearing white robes and were holding palm branches in their hands. And they cried out in a loud voice: "Salvation belongs to our God, who sits on the throne, and to the Lamb" (Revelation 7:9-10).

In Revelation, there is a multitude of people wearing white robes washed in the blood of the Lamb. They hold palm branches and cry out *Hosanna* just as those who accompanied Yeshua into Jerusalem. This is an enormous group of people from every generation who received salvation through faith in the Messiah. They are from every nation, tribe, and language. They are overjoyed and sing at the throne of Yeshua. These men, women, and children are the invited guests at the wedding feast of the Lamb.

Yeshua also says that not everyone invited to the wedding feast will attend. Some make excuses like having just bought property or a cow (Luke 14). Others will excuse themselves because the 'Jewish' feast isn't for them. Some guests who thought they were important will find out they are not: *'the first shall be last and the last shall be first'* (Matthew 20:6). Other guests will be *'thrown out of the kingdom into outer darkness'* for not following protocol and wearing the proper wedding clothes (Matthew 22:11).

The Wedding of the Lamb

"Let us rejoice and be glad and give the glory to Him for the wedding of the Lamb has come, and his bride has made herself ready. Fine linen, bright and clean, was given her to wear. (Fine linen stands for the righteous acts of the saints)" (Revelation 19:8).

The wedding of the Lamb will take place in the Kingdom of God. The wedding hall will be filled with guests. The Bride's righteous way of life will be rewarded with a gown of fine linen, bright and clean, for her to wear in front of all the wedding guests. The Bridegroom will once again drink the fruit of the vine with his Bride.

Until her glorious wedding day, the wise Virgin will spend her life preparing herself with acts of righteousness. She will keep herself pure and holy and unspotted from the world through personal sanctification. She will keep her lamp full of oil waiting for the soon return of her Bridegroom at his 'appointed time.' Every year she will commemorate the Passover as the annual reminder of his words to her, *"Do this in remembrance of me"* while he is away preparing a place for them to live in his Father' (1 Corinthians 11:23-24).

Chapter Photo: My son and daughter-in-law sharing a cup of wine at their wedding ceremony after which they broke the glass.

Feast of Unleavened Bread - Matzah

"These are the LORD's appointed festivals, the sacred assemblies you are to proclaim at their appointed times: the LORD's Passover begins at twilight on the fourteenth day of the first month. On the fifteenth day of that month the LORD's Festival of Matzah  *Unleavened Bread begins; for seven days you must eat bread made without yeast. On the first day hold a sacred assembly and do no regular work"* (Leviticus 23:4-7).

The seven days of Unleavened Bread follow the Passover as a memorial to the Exodus when the Israelites were set free from slavery. The first day of unleavened bread when Israel left Egypt is the exact day that Jacob and his family entered Egypt centuries earlier. The Exodus marked the end of the prophecy given to Abraham that his descendants would be enslaved in a foreign land for 400 years (Genesis 15:13). Through the blessing of the God of Jacob, a family of 70 had grown to over one million.

After losing his firstborn son and the firstborn of all of his kingdom, Pharaoh set the people of Israel free. God made the Egyptians favorably disposed to the Israelites and they were more than willing for them to take whatever they wanted from livestock to gold just so they would leave their land. For seven days the children of Israel traveled from Egypt to Sukkoth during which time they ate only *matzah.*

"They baked matzah loaves from the dough they had brought out of Egypt, since it was unleavened; because they had been driven out of Egypt without time to prepare supplies for themselves" (Exodus 12:39).

Soured Dough - Chametz

"You are not to eat any chametz with it; for seven days [of Unleavened Bread] you are to eat with it matzah, the bread of affliction; for you came out of the land of Egypt in haste. Thus you will remember the day you left the land of Egypt as long as you live" (Deuteronomy 16:3).

'Leaven' in Hebrew is *chametz* and literally means 'soured dough.' In ancient times, leavening was done through a soured starter dough. The starter was a mixture of flour combined with water and allowed to sit for several days, souring the dough. A portion of this soured dough could be mixed with other flour creating a leavened dough. Then, a little more flour is added to the lump of starter to keep the wild yeast from dying. By removing the *chametz* from their homes, the Israelites were literally throwing away a 'lump of dough' in order to start over with a new batch.

"Get rid of the old lump, so that you can be a new batch of dough, because in reality you are unleavened..." (1 Corinthians 5:7).

Yeshua used the leaven of 'soured dough' to symbolize the false teachings and traditions of the elders that diluted the truth of the Scriptures. Just as a little leaven infects a whole loaf of bread, centuries of false teachings and manmade practices had contaminated the Word of God.

This is what happened to the Israelites in Egypt. Centuries of other gods and Egyptian culture had infiltrated their lives and their faith. God commanded His people to remove all 'soured dough' from their homes because He desired that His people would leave behind the leaven of Egypt and become decontaminated from the ways of that nation. For seven days they were to eat nothing but the 'bread of affliction' and search their souls. They were to turn away from everything that had soured their hearts and minds in that world of darkness and slavery.

The Bread of Affliction

Within the symbolism of the 'bread of affliction,' there is the idea of death and decay.   As the little yeasty bugs puff up the dough by souring it, they are actually dying and decaying. If the dough is allowed to rise too long, those little guys run out of energy and the loaf flattens or 'dies'. This is the essence of the new pure lump of dough where there has been affliction and the death of those yeasty bugs that puff up the dough with pride and unbelief.

When making unleavened bread or matzah, it is important to prick the dough. This allows all air and steam to escape and keep the dough flat. As it bakes, it turns brown between the piercings giving the bread the appearance of stripes.   In the traditional Passover seder, a piece of *matzah* is broken and half, wrapped in a white cloth and hidden. It is called the *afikomen* and means 'that which comes after.'

After the Passover supper, Yeshua used the *afikomen* to reveal himself as 'the coming one.'   He broke the pierced and striped bread, his 'bread of affliction', and gave it to his disciples to eat. He was arrested during the night, beaten in the morning, and hung on the cross in the afternoon where his broken and afflicted body died. (Mark 10:45).

"Also, taking a piece of matzah, he made the blessing, broke it, gave it to them and said, "This is my body, which is being given for you; do this in memory of me" (Luke 22:19).

Preparation Day

"It was Preparation Day [for Unleavened Bread], and the Jews did not want the bodies to remain on the stake on Shabbat, since it was an especially important Shabbat. In the vicinity of where he [Yeshua] had been executed was a garden, and in the garden was a new tomb in which no one had ever been buried. So, because it was Preparation Day [for Unleavened Bread] ..., and because the tomb was close by, that is where they buried Yeshua" (John 19:31, 41-42).

The day these events took place was the Preparation Day for Unleavened Bread and known as a 'high sabbath', different from the weekly Sabbath. Because sunset was approaching and the Feast of Unleavened Bread was arriving, Yeshua was immediately rubbed with myrrh, wrapped in linens and placed in a tomb. He was buried *hastily* and his 'appointed time ' in the grave began. For the first three days and three nights of the Feast of Unleavened Bread, Yeshua lay dead, left to decay in a tomb.

"You are to observe the festival of matzah, for on this very day I brought your divisions out of the land of Egypt. Therefore, you are to observe this day from generation to generation by a perpetual regulation" (Exodus 12:17).

The Feast of Unleavened Bread was a permanent regulation to be celebrated from generation to generation to remember Israel's hasty exodus from the land of Egypt. The 'appointed time' of *matzah* was fulfilled by the hasty burial of Yeshua, the unleavened bread from heaven, who was 'the coming one.' Paul tells the Corinthians that believers in Messiah are to remove the 'soured dough' lump of false teachings and celebrate the festivals of Unleavened Bread (and Passover) not with the puffed up bread of wickedness and evil, but with the *matzah* of purity and sincerity in the Truth of God's Word.

For our Pesach lamb, the Messiah, has been sacrificed. Therefore, let us keep the feast, not with old leaven, nor with leaven of vice and malice and wickedness, but with the unleavened [bread] of purity (nobility, honor) and sincerity and [unadulterated] truth" (1 Corinthians 5:7-8 The Amplified Bible).

Chapter Photo: Piece of Passover matzah with stripes and piercings.

Feast of Firstfruits - Yom Habikkurim

"The Lord said to Moses, "Speak to the Israelites and say to them: 'When you enter the land I am going to give you and you reap its harvest, bring to the priest a sheaf of the first grain you harvest. He is to wave the sheaf before the LORD so it will be accepted on your behalf; the priest is to wave it on the day after the Sabbath. On the day you wave the sheaf, you must sacrifice as a burnt offering to the LORD a lamb a year old without defect, together with its grain offering of two-tenths of an ephah of the finest flour mixed with olive oil—a food offering presented to the LORD, a  *pleasing aroma—and its drink offering of a quarter of a hin of wine. You must not eat any bread, or roasted or new grain, until the very day you bring this offering to your God. This is to be a lasting ordinance for the generations to come, wherever you live"* (Leviticus 23:9-14).

The Offerings

When Israel entered the Promised Land, they were to celebrate the day of Firstfruits by offering an individual sheaf of grain from their harvest. The sheaf was to be waved by the priest along with a burnt offering of a lamb, a fellowship offering of fine grain mixed with olive oil and a drinking offering of wine.

For the burnt offering, a lamb without defect was presented to the LORD. Laying hands on the animal's head was called *semichah*. It implied a physical 'leaning' on the animal so that the weight of the man was transferred to the animal. This was symbolic of transferring the identity of the man onto the lamb. In effect, the lamb represented him before God. The blood of the lamb was splattered on the sides of the Altar. Then the lamb was completely burnt up on the Altar as a food offering and a pleasing aroma to the LORD.

The grain offering was a free will offering. It was to be from kernels from fresh ears, dry roasted and covered in olive oil and frankincense or it could be a fine flour mixed with olive oil and frankincense poured over it. A grain offering could be baked in an oven like bread, cooked on a griddle like a pancake or boiled in a pot like a dumpling.

A *hin* of liquid was equal to about 1.5 gallons or 5.7 liters. The drink offering was a quarter of a *hin* of wine or close to one liter - the size of a modern-day Coke. It was to be poured out at the foot of the altar as part of the burnt and grain offering.

These three firstfruits offerings of the lamb, the grain, and the wine were Yeshua's reality within the Passover that had occurred several days earlier: the Lamb of God, his broken body and poured out blood. These offerings were presented to God by the priest bringing individual atonement for sin.

The Sheaf of Grain

"Those who go out weeping, carrying seed to sow, will return with songs of joy, carrying sheaves with them" (Psalm 126:6).

There was another offering on firstfruits, a sheaf of grain. According to *Zondervan's Bible Dictionary,* sheaves are the stalks of grain left behind by the reaper. It is gathered by the handfuls and bound by women or children in a joyful manner. Collected sheaves were carried by donkeys or on heavily loaded carts to the threshing floor. Some sheaves were left behind for the poor. The sheaves that were offered as Firstfruits were only the amount that an individual could hold, a handful.

According to the command, a handful of sheaves from the spring harvest was to be brought to the priest. He became the intercessor between the individual and God as he waved it before the LORD as an acceptable offering. Until the firstfruits sheaf was accepted by God, no one was to eat any roasted or new grain.

Yeshua, the Firstfruits

"Very truly I tell you, unless a kernel of wheat falls to the ground and dies, it remains only a single seed. But if it dies, it produces many seeds" (John 12:24).

In the beginning eternal fellowship with God was cut short by sin and death. God promised a Seed who would have victory over death and restore fellowship with Him. In order to have a sheaf of grain, there has to be a planting of one Seed. Once put into the ground, it dies and then produces a harvest. Yeshua is the promised Seed. He was buried in the ground and rose to life producing a firstfruits sheaf of grain becoming the firstfruits of those who have fallen asleep.

"But Messiah has indeed been raised from the dead, the firstfruits of those who have fallen asleep" (1 Corinthians 15:20).

Notice that he was the plural firstfruits of those raised from the dead, not the singular. According to the gospel of Matthew, at the moment of Yeshua's death, when the temple curtain was torn in two, the bodies of holy people who had died were raised to life. A firstfruits resurrection of the dead had occurred.

"At that moment the curtain of the temple was torn in two from top to bottom. The earth shook, the rocks split and the tombs broke open. The bodies of many holy people who had died were raised to life. They came out of the tombs after Yeshua's resurrection and went into the holy city and appeared to many people" (Matthew 27:52-23).

The Day After the Sabbath

Over the centuries a lot of confusion has developed over the meaning of the 'day after the Sabbath' because the first and last days of the Feast of Unleavened Bread are also called 'sabbaths'. God never called these days Sabbath even though He commanded complete rest. This subtlety is a manmade tradition that has caused the Feast of Firstfruits to fall on whatever day of the week the 'day after the sabbath' of Unleavened Bread begins. This rendering has blurred the tremendous differences between the Feast of Unleavened Bread and Firstfruits and put much less emphasis on the day of the firstfruits of those raised from the dead. If the sheaf were to be waved by the priest on the day after the weekly Sabbath during the week of Unleavened Bread, this would always put Firstfruits on the 'first day of the week' and put a powerful reality of Yeshua in another of God's 'appointed times!'

"When the Sabbath was over, on the first day of the week when it was still dark, Mary Magdalene, Mary the mother of James, and Salome bought spices so they might go anoint Yeshua's body. Just after sunrise, they were on the way to the tomb and they asked each other, 'Who will roll the stone away from the entrance of the tomb?' When they arrived at the tomb, they saw the stone had been removed from the entrance. They entered, but they did not find the body of Yeshua. While they were wondering about this, suddenly two men in clothes that gleamed like lightning stood beside them. In their fright the women bowed down with their faces to the ground, but the men said to them, "Why do you look for the living among the dead? He is not here; he has risen! Remember how he told you, while he was still with you in Galilee: The Son of Man must be delivered over to the hands of sinners, be crucified and on the third day be raised again.' Then they remembered his words. 'Go quickly and tell his disciples, 'He has risen from the dead....' They told this to the apostles, but they did not believe the women, because their words seemed to them like nonsense. Peter, however, got up and ran to the tomb. He saw the strips of linen lying there, as well as the cloth that had been wrapped around Yeshua's head. The cloth was still lying in its place, separate from the linen. Finally the other disciple, who had reached the tomb first, also went inside. He saw and believed" Matthew 28:7-10, Mark 16:1-3, Luke 24:1-8, John 20:1-8 15-16).

Yeshua's Sheaf

"Yeshua said, 'Do not hold on to me, for I have not yet ascended to the Father. Go instead to my brothers and tell them, 'I am ascending to my Father and your Father, to my God and your God'" (John 20:17).

In order for the sheaf of grain to be accepted, the priest had to wave it before God. As our High Priest, the risen Yeshua ascended to his

Father to offer his sheaf of firstfruits in our behalf. Once his sheaf of grain, filled with innumerable seeds was accepted, the spiritual harvest of souls could begin. Yeshua's family would not only include his brothers and sisters in Israel, but those brought forth in a harvest from the nations.

"...Because those whom he knew in advance, he also determined in advance would be conformed to the pattern of his Son, so that he might be the firstborn among many brothers..." (Romans 8:29).

While the priests were preparing for the Firstfruits offering in the Temple, the women found the empty tomb, met with angels, and spoke with their risen Lord. While the women ran to tell the disciples that Yeshua was alive, the men of Israel began to offer their lambs, grain and wine. As the individual sheaves of grain were taken by the priests, Yeshua ascended to his Father and presented himself as a sheaf offering. As the sheaf of grain was being waved, a gentle breeze drifted throughout the Temple. Yeshua's offering to His Father was accepted. The disciples entered the empty tomb and saw the strips of linen and the cloth that had been wrapped around Yeshua's head separate from the linen. They knew and believed he had risen from the dead. Yom Habikkurim, the day of Firstfuits had been become reality. It was time to begin counting the days to the celebration of the final spring harvest.

Chapter Photo: A sheaf of grain offering.

Counting the Omer

*"From the day after the Sabbath —
that is, from the day you bring the
sheaf for waving — you are to count
seven full weeks, until the day after
the seventh Sabbath; you are to count
fifty days; and then you are to
present a new grain offering to the
Lord"* (Leviticus 23:15-16).

Counting the weeks between the sheaf wave offering of the
Firstfruits of barley until the firstfruits harvest of wheat is called
Sefirat HaOmer meaning 'counting the omer.' The *omer*, also called a
sheaf, is an ancient Temple period unit of dry measure equal to 1/10
ephah or about 3.7 quarts (3.5 liters) of grain.

Hiking the Omer

The children of Israel were redeemed by the blood of the lamb on
Passover and the very next day, on the fifteenth day of month, they
began their Exodus out of Egypt. While they 'hiked the omer' from
Egypt to Mount Sinai, they experienced God's power as He molded
them into His treasured possession. They saw His holy presence in
the pillar of fire by night and the cloud by day. They saw His
complete deliverance as they walked through the Red Sea on dry
land and then watched Pharaoh's army drown. They saw His
faithfulness when they received living water from a rock that
followed them. They saw His provision as He gave them daily
manna and taught them about the double-portion on the Sabbath.
They saw His protection when they followed their Commander in
Chief and defeated the Amalekite armies. Fifty days later, they stood
at the foot of the mountain transformed from slaves into a free
people walking with the God of their fathers. They had been

prepared to receive God's teachings and instructions that would set them apart as a holy nation and a kingdom of priests.

"Now if you obey me fully and keep my covenant, then out of all the nations you will be my treasured possession. Although the whole earth is mine, you will be for me a kingdom of priests and a holy nation" (Exodus 19:5-6).

Ruth and the Omer

"So Naomi returned from Moab accompanied by Ruth the Moabite, her daughter-in-law, arriving in Bethlehem as the barley harvest was beginning" (Ruth 1:22).

When Naomi and Ruth returned to Bethlehem, it was the beginning of the barley harvest and the *counting of the omer.* Naomi was bitter because of all the pain she suffered in Moab with the death of her husband and sons. She had no vision or hope for the future. She had no idea how *counting the omer* would transform her life.

Naomi could never have imagined that within a mere fifty days her faithful daughter-in-law Ruth would be married to a relative named Boaz. She could never have anticipated that she would have a grandson named Obed who would become the grandfather of Israel's greatest King. She could never have envisioned that as the sheaf of barely was being waved in Jerusalem on the day of firstfruits when she called herself 'bitter' that one of her descendants would become the Redeemer of all Israel.

Yeshua and the Omer

"Let them both grow together until the harvest; and at harvest-time I will tell the reapers to collect the weeds first and tie them in bundles to be burned, but to gather the wheat into my barn'" (Matthew 13:30).

For the nation of Israel, the *days of the omer* were a time of great anticipation. The barley harvest would end and the wheat harvest would begin. They would gather, thresh and clean grain to store in their barns for the next year. For the disciples, this particular forty *days of the omer* were spent with their risen Lord, the final ten were spent waiting for the promise.

"In the first book, I [Luke] wrote about everything Yeshua set out to do and teach, until the day when, after giving instructions through the Holy Spirit to the emissaries whom he had chosen, he was taken up into heaven. After his death he showed himself to them and gave many convincing proofs that he was alive. During a period of forty days they saw him, and he spoke with them about the Kingdom of God" (Acts 1:1-3).

On the *first day of counting the omer*, Yeshua fulfilled the 'appointed time' of Firstfruits. As the firstfruits sheaves of barley were being waved in the Temple, Messiah ascended to his Father and became the firstfruits sheaf offering for those to be resurrected at a later harvest.

"Yeshua said [to Mary], "Do not hold on to me, for I have not yet ascended to the Father. Go instead to my brothers and tell them, 'I am ascending to my Father and your Father, to my God and your God'" (John 20:17).

That evening, at the beginning of *second day of counting the omer*, Yeshua miraculously appeared in a locked room where his disciples were hiding.

"On the evening of that first day of the week, when the disciples were together, with the doors locked for fear of the Jewish leaders, Yeshua came and stood among them and said, "Peace be with you!" After he said this, he showed them his hands and side. The disciples were overjoyed when they saw the Lord" (John 20:19-20).

There was no denying it now. Yeshua was alive and standing in front of them. He had put his peace upon them and showed them his hands and feet. Their sorrow turned to joy. What would happen now?

"Shalom aleikhem!" Yeshua repeated. "Just as the Father sent me, I myself am also sending you." Having said this, he breathed on them and said to them, "Receive the Ruach HaKodesh! If you forgive someone's sins, their sins are forgiven; if you hold them, they are held" (John 20:21-23).

Yeshua was sending them into the world as his Father had sent him. They weren't to remain in hiding, they were to go out and be witnesses to his Father and the resurrection of the dead. He breathed on them with the 'breath of God'. He anointed them with the same Spirit that was in him giving testimony that he and his Father are one. When the Spirit of his Father was poured out in seven weeks, they would understand that the power was from him and they would go into the world with the same authority that he had been given: to forgive sins.

They had witnessed what forgiveness of sins had brought to the people of Israel: miracles. Forgiveness of sins was also part of God's promised new covenant to Israel. He would forgive their sins and no longer remember their lawless deeds (Jeremiah 31:34). God was beginning to harvest other sheaves of grain. Salvation was going to be proclaimed by Yeshua's disciples to the world.

On the *eighth day of counting the omer*, Yeshua appeared to Thomas and showed him his scars.

"A week later his disciples were in the house again, and Thomas was with them. Though the doors were locked, Yeshua came and stood among them and said, "Peace be with you!" Then he said to Thomas, "Put your finger here; see my hands. Reach out your hand and put it into my side. Stop doubting and believe" (John 20:26-27).

On another day of *counting the omer,* Yeshua appeared to the disciples at the Sea of Galilee. After fishing all night and catching nothing, Yeshua told them to throw their nets over the right side of the boat. Though they did not recognize him, they did what he said. The net filled with fish, 153 fish to be exact. In Hebrew the numerical value of one hundred and fifty three means "I Am *Yod Hey Vav Hey*".

Throughout the days of *counting the omer* Yeshua appeared to more than 500 people including James and the rest of the apostles.

"After that, he appeared to more than five hundred of the brothers and sisters at the same time, most of whom are still living, though some have fallen asleep. Then he appeared to James, then to all the apostles ...
(1 Corinthians 15:7-8).

The Fortieth Day

"After his suffering, he presented himself to them and gave many convincing proofs that he was alive. He appeared to them over a period of forty days and spoke about the kingdom of God. On one occasion, while he was eating with them, he gave them this command: "Do not leave Jerusalem, but wait for the gift my Father promised, which you have heard me speak about. For John baptized with water, but in a few days you will be baptized with the Holy Spirit" (Acts 1:3-5).

Day forty of *counting the omer* arrives. The day that Yeshua ascends into the clouds, into the heavenly realm.

"Then they gathered around him and asked him, "Lord, are you at this time going to restore the kingdom to Israel?" (Acts 1:6).

Before Yeshua ascends, the disciples have two questions. First, they want to know when the Kingdom would be restored to Israel. It is obvious they understood that the Kingdom the Messiah establishes would be with Israel in the Promised Land. From centuries of anti-semitism, this understanding of the coming Kingdom has been distorted. The Kingdom of God will not be Roman Catholic, Evangelical Christian, Protestant, Islamic, Buddhist, Hindu or even Palestinian. It will be established with the children of Israel and those who have joined the commonwealth of Israel.

Second, they wanted to know the timing of the coming Kingdom. Though the actual year of Yeshua's return is only known by the Father, there is an 'appointed time' established for his return. We are supposed to be children of the light and, according to 1 Thessalonians 5, we should know the signs and the seasons *mo'edim* established by God.

He said to them: "It is not for you to know the times or dates the Father has set by his own authority. But you will receive power when the Holy Spirit comes on you; and you will be my witnesses in Jerusalem, and in all Judea and Samaria, and to the ends of the earth" (Acts 1:7-8).

Though the disciples didn't receive definitive answers to their questions, they learned that they were going to receive power. The

Holy Spirit would come upon them and they would be witnesses of Messiah in Jerusalem, Judea, Samaria and to the ends of the earth. These words must have seemed incredible. The message of salvation would go to the ends of the earth through their testimony!

Yeshua was taken up and hidden in a cloud. They could no longer see him. As they stared into space, two men dressed in white appeared and told them that Yeshua would return in the clouds the same way he left.

"After saying this, he was taken up before their eyes; and a cloud hid him from their sight. As they were staring into the sky after him, suddenly they saw two men dressed in white standing next to them. The men said, "You Galileans! Why are you standing, staring into space? This Yeshua, who has been taken away from you into heaven, will come back to you in just the same way as you saw him go into heaven" (Acts 1:9-10).

Counting down 10, 9, 8 ...

"If you love me, you will keep my commands; and I will ask the Father, and he will give you another comforting Counselor like me, the Spirit of Truth, to be with you forever. The world cannot receive him, because it neither sees nor knows him. You know him, because he is staying with you and will be united with you. I will not leave you orphans — I am coming to you" (John 14:15-17).

At Passover weeks earlier, the disciples understood that Yeshua was instituting the new covenant prophesied by Ezekiel, but they didn't know when the Spirit would arrive and change their hearts. Now they did. The only thing left to do was to obey Yeshua's command to return to Jerusalem, wait for the promise and continue *counting the last ten days of the omer.*

Chapter Photo: Grains of barley.

Feast of Weeks - Shavuot

"From the day after the Sabbath, the day you brought the sheaf of the wave offering (Firstfruits), count off seven full weeks. Count off fifty days up to the day after the seventh Sabbath, and then present an offering of new grain to the Lord. From wherever you live, bring two loaves made of two-tenths of an ephah of a fine flour, baked with yeast, as a wave offering of Firstfruits to the Lord.... This is to be a lasting ordinance for the generations to come, wherever you live" (Leviticus 23:15-21).

The Feast of Weeks in Hebrew is *Shavuot*. In Greek it is known as *Pentecost*. Fifty days after leaving Egypt, the Israelites arrived at Mount Sinai. God descended to the top of the mountain to meet with His people who were waiting at its base in order to give them His commandments. There was thunder and lightning and a thick cloud covered the mountain along with a long shofar blast. The people trembled with fear and asked that Moses be their mediator for they feared dying. Ten days after Yeshua's ascension, on the exact same day that God gave Israel His commandments, *Shavuot* arrived.

Rushing Wind and Tongues of Fire

"The festival of Shavuot arrived, and the believers all gathered together in one place. Suddenly there came a sound from the sky like the roar of a violent wind, and it filled the whole place where they were sitting. Then they saw what looked like tongues of fire, which separated and came to rest on each one of them. They were all filled with the Ruach HaKodesh and began to talk in different languages, as the Spirit enabled them to speak" (Acts 2:1-4).

In Hebrew the word for Holy Spirit is *Ruach haKodesh*. The word *ruach* means 'breath or wind'; the word *kodesh* means 'holy'. The Holy Spirit is the 'holy breath of God'.

Hebrew Word Pictures

Holy Spirit - Ruach HaKodesh רוח הקודש

Resh ר - A Head means 'what is most important'

Vav ו - A Nail means 'to bind or join together, and'

Chet ח - A Fence means 'inner room'

Hey ה - A Window means 'behold or reveal, the'

Qof ק - A Back of the Head means 'what is final'

Vav ו - A Nail means 'to bind or tie together, and'

Dalet ד - A Door means 'pathway'

Shin ש - A Tooth means 'consume' or Shekinah, 'the Divine Presence of God'

The Hebrew word picture for *Ruach HaKodesh*: *"The inner chamber joined to what is most important, the final pathway to the divine presence of God."*

Tongues of fire separated and came to rest on each of the disciples. Through the power of the *holy breath of God*, they began to speak in other languages.

Hebrew Word Pictures

Fire - Esh אש

Aleph א - An Ox means 'strength'

Shin ש - A Tooth means 'consume' or Shekinah, 'the Divine Presence of God'

The Hebrew word picture for *esh*: *"The divine presence and strength of God."*

In Greek the word *glossa* is 'tongue' and means 'a nation distinguished by its speech.' As the disciples spoke, Jews from every nation heard the message in their own 'tongue.'

Tongues - Lashon - לשון

Lamed ל - A Shepherd's Staff means 'to urge forward'

Shin ש - A Tooth means 'consume' or Shekinah, 'the Divine Presence of God'

Vav ו - A Nail means 'to bind or join together, and'

Nun נ - A Fish means 'action and life'

The Hebrew word picture for *lashon: "To urge forward the divine presence of God joining action and life."*

In the Temple

Traditionally, Ezekiel's vision of the four living creatures is read on Shavuot:

"I looked, and I saw a windstorm coming out of the north—an immense cloud with flashing lightning and surrounded by brilliant light. The center of the fire looked like glowing metal…" (Ezekiel 1:4).

Feast of Weeks was one of the pilgrimage festivals and thousands of Jewish people from every nation gathered in Jerusalem. They went to the Temple with two loaves of leavened bread for a wave offering. Thousands of Jewish people heard the passage of Ezekiel read aloud. While the priest waved their offerings, the *holy wind of God* began to roar violently and before their eyes, a small group of seventy people had tongues of fire appearing over their heads.

"Now there were staying in Jerusalem religious Jews from every nation under heaven. When they heard this sound, a crowd gathered; they were confused, because each one heard the believers speaking in his own language. Totally amazed, they asked, "How is this possible? Aren't all these people who are speaking from the Galilee? How is it that we hear them speaking in our native languages? We are Parthians, Medes, Elamites; residents of Mesopotamia, Judah, Cappadocia, Pontus, Asia, Phrygia, Pamphylia, Egypt, the parts of Libya near Cyrene; visitors from Rome; all Jews by birth and proselytes; Jews from Crete and from Arabia. . . ! How is it that we hear them speaking in our own languages about the great things God has done?" Amazed and confused, they all went on asking each other, "What can this mean? ..." (Acts 2:5-13).

Two millennia earlier, God's made His holy presence known to the Israelites through wind and lightning. He revealed His holy presence to through wind and fire to Ezekiel. Could it be that God was now revealing His holy presence again through *wind* and *tongues of fire?* The Jewish crowds in Jerusalem from all over the known world were hearing the impossible. They were confused and amazed. The disciples of Yeshua were speaking in each of their different languages with such perfection that they knew it was a miracle.

"I will pour out my Spirit on all people. Your sons and daughters will prophesy, your old men will dream dreams, your young men will see visions. Even on my servants, both men and women, I will pour out my Spirit in those days" (Joel 2:28-29).

Peter stood up. The man who had publicly denied knowing Yeshua only seven weeks earlier raised his voice and addressed the crowd. He tells them they are witnessing the fulfillment of a prophecy of Joel and begins to testify about Yeshua, the Messiah of Israel.

Pierced Hearts

"Men of Israel! Listen to this! Yeshua from Natzeret was a man demonstrated to you to have been from God by the powerful works, miracles and signs that God performed through him in your presence. You yourselves know this. This man was arrested in accordance with God's predetermined plan and foreknowledge; and, through the agency of persons not bound by

the Torah, you nailed him up on a stake and killed him! But God raised him from the dead, freeing him from the agony of death, because it was impossible for death to keep its hold on him. ... Therefore let all Israel be assured of this: God has made this Yeshua, whom you crucified, both Lord and Messiah" (Acts 2:22-24).

When the Jews heard the testimony of Peter about Yeshua, they were *cut to the heart*. The *Orthodox Jewish Bible* says they were *'pierced with conviction in their hearts.'* The Hebrew word for 'cut' is *brit*, the word used for *cutting a covenant*.

The people asked what they should do regarding this 'new' covenant. Peter and the apostles responded with the Hebrew word *shuv*. This Hebrew word means 'turn back' or 'return' in the sense of making a 180 degree turn around. It is translated into English as *repent*.

"Repent (change your views and purpose to accept the will of God in your inner selves instead of rejecting it) and be baptized, every one of you, in the name of Messiah Yeshua for the forgiveness of and release from your sins; and you shall receive the gift of the Holy Spirit" (Acts 2:29 The Amplified Bible).

The people of Israel needed to return to faith in God and repent from their disobedience and sin. They were to be immersed (or baptized) into the name of Yeshua the Messiah for the forgiveness of their sins and receive the gift of God's Spirit. Three thousand Jewish men and women repented, obtained forgiveness of their sins and received the the gift of the Holy Spirit (Acts 2:41). Hearts of stone were transformed to hearts of flesh. The new covenant prophesied by Ezekiel and Jeremiah, instituted and promised by Yeshua, had begun with Israel.

"This is the [new] covenant I will make with the House of Israel after that time," declares the LORD. "I will put my law in their minds and write it on their hearts. I will be their God, and they will be my people.... For I will forgive their wickedness and will remember their sins no more" (Jeremiah 31:33-34).

"I will give you a new heart and put a new spirit inside you; I will take the stony heart out of your flesh and give you a heart of flesh. I will put my

Spirit inside you and cause you to live by my laws, respect my rulings and obey them" (Ezekiel 36:24).

Two Loaves of Leavened Bread

"And he [Yeshua] told them yet another parable. "The Kingdom of Heaven is like chametz that a woman took and mixed with a bushel of flour, then waited until the whole batch of dough rose" (Matthew 13:33).

Chametz or 'soured dough' that is used for raising bread is always symbolic of the leavened teachings of Israel's leaders yet Yeshua uses it to describe the Kingdom of Heaven in his Parable. 'Soured dough' is the ingredient the woman takes and mixes with flour to make her dough rise. When the leavened dough rose to its fullest extent, the woman would have enough dough from a single bushel of flour for a feast of bread.

The commandment for *Shavuot* included an offering of grain along with two loaves of leavened bread made from finely ground flour. The two leavened loaves were to be waved before God by the high priest. For centuries, as the two loaves were waved, the people hoped in the coming Messiah promised by the two witnesses of the Torah and the Prophets.

When Yeshua walked on the Road to Emmaus after his resurrection, he told the two men with him everything that the Torah and Prophets had spoken about him. This witness of two established him as the Messiah of Israel. Forty days later he ascended to the right hand of His Father.

Ten days after his ascension *Shavuot* arrived. Jewish men and women were empowered to be witnesses of God's forgiveness and salvation to the nations. The Kingdom of Heaven began to grow. The Jews who had been 'cut to the heart' would take the message of Yeshua of Nazareth to their own countries in their own languages. They would become the first missionaries to proclaim salvation to the Jew first, then to the gentiles in their nations (Romans 1:16).

Within a few years the Spirit of God would come upon the gentiles, change their hearts, and make them praisers of God along with

Israel. As the two leavened loaves of bread were being waved by the high priest in the Temple, the Body of Messiah, made up of Jews and gentiles was born. God's Spirit had been poured into a small lump of dough, the Jewish people. His Spirit, like the woman's leaven would continue to spread from them to the nations of the world until the Kingdom of heaven was established on earth with the returning King Messiah.

The Promise of Yeshua

"... I will ask the Father, and he will give you another advocate (Counselor, Helper, Intercessor, and Strengthener), to help you and be with you forever— the Spirit of truth.... I will not leave you as orphans; I will come to you. ... Because I live, you also will live. On that day you will realize that I am in my Father, and you are in me, and I am in you" (John 14:14-20).

Yeshua kept his promise. He ascended to his Father and asked Him to send the Counselor, the Spirit of Truth. On the 'appointed time' of Feast of Weeks, God poured out His Spirit not just by breathing on the disciples, but breathing in them. They immediately knew and understood that Yeshua and his Father were One and they were joined with them through the Spirit. They were no longer fatherless,; they had God as their *Abba* Father just as Yeshua did. They were given the same authority to forgive sins and the anointing power to be witnesses of Yeshua's salvation to the world.

They were sealed with God's Spirit along with thousands of Jews and those of the nations who would also believe their message. They were reborn by water immersion and the Spirit of God and had entered His Kingdom as adopted children with the promise of a final redemption of their bodies from mortal to immortality. With God's mark of ownership, they became the latter firstfruits of the wheat harvest, a guarantee that the same *Ruach haKodesh* that brought Yeshua from the dead would raise them to life (Ephesians 1:13-14).

Chapter Photo: Inner Court Dancers leading worship at Shavuot, Loveland, Colorado.

Feast of Trumpets - Yom Teruah

"The LORD said to Moses, "Say to the Israelites: 'On the first day of the seventh month you are to have a day of sabbath rest, a sacred assembly commemorated with trumpet blasts. Do no regular work, but present a food offering to the LORD" (Leviticus 23:23-25).

The Feast of Trumpets begins the fall Feasts of the LORD. Unlike the spring festivals, the fall 'appointed times' have yet to be fulfilled by Yeshua. In Hebrew Feast of Trumpets is *Yom Teruah*. *Yom* means 'day' and *teruah* means 'blowing' making this festival 'a day of blowing.' A smaller word within *teruah* is *ruach* and means 'breath of God' or signifying God's Spirit. *Yom Teruah* is a day of blowing trumpets that sends the Spirit of God around the world.

New Moon Festival

"Blow the shofar on the concealed, hidden moon on the festival day..." (Psalm 81:3, Hebrew translation).

Yom Teruah begins 'on the first day of the seventh month' as a New Moon festival. This means that until the new moon is sighted, the festival cannot begin. When there was a ruling body in Israel, known as the Sanhedrin, a visual sighting of the new dark moon was done by two witnesses. The high priest would then have the shofar sounded to establish the beginning of the New Moon feast day. Until that moment, 'no one knew the day or the hour' that *Yom Teruah* began.

Yeshua used the same terminology in Matthew 24:36 when he told his disciples about the timing of His return: *"No one knows the day or the hour except my Father in heaven."* As a Jewish man, Yeshua understood that *'no one knows the day or the hour'* to be an idiom for *Yom Teruah* like we understand the Fourth of July as Independence Day. While living in the flesh as a son of man, he could not know the year for the prophetic fulfillment of *Yom Teruah*, but he did know in what season it would occur. Paul did too.

"Now, brothers and sisters, about times and dates we do not need to write to you, for you know very well that the day of the Lord will come like a thief in the night" (1 Thessalonians 5:1).

Paul wrote these words to gentile believers in Messiah who had been taught God's appointed seasons, the *mo'edim*. They would also have understood the imagery of a bridegroom coming for his bride. For those believers who were unaware of the 'appointed times', who were in darkness and not walking in the light of Torah, the Messiah's return would be like *a thief in the night*.

The Trumpets

There are two types of trumpets that are blown at *Yom Teruah*. The first are trumpets made of hammered silver that God commanded Israel to make in Numbers chapter 10. The priests blew these two trumpets on numerous occasions: when they were assembling the community and setting out from their camps in the wilderness, when they went into battle so that the LORD would remember them and rescue them, when they had burnt offerings and fellowship offerings, and when they rejoiced at the 'appointed times' like the New Moon festival of *Yom Teruah*.

The other trumpet is the *shofar*. A shofar is made from a ram's horn or any other clean animal such as a goat, antelope, kudu, or gazelle. This type of horn is mentioned 69 times in the Hebrew Scriptures and was symbolic of the ram that was caught in the thicket when Abraham was going to sacrifice Isaac. There are many resources on the internet where shofars can be purchased. There are small and medium sized ones that come from rams and goats known as a ram's horn. Extra long ones with one or two twists come from an African kudu and are called *yeminite shofars*. One way to experience the joy and celebration of 'the day of blowing' is to blow a shofar.

Hebrew Word Pictures

Trumpet - *Shofar* שופר

Shin שׁ - A Tooth means 'consume' or Shekinah, 'the Divine Presence of God'

Vav ו - A Nail means 'to bind or tie together'

Peh פ - A Mouth means 'to speak or blow'

Resh ר - A Head means 'what is most important'

The Hebrew word picture for *shofar*: "*The Divine Presence of God is tied to the blowing what is most important.*"

The Shofar Blasts

Though Scripture doesn't indicate what sound patterns to make, over the millennia the rabbis came up with three that are blown in a certain order. This is the tradition that was most likely being done when Yeshua lived in Israel as Paul also used these different sounds when he wrote his letter to the Thessalonians. These traditional sounds are still used today when celebrating the *day of blowing*.

Tekiah

The *tekiah* means to 'blow or to blast'. It is a call to worship. This blast gathers Israel and those who join with them around the world to celebrate the Feast of Trumpets. The blast is medium length with a low to high pitch transition. It starts with a hard, short push on low pitch and a slight sustain on high pitch and ends with a short higher pitched burst. It is considered by many as the blast to praise the Lord's creative acts as well as for the coronation of a King.

"Praise him with a blast on the shofar! Praise him with lute and lyre!" (Psalm 150:3).

"Then David danced and spun around with abandon before the LORD, wearing a linen ritual vest. So David and all the house of Israel brought up the ark of the LORD with shouting and the sound of the shofar" (2 Samuel 6:14-16).

Shevarim

The second blast of the shofar is the *shevarim* and means 'broken.' This is the call to repentance. This blast reaches into men's souls to convict them to turn back to God with a broken and penitent heart. It consists of three blasts each low-to-high pitch making a wave-like sound.

"Shout out loud! Don't hold back! Raise your voice like a shofar! Proclaim to my people what rebels they are to the house of Jacob their sins" (Isaiah 58:1).

"Put the shofar to your lips! Like a vulture [he swoops down] on the house of the LORD, because they have violated my covenant and sinned intentionally against my Torah" (Hosea 8:1).

Teruah

The third blast is the *teruah* and means 'blowing' as in *Yom Teruah*. This blast is a battle alarm. It is made with nine short one-second staccato bursts of sound. This is the sound that Jeremiah heard as the Assyrians began their attack against Jerusalem. It will be the sound that begins the judgment Day of the LORD.

"My guts! My guts! I'm writhing in pain! My heart! It beats wildly — I can't stay still! — because I have heard the shofar sound; it's the call to war" (Jeremiah 4:19).

"Blow the shofar in Tziyon! Sound an alarm on my holy mountain!" Let all living in the land tremble, for the Day of the LORD is coming! It's upon us!" (Joel 2:1).

Hebrew Word Pictures

Blowing - *Teruah* תרועה

Tav ת – Crossed Sticks means 'sign or mark'

Resh ר - A Head means 'the most important'

Vav ו - A Nail means 'joined or bound together, and'

Hey ה - A Window means 'to reveal'

The Hebrew word picture for *teruah*: *"The sign of the most important revelation."*

Tekiah Gadolah

The final blast is called the *tekiah gadolah* and is the long great blast known in Scripture as *The Great Shofar*. It is similar to the *tekiah* except that the high note is sustained for the longest possible breath. It also ends with a violent, short, pushed out breath and an even higher-pitched note. This is the blast of hope prophesied by Isaiah that will raise the dead from the dust of the earth.

"But your dead will live; their bodies will rise. You who dwell in the dust, wake up and shout for joy. Your dew is like the dew of the morning; the earth will give birth to her dead" (Isaiah 26:19).

Let's Throw Stones

"Who is a God like you, who pardons sin and forgives the transgression of the remnant of his inheritance? You do not stay angry forever but delight to show mercy. You will again have compassion on us; you will tread our sins underfoot and hurl all our iniquities into the depths of the sea" (Micah 7:19).

Tashlich comes from the Hebrew word meaning 'to cast'. After the Temple in Jerusalem was destroyed and there could be no atonement for Israel on *Yom Kippur*, a tradition of 'casting stones' was created. The traditional ceremony involved filling your pockets with small pebbles or stones and 'casting' them into a body of water. The body of water was to be 'living water' or a place where fish were able to live.

To celebrate *tashlich,* stones are gathered representing the sins that individuals have committed either willfully or unknowingly. They can be little pebbles or larger rocks depending on the situation and the personal view of that sin against God. The gathered stones are then placed into the person's pockets to remind them that sin hinders and becomes a burden in our lives when it remains unconfessed. As each stone is taken from the pocket and thrown into the water, it is symbolic of not only confessing those sins, but also repenting from those sins. Some people yell out their sins while others remain contemplative.

Tashlich is a fun and memorable way to act out Yeshua's atonement for sin with God *hurling all of our iniquities and sins into the bottom of the sea.* It is also holds the powerful reminder that like the stone which remains in the bottom of the sea, our sins do not float back to the top and return to us. They remain 'cast away' forever.

"For if you forgive other people when they sin against you, your heavenly Father will also for give you. But if you do not forgive others their sins, your Father will not forgive your sins" (Matthew 6:14).

Tashlich is more than just a time for us to repent to God for our sins and turn back to Him, it is also a time for us to forgive one another. Yeshua says that we are to forgive a brother (or sister) seventy times seven. It is up to us to forgive those who have offended us whether its 490 times or 490,000 times. It is important to live with a clear conscience with our family, friends and acquaintances. As stones are thrown into the water, we can 'cast away' all offenses that may have been committed against us so we can live in peace with each other as well as God.

"...Because his mercy toward those who fear him is as far above earth as heaven. He has removed our sins from us as far as the east is from the west. Just as a father has compassion on his children, the LORD has compassion on those who fear him" (Psalm 103:11-13).

A Mysterious Memorial

"'In the seventh month, on the first day of the month, you are to have a holy convocation; do not do any kind of ordinary work; it is a day of blowing the shofar for you" (Numbers 29:1).

As commanded in Scripture, the Feast of Trumpets is a day of blowing the shofar; however God gives no reason for doing it. Perhaps through this annual blowing of the shofar, God's people learn to recognize the sounds preparing them for an event that has not yet happened.

"Listen, I tell you a mystery: We will not all sleep, but we will all be changed— in a flash, in the twinkling of an eye, at the last trumpet. For the trumpet will sound, the dead will be raised imperishable, and we will be changed. For the perishable must clothe itself with the imperishable, and the mortal with immortality. When the perishable has been clothed with the imperishable, and the mortal with immortality, then the saying that is written will come true: "Death has been swallowed up in victory" (1 Corinthians 15:51-54).

Paul describes the trumpet blast of God as a *Teruah Gadolah*. On *Yom Teruah* the eternal hope of everyone from Adam to Abraham to the Prophets and Israel to the redeemed Body of Messiah will be reality. When this *shofar* blast is sounded, the dead in Messiah will rise and those who are living will be changed from mortal into immortality and live with Yeshua forever.

"For the Lord himself will come down from heaven with a loud command, teruah gadolah with the voice of the archangel and with the trumpet call of God, and the dead in Messiah will rise first. After that, we who are still alive and are left will be caught up with them in the clouds to meet the Lord in the air. And so we will be with Yeshua forever" (1 Thessalonians 4:15-16).

There are no New Testament accounts of Yeshua celebrating the Feast of Trumpets. Though he was revealed as the Messiah of Israel, he still remains 'concealed' in the heavenly realm just like the New Moon until his next 'appointed time' arrives. Until that 'unknown day and hour' comes, Israel and those joined to her are commanded to gather once a year to blow the shofar and prepare for a mysterious event. When the Spirit of God blows the Great Shofar on the Day of the Lord, the concealed mystery of *Yom Teruah* will be revealed.

Chapter Photo: Blowing the shofar at Feast of Trumpets, Chappell Lake, Nebraska.

A Shofar and A Crown

"Daughters of Zion, come out, and gaze upon King Solomon, wearing the crown with which his mother crowned him on his wedding day, his day of joy!" (Song of Solomon 3:11).

The Jewish New Year, also known as *Rosh Hashanah* or the 'head of the year,' occurs in the fall on the common Gregorian calendar. It is also the same day as the Feast of Trumpets. According to Leviticus 23, the Feast of Trumpets occurs on the first day of the seventh month of the Hebrew calendar, so how can it be the 'new year'?

The first of months is given in Exodus 1:2 in the spring month of Nisan around the time of Passover. Counting ahead brings us to the seventh month of Tishri and *Rosh Hashanah.* There is another consideration, however, regarding the new year. It is found in the command for the Feast of Trumpets. It was to be celebrated on the new moon. Since all Biblical months are determined by the new moon, it could be that Tishri 1 begins a new year with a new month.

Jewish tradition states that the earth was created on Tishri 1. Ten days later when Adam and Eve sinned, there needed to be atonement. That idea works for Nisan 1 as well with the lamb being brought into the home on the tenth day of the first month in preparation for Passover. In both Nisan and Tishri, a lamb was connected to redemption, Nisan for individuals in Israel, Tishri for corporate Israel.

However and whenever the confusion started, there are now two 'new years'. The first is referred to as the spiritual new year that begins with the events surrounding Passover. From this new year all Biblical months and festivals are set. The other new year, referred to as the civil new year, is used to number days and count the years. For example, every 50 years on the tenth day of the seventh month, the trumpet was sounded and a Year of Jubilee began. Property was returned to its original owners and people went back home to their Tribal lands to begin the 50-year cycle again. It was a new year with a new beginning. A similar command was given for every seven years when slaves would be released, debts would be dissolved, and the land would be given a rest from planting. This 'year of release' was called the *shemitah* and ended before sunset on Tishri 1, before the new year began on *Rosh Hashanah*.

Does this tradition of having two 'new years' nullify the commands of God? Biblical days are still sunset to sunset, months are still rendered new moon to new moon, 'appointed times' of the LORD are celebrated in the spring and fall as commanded, and years are counted for the releasing of land and debt and the Jubilee. Scriptures that could be interpreted with either month as the beginning of the year were studied and *midrashed* out by elders in Israel who centuries ago established the two 'new year' Hebrew calendar.

A King's Coronation

One of the most familiar types and shadows of *Rosh Hashanah* involves the coronation of a king. The day when kings in Israel were coronated, that day was the new year's day of that king's reign. The counting of the days, weeks, months and years of the monarch's royal rule began on his *Rosh Hashanah*. Prophets, priests, and royal officials along with the people of the kingdom cheered and rejoiced. Shofars were blown. It was a time of great rejoicing. First Kings describes the coronation day of King Solomon:

"The king has sent with him Zadok the priest, Nathan the prophet, Benaiah son of Jehoiada, the Kerethites and the Pelethites, and they have put him on the king's mule, and Zadok the priest and Nathan the prophet have anointed him king at Gihon. From there they have gone up cheering, and the city resounds with it. That's the noise you hear. Moreover, Solomon has taken

his seat on the royal throne. Also, the royal officials have come to congratulate our lord King David, saying, 'May your God make Solomon's name more famous than yours and his throne greater than yours!' And the king bowed in worship on his bed and said, 'Praise be to the Lord, the God of Israel, who has allowed my eyes to see a successor on my throne today'" (1 Kings 1:44-48).

According to the Scriptures, Yeshua will return to Jerusalem to begin a one thousand year reign. With the blast of shofars, he will be coronated as King over all the earth and sit on David's throne. At that moment the dead in Messiah will rise and those who are alive will be transformed into immortality. They will become his Kingdom of royal priests and rule and reign with him for one thousand years.

The prophetic picture of the Feast of Trumpets is the blowing of a shofar for something that has not yet taken place. As of this day, Yeshua has not returned to Israel, has not been coronated King over all the nations, has not taken up his throne in Jerusalem. There also has not been a resurrection of the dead.

"I saw thrones on which were seated those who had been given authority to judge. And I saw the souls of those who had been beheaded because of their testimony about Yeshua and because of the word of God. ... They came to life and reigned with Messiah a thousand years. ...Blessed and holy are those who share in the first resurrection... they will be priests of God and of Messiah and will reign with him for a thousand years" (Revelation 20:4-6).

According to tradition, Kings of Judah were coronated on the new year day in the spring and gentile kings coronated on the new year day in the fall. Yeshua was 'crowned' King of the Jews at Passover when he hung on the cross with the sign "King of the Jews." When he returns, he will be more than the King of the Jews, he will be King over Jews as well as gentiles. His coronation as King of the nations of the world will most likely occur on the combined new year of *Rosh Hashanah* and Feast of Trumpets.

"Clap your hands, all you nations; shout to God with cries of joy. For the Lord Most High is awesome, the great King over all the earth. ...God has ascended amid shouts of joy, the Lord amid the sounding of trumpets. Sing

praises to God, sing praises; sing praises to our King, sing praises. For God is the King of all the earth; sing to him a psalm of praise. God reigns over the nations; God is seated on his holy throne. The nobles of the nations assemble as the people of the God of Abraham, for the kings of the earth belong to God; he is greatly exalted" (Psalm 47).

Books are Opened

According to another Jewish tradition, two books are opened on *Rosh Hashanah.* The destiny of the righteous is written in the Book of Life and the destiny of the wicked is written in the Book of Death. According to Moses, David and Yeshua, these books do exist and names can be blotted out of the Book of Life (Exodus 32:32, Psalm 69:29, Revelation 3:5). Anyone whose name is not found in the Book of Life will face serious consequences. According to Revelation 20:12-15, those whose names are not found in the Book of Life will be thrown into the lake of fire where there is eternal torment.

For this reason, Jewish men and women spend the month of Elul (the month before Tishri and new year's day) preparing themselves through repentance and immersion so that their names are not blotted out of the Book of Life and they face the same judgment as the wicked. It was during the month of Elul that John was immersing people in the Jordan for repentance of sins so they would be ready for the coming day of atonement.

Feast of Trumpets or Rosh Hashanah

In the past few years, a trend has come about where non-Jewish believers in Yeshua condemn the new year celebration of *Rosh Hashanah* as a 'tradition of men' and not God's 'appointed time' of Feast of Trumpets. This is grievous because both celebrations have prophetic and Biblical significance.

According to Yeshua, some traditions do nullify the commands of God, but the error of the Christian church over the centuries has been the belief that all Jewish traditions nullify the commands and even faith in Messiah. They not only cut themselves off from the Biblically Jewish roots of their faith, they cut themselves off from being a witness of the Messiah to the Jewish people, the 'lost sheep of the House of Israel' Yeshua came to find.

Messianic gentiles should not make the blanket statement that *Rosh Hashanah* is a manmade tradition and therefore should be avoided. It is not, and even if it were, Paul commends the Corinthians for 'holding onto the traditions' he passed onto them (1 Corinthians 11:1). Gentile believers in Messiah should use every opportunity to make Israel envious for their Messiah. This is the purpose for being grafted into the Olive Tree of Israel. The unnatural branches are not to be arrogant over the natural especially when it comes to 'traditions' they don't understand. As foreigners, gentiles need to learn about some of the traditions Paul may have been passing on as they may be the very traditions that bring the Jewish people to faith in Yeshua. It is only when the Jews and their brothers cry out for the Messiah that those shofars will sound and there will be life from the dead. This is a mystery that has many allusions to the first day of Tishri no matter what name you call it.

Rosh Hashanah and Feast of Trumpets are two different names for the same event reasoned from different perspectives of Scripture. One perspective is from God's point of view; the other from man's. Both cast great light into the reality of a coming King and his Kingdom. On a future 'first day of the seventh month' with the blasts of shofars and a miraculous gathering of his royal priesthood, King Yeshua will be crowned King of the nations in Jerusalem. His coronation will occur on the 'appointed time' of Trumpets and his Millennial Kingdom established on a new year's day called *Rosh Hashanah.*

Chapter Photo: A small shofar that my husband made along with the crown flag I made for a festival table centerpiece.

Day of Atonement - Yom Kippur

"The LORD said to Moshe, 'The tenth day of this seventh month is Yom-Kippur, you are to have a holy convocation, you are to deny yourselves, and you are to bring an offering made by fire to the LORD. You are not to do any kind of work on that day, because it is Yom-Kippur, to make atonement for you before the LORD your God. Anyone who does not deny himself on that day is to be cut off from his people; and anyone who does any kind of work on that day, I will destroy from among his people... (Leviticus 23:26-32).

Ten days after the Feast of Trumpets is the Day of Atonement or *Yom Kippur.* The Hebrew word *kippur* comes from the word *kapparah* meaning 'covering or atonement.' The root for the word probably derives from the word *kofer* meaning 'to ransom' or 'atone by offering a substitute.' According to Torah, an animal, a lamb or goat, was required as a substitute offering for sin. The offerer would put his hands on the head of the animal, confess his sins over the animal which was then killed. Its blood was sprinkled on the Altar by the priest to remove the person's sin and defilement.

The *Day of Atonement* was a unique day of sacrifices and offerings. It was on this one day of the year that the the high priest would enter the Holy of Holies in the Temple to make atonement for the entire nation of Israel. His priestly duties were specifically outlined in the Torah and it was vitally important that he follow them precisely or he would lose his life. It was also on this day, and only on this day, that the high priest would speak the memorial name of God - the *Yod Hey Vav Hey.*

Wearing 'the armor of God' consisting of a golden crown, a breastplate, an outer robe decorated with pomegranates and bells, an apron, four linen garments, a belt, turban and pants, the high priest would offer a bull for a sin offering and a ram for a burnt offering. He would then enter the Holy of Holies where he would burn incense which rose in a cloud of smoke enveloping the Ark of the Covenant. It was on the *kapparah* or covering of the Ark where atonement would be made. Using his fingers, the priest would sprinkle some of the blood from the burnt offering on the mercy seat between the cherubim and on the ground in front of the Ark. He was to do this seven times in order to purify the Holy of Holies. According to the commands set out in the Torah and outlined in the Talmud (the oral laws written down), the high priest made 43 trips between the Outer Court and the Holy of Holies on *Yom Kippur*.

"God put Yeshua forward as the kapparah for sin through his faithfulness in respect to his bloody sacrificial death. This vindicated God's righteousness; because, in his forbearance, he had passed over [with neither punishment nor remission] the sins people had committed in the past; and it vindicates his righteousness in the present age by showing that he is righteous himself and is also the one who makes people righteous on the ground of Yeshua's faithfulness" (Romans 3:24-25).

The Tabernacle and its system of worship was how God taught Israel that sin hinders access to His presence. Their sacrifices and offerings covered only their outward sins and so they remained 'out' of the Tabernacle in the Outer Court. The blood of bulls, goats and sheep on the Altar of Sacrifice could not bring about an inward purification that would remove the iniquity of sin in their hearts and allow them to enter the Holy Place and the Holy of Holies.

Two Goats

Another *Day of Atonement* offering centered around two goats. By casting lots, one goat was sacrificed to the LORD and its blood sprinkled on the Altar of Sacrifice cleansing it from all of Israel's sins. The other goat was called the scapegoat. The priest would lay his hands on the head of the goat as he confessed the sins of the people. This goat would not be sacrificed, but be set free in the wilderness to take the sins of Israel far away. These two goats were a picture of

God's plan of salvation for Israel through Yeshua. The sacrificed goat's blood made atonement for their national sins; the scapegoat took their sins far away into the wilderness until it died.

During the day of Passover, Pilate had two prisoners, Yeshua and Barabbas. He offered to set one prisoner free. Yeshua who was the 'Son of the Father' was chosen as the imprisoned goat to be sacrificed. Barabbas whose name meant 'son of the father' was the scapegoat released into the world to die a natural death.

The Talmud says that the priest would tie a red wool cord to one of the horns of the scapegoat before it was released. He would also put a red wool cord on the outside of the door to the Temple. When the cord turned white, it was a sign that the goat had died and God had forgiven the sins of Israel. There would be a great celebration. If it stayed red, they were filled with sorrow for their guilt had not been removed.

Josephus, a Jewish historian, states that 40 years before the destruction of the Temple by the Romans in 70 C.E., the red wool no longer supernaturally turned white. The priesthood had not only become completely corrupt before and during this time, but as the spiritual leadership representing Israel, they had rejected Yeshua as the Messiah of Israel. Each year that the red wool remained red, they became increasingly aware that God was no longer accepting atonement for their sins through the sacrifices of *Yom Kippur.*

"Come now," says the LORD, "let's talk this over together. Even if your sins are like scarlet, they will be white as snow; even if they are red as crimson, they will be like wool" (Isaiah 1:18).

Our High Priest

"But when Messiah appeared as High Priest of the good things that are happening already, then, through the greater and more perfect Tabernacle which is not man-made (that is, it is not of this created world), he entered the Holiest Place once and for all. He entered not by means of the blood of goats and calves, but by means of his own blood, thus setting people free forever. For if sprinkling ceremonially unclean persons with the blood of goats and bulls and the ashes of a heifer restores their outward purity; then

how much more the blood of the Messiah, who, through the eternal Spirit, offered himself to God as a sacrifice without blemish, will purify our conscience from works that lead to death, so that we can serve the living God!" (Hebrews 9:11-14).

Yom Kippur holds valuable truths about Yeshua, our High Priest, who made atonement for not only for corporate Israel, but for the world. He entered the heavenly Tabernacle and offered his blood on the heavenly Ark as a substitute for ours. Because he was sinless, he only had to enter the Tabernacle one time for all eternity. His blood brought forgiveness of sin to anyone who trusts in his atoning sacrifice. His blood purifies men by removing the iniquity in their hearts and sending their sins far away, *"as far away as the east is from the west, so far he has removed our transgressions from us"* (Psalm 103:12).

"Unlike the other high priests, he [Yeshua] does not need to offer sacrifices day after day, first for his own sins, and then for the sins of the people. He sacrificed for their sins once for all when he offered himself" (Hebrews 7:27).

While many Jewish people accepted and still do accept Yeshua's atonement for their individual atonement, corporate Israel through their leadership rejected it. It is this corporate rejection that brought reconciliation to the nations. Some day soon Israel will corporately repent and accept Messiah's sacrifice on a future day of atonement.

Israel's Day of Atonement

"When that day comes, I will seek to destroy all nations attacking Jerusalem; and I will pour out on the house of David and on those living in Jerusalem a spirit of grace and prayer; and they will look to me, whom they pierced. They will mourn for him as one mourns for an only son; they will be in bitterness on his behalf like the bitterness for a firstborn son ..." (Zechariah 12:10).

The prophet Zechariah speaks of a coming *Day of Atonement* when God will pour out His Spirit on unbelieving Israel. He will lift the veil from their eyes and corporately change their blinded hearts. They will see the one they pierced and mourn for him as one mourns for the death of a firstborn son. They will receive the *kapparah* of

Yeshua and he will become their High Priest. At that time, in that moment, all Israel will be saved.

Eternal Destiny Determined

"For we must all appear before the judgment seat of Messiah; that everyone may receive the things done in his body, according to what he has done, whether it be good or bad" (2 Corinthians 5:10).

There is a final Day of Atonement to come. Everyone who has ever lived will appear before the judgment seat of Yeshua and give an account of their lives whether they died in the sea or were kept in Hades for this final day of reckoning. Those who names are found in the Book of Life will be rewarded with crowns for their faith expressed in works. Those who names are written in the Book of Death, whose faith and works fall short, will experience the second death and receive the judgment of eternal torture in the lake of burning fire (Revelation 20:14-15).

"Yet you have a few people in Sardis who have not soiled their clothes. They will walk with me, dressed in white, for they are worthy. He who overcomes will, like them, be dressed in white. I will never blot out his name from the book of life, but will acknowledge his name before my Father and his angels" (Revelation 3:4-6).

The Days of Awe or the ten days between the Feast of Trumpets and *Yom Kippur* are the time when Jewish individuals search their hearts and lives to see what sin and rebellion may be lurking that separates them from God. They are to search out what has soiled their spiritual garments in unrighteous living and be overcomers so that their names are not blotted out of the Book of Life. Those who have received Yeshua as the *kapparah* for their sins will be especially blessed. Their sins will be forgiven and will not go against their account in the Book of Life. They will not experience the second death but receive eternal life in the new heavens and new earth.

"Blessed are those whose transgressions are forgiven, whose sins are covered over; Blessed is the man whose sin the LORD will not reckon against his account" (Psalm 32:1-2, Romans 4:7-8).

The Fast of Atonement

"Rend your heart and not your garments. Return to the Lord your God, for he is gracious and compassionate, slow to anger and abounding in love... Blow the trumpet in Zion, declare a holy fast, call a sacred assembly" (Joel 2:13-15).

The basis for atonement is already settled in the blood sacrifice of Yeshua. However, even as believers, we can always use the 'appointed time' of *Yom Kippur* to remember the atonement through the two goats: the one that was sacrificed for sin and the one that took that sin away.

Each of us still sins and needs to confess those sins in order to receive the forgiveness offered by Yeshua. We need to repent from those sins and return to a sanctified walk with God. 'Denying oneself' is part of the Biblical command for *Yom Kippur*. Fasting can sensitize our spirits to what God desires in our hearts and lives. It can become a time of internal reflection and spiritual purification that keeps us unspotted from the world.

We can also fast for the Jewish people around the world. They pack synagogues on *Yom Kippur* praying and confessing their sins. It is on *Yom Kippur* that they face a serious reality. Without a Temple there is no Altar for sacrifice; without a priesthood there is no high priest for the sacrificial system. There are no bulls, no goats, no blood. It is a day of sorrow, a day of despair. Through the Messianic believer's intercession and fasting, *'they may see one they have pierced'* before the Lamb's Book of Life is opened. Their veil may be removed and they may see their High Priest and receive the atonement they have desired for millennia.

"We have this hope as a sure and safe anchor for ourselves, a hope that goes right on through to what is inside the the Holy of Holies behind the curtain, where a forerunner has entered on our behalf, namely, Yeshua, who has become a High Priest forever..." (Hebrews 6:19).

Feast of Tabernacles - Sukkot

"The Lord said to Moses, "Say to the Israelites: 'On the fifteenth day of the seventh month the LORD's Festival of Tabernacles begins, and it lasts for seven days. The first day is a sacred assembly; do no regular work. For seven days present food offerings to the LORD, and on the eighth day hold a sacred assembly and present a food offering to the LORD. It is the closing special assembly; do no regular work" (Leviticus 23:33-36).

The Feast of Tabernacles is the last of the seven 'appointed times' given to Israel. In Hebrew the Feast of Tabernacles is *sukkot* meaning 'shelters or booths'. *Sukkot* is the eight-day fall festival of ingathering that follows the solemn days of awe and the Day of Atonement. It is known as the 'season of our joy' when everyone dances with lulavs and builds temporary shelters with roofs made from branches of trees. Like the other fall festivals, the Feast of Tabernacles has yet to be fulfilled by Messiah. Its shadow contains the vision of the coming Millennial Kingdom when Yeshua will once again tabernacle with His people Israel. The final culmination of the Feast of Tabernacles will occur in eternity when there is a new heavens, new earth and the New Jerusalem where Yahweh will sit on His throne.

"And I heard a loud voice from the throne saying, "Look! God's dwelling place (the Mishkan) is now among the people, and he will dwell (tabernacle) with them. They will be his people, and God himself will be with them and be their God" (Revelation 21:3 NIV and Orthodox Jewish Bible).

Hebrew Word Pictures

Booth - *Sukkah*, the singular of *sukkot* סכה

Samech ס - A Prop means 'to support and protect'

Kaf כ - An Open Palm means 'to allow, to open'

Hey ה - A Window means 'to reveal'

The Hebrew word picture for *sukkah*: *"A protection opening revelation."*

Abraham's Faith

"By faith he [Abraham] made his home in the promised land like a stranger in a foreign country; he lived in tents as did Isaac and Jacob, who were heirs with him of the same promise. For he was looking forward to the city with permanent foundations, of which the architect and builder is God" (Hebrews 11:9-10).

Abraham was called a friend of God because he believed God. He had faith in God's promises to make him a great nation through a promised seed. Though he had to live in a tent in this world, he had the hope of an eternal city built by God, the the New Jerusalem.

Jacob's Sukkah

"Jacob went on to Sukkoth, where he built himself a house and put up shelters for his animals. This is why the place is called Sukkoth (shelters)" (Genesis 33:17).

When the Israelites left Egypt, their first stop on their way to Mount Sinai was Takut, the Egyptian name for Sukkoth. Hundreds of years earlier, Jacob, whose name had been changed to Israel, stopped at this exact place after he reunited with his brother Esau. He built 'temporary dwellings' for his family and livestock and called it *Sukkoth.*

Sukkot

"You are to live in sukkot for seven days ... so that generation after generation of you will know that I made the children of Israel live in sukkot when I brought them out of the land of Egypt; I am the LORD your God" (Leviticus 23:42).

In the LORD's command for the Feast of Tabernacles, the Israelites were to live in *sukkot* as a reminder of the 40 years they traveled in the wilderness and lived in temporary shelters. Throughout their generations, the nation of Israel (specifically the Jewish people) has built *sukkot* no matter where they have lived.

A *sukkah* can be built in a yard or on a porch or balcony. It generally has three walls with all or part of its roof open to the sky. Any roof covering is usually branches from trees. Lights may be hung in the *sukkah* along with interior decorations such as pictures, flowers, leaves or fruit. Some families line the interior walls with white in order to remember the 'clouds of Glory' that surrounded them as they traveled in the desert. For seven days the *sukkah*, the personal or family dwelling place, is used for eating, sleeping and inviting special guests for the season of joy.

The Lulav

"On the first day you are to take branches from luxuriant trees—from palms, willows and other leafy trees—and rejoice before the Lord your God for seven days. Celebrate this as a festival to the LORD for seven days each year" (Leviticus 23:40-42).

On the first day of *Sukkot*, branches from palms, willows and myrtles along with a large fragrant citrus fruit called the etrog are bound together in what is called the *lulav* or the Four Species representing the nations of the world. On each day of the Feast of Tabernacles, the *lulav* is waved facing north, south, east and west while proclaiming the coming Kingdom of God to the nations.

Several other symbolic meanings developed from the four species creating the *lulav*. Some believe the four species represent the memorial name of God: *Yod Hey Vav Hey* which is why they species are bound together as one. Others believe the fruit and the aroma of the trees relate to different people and how they respond to God's Torah very similar to the Parable of the Sower and how different people's hearts respond to the Word of God. Still others believe that the branches and the fruit represent the parts of our bodies, our temporary dwellings, that we are to offer to God as *"instruments of righteousness"* (Romans 6:12-13).

The Tabernacle

"On the first day of the first month of the second year, the tabernacle was set up" (Exodus 40:17). The Hebrew word for tabernacle is *mishkan and* this is what the the Tabernacle or 'tent of meeting' was called in the wilderness.

Hebrew Word Pictures

Tabernacle - *Mishkan* משכן

Mem מ- Water means 'to come down from, immense'

Shin ש - A Tooth means 'consumed' or Shekinah, 'the Divine Presence of God'

Kaf כ- A Palm or Wing means 'to cover or allow'

Nun נ - A Fish means ' action and life'

The Hebrew word picture for *mishkan*: *"The immense consuming [divine presence of God] cover of life."*

After the children of Israel were delivered from Egypt, they ended up at Mount Sinai where Moses received God's instructions for constructing His portable 'dwelling place', His *mishkan.* It took a long time for all of its posts, curtains, and holy articles to be made. Gold, silver and bronze objects that were taken from Egypt had to be melted down or beaten and formed into shapes. Acacia wood had to be gathered, cut and built into boxes. Animals had to be slaughtered for their skins. Fabric had to be spun from flax and wool.

Eventually the articles became a the Altar of Sacrifice, a hammered golden Menorah, an Altar of Incense, a Table of pPresence and the Ark of the Testimony. Mirrors were collected from the women to cover the large basin for priestly washing and purification. Tabernacle coverings were stitched together and mounted on the posts. Curtains from finely twisted linen with blue, purple and scarlet yarn were hung in the Holy Place. By the time of their two-year anniversary of leaving Egypt, the *Mishkan* was set up and the glory of the LORD filled it with a cloud. Yahweh had His 'temporary dwelling' that could be transported when He moved His people.

"Then the cloud covered the tent of meeting, and the glory of the LORD filled the tabernacle. Moses was unable to enter the tent of meeting, because the cloud remained on it, and the glory of the LORD filled the tabernacle. Whenever the cloud was taken up from over the tabernacle, the people of Israel continued with all their travels. But if the cloud was not taken up, they did not travel onward until the day with it was taken up. For the cloud of the LORD was above the tabernacle during the day, and the fire was (in the cloud) at night, so that all the house of Israel could see it throughout all their travels" (Exodus 40:34-38).

The Living Tabernacle

Yeshua is the living *tabernacle* of God's divine presence on earth. According to the details given in the first two chapters of Luke, it can be determined that Yeshua was born on the first day of the Feast of Tabernacles. In a 'temporary dwelling' outside of Bethlehem, the Word became flesh and was placed in a *sukkah*. His heavenly Father, the angels in heaven, the shepherds watching their flocks, his mother Miriam and his earthly father celebrated in the birth of the Son of God. While all Israel commemorated the festival of ingathering, Yeshua became the reason for the season of our joy.

"The Word became flesh and tabernacled with us, we saw his glory, the glory of the Father's only Son, full of grace and truth ... for it pleased God to have his full being live in His Son..." (John 1:14, Colossians 1:19).

Yeshua celebrates Feast of Tabernacles in John chapter 7, though he didn't go to Jerusalem until the festival was half over. When he arrived and began to teach in the Temple, the people were astonished and and wondered how he knew so much. He gave credit to his Father who had sent him to find the lost sheep of Israel and told them to search the Scriptures to know if his teachings were from God or himself.

"So Yeshua gave them an answer: 'My teaching is not my own, it comes from the one who sent me. If anyone wants to do his will, he will know whether my teaching is from God or I speak on my own. A person who speaks on his own is trying to win praise for himself; but a person who tries to win praise for the one who sent him is honest, there is nothing false about him" (John 7:16-18).

Streams of Living Water

The Levitical priesthood officiated the sacrifices in the Temple during the Feasts as well as led other traditions rooted in celebrating the 'appointed times.' The highlight each day of the Feast of Tabernacles was the Water Pouring Ceremony. A white-robed priest would lead a procession through the city of Jerusalem carrying a golden pitcher. The people would follow him through the Water Gate to the Pool of Siloam where he filled the pitcher with water. He would return to the Temple with the filled pitcher while the people would follow him singing, waving their *lulavs* and dancing in the streets. When the priest arrived at the Temple, he would pour the water on the Altar. As he poured the water from the golden pitcher, he would cry out in a loud voice words from the prophet Isaiah, *"Therefore with joy you will draw water from the wells of salvation"* (Isaiah 12:3).

The multitude of people who gathered in Jerusalem for this festival would respond with *"LORD, save us! LORD, grant us success! Blessed is he who comes in the name of the LORD. From the house of the LORD we bless you"* (Psalm 118).

The last and greatest day of the Feast of Tabernacles was called *Hoshana Rabbah* and means 'The Great Salvation.' It was the culmination of the week-long celebration of the Feast and was a vision of the final judgments to come before the restoration of God's eternal Kingdom when He would *tabernacle* with mankind again.

It was on this day of the *Great Salvation* that Yeshua responds to the nation's cry for salvation. As the *Great Salvation*, he delivered a message not of judgment, but of freedom and fullness of life in the Spirit. If they would come to him and put their faith in him, the Spirit of God would be poured out into their hearts and their spiritual thirst would be quenched. Living waters would flow from within them and they would receive their *Great Salvation*.

"Now on the last day and greatest day of the festival, Hoshana Rabbah, Yeshua stood and cried out, 'If a man is thirsty, let him keep coming to me and drink! Whoever puts his trust in me, as the Scripture says, rivers of living water will flow from his inmost being.'" (Now he said this about the Spirit, whom those who trusted in him were to receive later. The Spirit had not yet been given, because Yeshua had not yet been glorified") (John 7:37-39).

Our Earthly Sukkah

"I think it is right to refresh your memory as long as I live in the tent of this body, because I know that I will soon put it aside, as our Lord Messiah Yeshua has made clear to me" (2 Peter 1:13).

While we live on the earth, we have an earth suit. Peter and Paul called it our *earthly tent*. Our *earthly tent* is mortal, decaying and dying. It is only a temporary physical dwelling for our spirits and will one day be destroyed through death. We will return to the dust of the ground from where we came. While we live in our mortal *sukkot*, we know that we are naked and unclothed in the eyes of God. We cry out in our temporary sufferings and affliction while we wait for the redemption of our bodies and receive our immortal clothes.

"For we know that if the earthly tent we live in is destroyed, we have a building from God, an eternal house in heaven, not built by human hands. Meanwhile we groan, longing to be clothed instead with our heavenly dwelling, because when we are clothed, we will not be found naked. For while we are in this tent, we groan and are burdened, because we do not wish to be unclothed but to be clothed instead with our heavenly dwelling, so that what is mortal may be swallowed up by life. Now the one who has

fashioned us for this very purpose is God, who has given us the Spirit as a deposit, guaranteeing what is to come" (2 Corinthians 5:1-5).

Once we are born again, our earth tents become the dwelling place for God's Spirit. He seals us with His Spirit as a guarantee that we will be released from our mortal bodies and given heavenly tents. When we receive our glorified bodies, they will never decay or die because they are eternal. Until that day arrives, we live in our earthly tents by faith as our father Abraham looking forward to what is to come.

"Do you not know that your bodies are temples of the Holy Spirit, who is in you, whom you have received from God? You are not your own; you were bought at a price. Therefore honor God with your bodies" (1 Corinthians 16:19-20).

Feast of Ingathering

"... Celebrate the Feast of Ingathering at the end of the year, when you gather in your crops from the field" (Exodus 23:16).

The Feast of Tabernacles is also called the *Feast of Ingathering*. It is celebrated after the harvest of grain and grapes, however, the olive harvest is still in process.

It foreshadows the time when the House of Judah and the House of Israel are gathered from the nations back to the Promised Land. This ingathering of God's chosen people will be so divinely inspired that it will be celebrated as a 'greater exodus' than when the Israelites left Egypt. The Ingathering has only just begun with a modern-day movement of Jewish people returning to Israel from all the nations of the world. It is called *aliyah* and means 'going up'.

"'Therefore,' says The LORD, 'the day will come when people will not longer swear, "As The LORD lives, who brought the nation of Israel out of the land of Egypt," but, 'As The LORD lives, who brought the people of Israel out of the land to the north and all the countries where he drove them,' for I will bring them back to their own land which I gave their ancestors'" (Jeremiah 16:14-15).

"They found written in the Law, which the Lord had commanded through Moses, that the Israelites were to live in temporary shelters during the festival of the seventh month and that they should proclaim this word and spread it throughout their towns and in Jerusalem: "Go out into the hill country and bring back branches from olive and wild olive trees, and from myrtles, palms and shade trees, to make temporary shelters"—as it is written" (Nehemiah 8:14-15).

When Israel returned from captivity in the days of Nehemiah, they found the book of Torah that commanded collecting branches to make their *sukkot*. In addition to branches from palms, willows, and myrtles, they also collected branches from *olive and wild olive trees* (Nehemiah 8:14-15). Because the Feast of Ingathering is a shadow of the coming Kingdom of God, the olive and wild olive tree branches hold significance to its fulfillment.

The first mention of the olive tree is in Genesis after the flood when Noah sends out a dove and it brings back a leaf, a symbol of new life. In Exodus Moses is given pure olive oil as one of the ingredients for the anointing oil, a symbol of the Spirit. In Deuteronomy, the land flowing with milk and honey also flowed with olive oil indicating the abundance of provision in the Promised Land. The doors of Solomon's Temple were made from olive wood on which were carved the cherubim that guarded the entrance to the Garden of Eden (1 Kings 6:32). In the Psalms, children are like olive shoots around a blessed man's table. Jeremiah and Hosea call Israel 'a thriving olive tree with great splendor'.

When Paul discusses the olive tree in Romans 11, he sees natural olive branches and wild olive branches attached to the same tree. He tells the gentiles that they are the wild olive branches which have been grafted into the olive tree with the natural branches of Israel.

When a branch is grafted into a tree, it gets its nourishment from the roots and sap of the tree. It will still bear its unique fruit, but only through its dependence on the natural tree. If the grafting doesn't take and the branch doesn't get its nourishment, it will die and fall off the tree.

Paul reminds the gentiles that as wild olive branches they can be cut off the olive tree if they become arrogant over the natural branches. They are to remember that the living water of the Spirit that comes from Messiah, the root of David, and the nourishing sap of the Scriptures supports them both by faith. Though some of the natural branches may have been broken off due to a lack of faith, they are easily grafted back into their own olive tree (Romans 11:13-24).

The addition of *olive and wild olive* branches to the *sukkah* in Nehemiah's time suggests that the Ingathering will not only include the natural olive branches of Israel, but also the wild olive branches of gentiles who have joined the covenant that God made with Israel. When both branches of olives live by faith in Yeshua trusting in him as the root of the tree, living water will bring nourishing sap to both branches. They will finally thrive with splendor as God intended for the Olive Tree of Israel.

The Millennial Kingdom

"In the last days the mountain of the LORD's temple will be established as the highest of the mountains; it will be exalted above the hills, and peoples will stream to it. ...Everyone will sit under their own vine and under their own fig tree, and no one will make them afraid, for the LORD Almighty has spoken" (Micah 4:1, 3).

Yeshua's teachings centered around the Kingdom of God or the Kingdom of Heaven. Though it was near, it had not yet fully arrived and would not until he had been glorified and crowned King. During a one thousand year 'season of our joy,' the nations of the world will come to the mountain of the LORD in Jerusalem. Yeshua will sit on his throne in the Temple and rule the nations from Israel. His reign will join the present world and mortal men with immortal men in a unique time in history. With an iron scepter, he will rule the earth and prepare its people for his Father's eternal kingdom.

"After six days Yeshua took Peter, James and his brother John and led them up a high mountain privately. As they watched, he began to change form - his face shone like the sun, and his clothing became as white as light. Then they looked and saw Moses and Elijah speaking with him. Peter said to Yeshua, 'It's good that we're here, Lord. I'll put up three sukkot [temporary

*dwellings] if you want - one for you, one for Moses, and one for Elijah.'
While he was still speaking, a bright cloud enveloped them; and a voice from
the cloud said, 'This is my Son, whom I love, with whom I am well pleased.
Listen to him'!* (Matthew 17:1-5).

Yeshua had just days before told the disciples that some of them
would not die until they saw the Son of Man coming in his kingdom
(Matthew 16:28). They were waiting for this kingdom to arrive with
great expectation. Six days later Yeshua took Peter, James and John
up a mountain.

The three disciples watched as Yeshua changed into glory in front of
them. They saw him speaking with Moses and Elijah establishing a
witness of three to the transfiguration. They didn't realize that were
receiving only a glimpse at the coming Kingdom, but believed that
Yeshua was establishing his Kingdom rule on earth at that 'appointed
time.' They believed that Yeshua was going to take up his throne in
Jerusalem and reign as King of Kings. They weren't being stupid;
they knew the prophecies. Peter responded with his great faith in
Yeshua's words about the Kingdom of God when he offered to build
these three glorified men, Moses, Elijah and Yeshua shelters or *sukkot*.

The Eternal Tabernacle

*"I heard a loud voice from the throne say, "Behold, the tabernacle of God is
with men, and he will dwell with them .... They will be his people, and he
himself, will be their God"* (Revelation 21:3).

At the end of Yeshua's Millennial reign, a new heaven and a new
earth will appear. Everything from the old heaven and earth will
pass away. The New Jerusalem will come down out of the restored
heavens and descend to the renewed earth. There won't be a Temple
in the New Jerusalem because God will be the Temple. There will be
no sun or moon to shine on it because the glory of God gives it its
light. It's lamp will be Yeshua.

The river of the water of life will flow from the throne of God
producing fruit for each month and healing leaves for the nations. The
servants of God will worship Him as His throne will be in the city.
The eternally redeemed will see His face and His name will be written

on their foreheads. They will reign as kings forever and ever. When the New Jerusalem descends from heaven, Yahweh, the Father, the Creator, the great I AM will eternally Tabernacle with His people.

"All of these people kept on trusting until they died, without receiving what had been promised. They had only seen it and welcomed it from a distance, while acknowledging that they were aliens and temporary residents on the earth. ...As it is, they aspire to a better homeland, a heavenly one. This is why God is not ashamed to be called their God, for he has prepared for them a city" (Hebrews 11:13-15).

Our father Abraham lived in a tent. As Abraham's children by faith and heirs to the same promises, we also live in earth tents like he did. Until the day of our redemption, we will live as strangers and foreigners on this earth. We can celebrate *Sukkot* with the hope of our future glory by building a *sukkah*. As we feast in our 'temporary dwelling', we can identify with the children of Israel who lived in tents with the *Mishkan* of Yahweh in their midst.

Yeshua took on the tent of a human body to live with us. As the Messiah of Israel, he will soon return to Jerusalem as King to prepare the nations for the eternal Kingdom of Heaven. When we keep our eyes on the promises of God and the the New Jerusalem we will truly understand the 'season of our joy' and the Feast of Tabernacles.

"Celebrate the Festival of Tabernacles for seven days after you have gathered the produce of your threshing floor and your winepress. Be joyful at your festival—you, your sons and daughters, your male and female servants, and the Levites, the foreigners, the fatherless and the widows who live in your towns. For seven days celebrate the festival to the Lord your God at the place the Lord will choose. For the Lord your God will bless you in all your harvest and in all the work of your hands, and your joy will be complete" (Deuteronomy 16:13-15).

Chapter Photo: Our family sukkah.

Rejoicing in the Torah

"Tell the people of Israel, 'On the fifteenth day of this seventh month is the feast of Sukkot for seven days to the LORD ... on the eighth day you are to have a holy convocation and bring an offering made by fire to the LORD; it is a day of public assembly; do not do any kind of ordinary work" (Leviticus 23:34-36).

The Feast of Tabernacles lasted seven days with an added day at its conclusion called *Shemini Atzeret* or the 'eighth day assembly'. *Simchat Torah,* Hebrew words meaning 'Rejoicing in the Torah' is celebrated as part of this assembly.

Simchat Torah is a joyful celebration with dancing and flags which surpasses even the 'season of our joy' in the entire Feast of Tabernacles. On this day, the yearly cycle of reading the Torah concludes. The scroll is rolled from the end of Deuteronomy back to the beginning of Genesis in order to begin a new cycle of studying God's teachings and instructions.

In synagogues the Torah scroll is removed from the ark and given to a group in the congregation to hold. It is marched around or *hakafot* while people touch and kiss the cherished Scriptures. Once the Torah is returned to the ark, everyone dances in circles. Children wave flags and hand out candy. This *hakafot* is done seven times as the scroll is given to other groups until everyone has taken part in the celebration.

The Eighth Day

The number eight holds the the Biblical vision for 'new beginnings' as in the Simchat Torah celebration. Dedication ceremonies for the Temple, the anointing oil and the Altar also lasted eight days hence the re-dedication of the Altar at Hanukkah lasting for eight days. Jewish baby boys were, and still are, circumcised and named on the eighth day in a ceremony called a *brit milah*.

A *brit milah* is the Hebrew terminology for 'covenant of cutting' or circumcision. Circumcision was the covenant sign, a symbol of a blood sacrifice, given to Abraham as God's promise to make him the father of many nations. Abraham believed God and trusted in the promise of a son, an heir.

Because of Abraham's faith, a *brit milah* was always to be in unity with the circumcision of the heart. When God told the Israelites to *'circumcise the foreskin of their hearts,'* He was directing them back to Abraham, the father of their faith to whom circumcision was given. He was also alluding back to the Garden of Eden and the hope in the coming Seed of woman who would become the blood sacrifice for sin.

From the details given in the first two chapters of Luke, we can reason that Yeshua was born on the first day of the Feast of Tabernacles. This means that on the eighth day, the *Shemini Atzeret,* while he was being circumcised in the Temple of Jerusalem, the Jewish people were dancing and celebrating *Simchat Torah*. As Israel and the priests were rejoicing in the Torah that held all the prophecies of their coming redemption, the Living Torah, a little baby was being circumcised and given the name *salvation* in their very presence. What a *brit milah* Yeshua had with his entire family of Jewish and Israeli brothers and sisters!

"On the eighth day, when it was time for his b'rit-milah, he was given the name Yeshua, which is what the angel had called him before his conception" (Luke 2:21).

In the modern spoken Hebrew language, *milah* also means 'word'. Thus a *brit milah* can also mean "the cutting of the Word' or 'the covenant of the Word.' With a *brit milah* every Jewish baby boy enters into a covenant with the the Word. Who is the Word of God? Whose blood became the 'cutting of the covenant'? Yeshua!

Though circumcision of the flesh is commanded for Israel and is vitally important to the covenant made with Abraham, it is even more important that one enters into the covenant of the Word by faith and receive a circumcised heart. Without faith it is impossible to please God; without a circumcised heart, it is impossible to obey God.

Years ago I remember a Messianic pastor saying that the circumcision of a baby boy was not so much for the baby as the father who gives the child to be circumcised and witnesses the event. It is at the moment when the beloved son's foreskin of his flesh is 'cut', that the father is 'cut to the heart' and remembers the promises given to Abraham and his descendants. It this the sign of the covenant in the flesh, the *brit milah,* that is a reminder of the promised Seed, salvation that would come from Israel and the Jewish people.

"A person is not a Jew who is one only outwardly, nor is circumcision merely outward and physical. No, a person is a Jew who is one inwardly; and circumcision is circumcision of the heart, by the Spirit, not by the written code. Such a person's praise is not from other people, but from God" (Romans 2:28-29).

Simchat Torah is the joyful celebration of the Torah, the written covenant God gave to Israel so they would be a light to the nations. On the eighth day when everyone in Israel was celebrating the Word of God, Yeshua had his *brit milah* and entered into the covenant of the Word. As his Father watched, He remembered His covenant with Abraham. One cycle of Torah ended and another began. The Word had become flesh and was 'cut'. Yeshua became the Living Torah, the covenant of the Word that would bring the circumcision of the heart to Israel and the nations.

Chapter Photo: Our children waving flags during Simchat Torah.

The Days of Dedication - Hanukkah

"Even if all the nations that live under the rule of the king obey him, and have chosen to do his commandments, departing each one from the religion of his fathers, yet I and my sons and my brothers will live by the covenant of our fathers.... We will not obey the king's word by turning aside from our religion to the right hand or to the left" (Septuagint*, 1 Maccabees 2:19-22).

Most people have heard of the holiday called Hanukkah. Some actually think that it is the Jewish alternative to Christmas. However, these two celebrations have nothing in common.

In Hebrew the word *chanak* means 'dedicate' making Hanukkah an an eight-day celebration centering around the *days of dedication.* During Hanukkah, a special menorah called a *hanukkiah* is lit and put in the window of Jewish homes. It holds nine candles. Each of the eight nights of Hanukkah one candle is lit by using the 'extra helper candle' or *shamash* until all eight (nine) candles are burning brightly.

The account of Hanukkah is not found in our modern Bibles because is was removed from the canon of Scriptures by Martin Luther due to the fact they conflicted with his anti-semitic theological views. However, the complete events surrounding the days of dedication are recorded by the historian Josephus and the Septuagint book of Maccabees. According to both accounts, the eight *days of dedication* were to be held every year in memory of the cleansing and re-dedication of the Temple and the Altar of Sacrifice.

"So they celebrated the dedication of the altar for eight days, and offered burnt offerings with gladness; they offered a sacrifice of deliverance and praise. ... Then Judas and his brothers and all the assembly of Israel determined that every year at that season the days of dedication of the altar should be observed with gladness and joy for eight days, beginning with the twenty-fifth day of the month of Chislev" (1 Maccabees 4:56-59).

"Now Judas celebrated the festival of the restoration of the sacrifices of the temple for eight days; and omitted no sort of pleasures thereon: but he feasted them upon very rich and splendid sacrifices; and he honoured God, and delighted them by hymns and psalms. Nay, they were so very glad at the revival of their customs, when, after a long time of intermission, they unexpectedly had regained the freedom of their worship, that they made it a law for their posterity that they should keep a festival, on account of the restoration of their temple worship, for eight days. And from that time to this we celebrate this festival, and call it Lights. I suppose the reason was, because this liberty beyond our hopes appeared to us; and that hence was the name given to that festival" (Josephus 12:5).

A Little History

Hanukkah is the memorial to a period of time beginning in 167 B.C.E. when the Greek Antiochus Epiphanes became king over the Seleucid Empire that included Israel. His name meant 'antichrist god incarnate', and as such, he attacked the God of Israel. In order to have a one-world religious and cultural system, his goal was to force Hellenistic pagan gods and customs on everyone in his empire including the Jewish people. He wanted to   nullify the Torah, invalidate the Levitical priesthood, cancel dietary laws, outlaw circumcision, and remove the Sabbath... everything Jewish.

The battle for independence from Syrian Greek rule began when a Levitical priest named Mattathias was commanded by a Greek official to make a sacrifice to a Greek god. He not only refused, but killed a Jewish man with him who began to do so. He also killed the official. When an edict for his arrest was sent out, Mattathias hid in the Judean wilderness with his five sons and called for other Jews to join him. Many did follow him into the wilderness and with the leadership of his son Judah, a small band of Jewish men began to revolt.

"Let everyone who has zeal for the Torah and who stands by the covenant follow me!" (Septuagint 1 Maccabees 2:17).

As the Greek armies went on their conquest, other Jewish men, women and children succumbed to Antiochus' commands. Those who didn't follow his orders were imprisoned or murdered. The Jewish people feared for their very existence. *Blessed be the Lord God of Israel*, this lawless man didn't succeed with his ultimate plan or there would have been no lineage from which the Messiah could come!

Judah was given the nickname 'hammer' or *Maccabee,* also an acronym for *mi komocho ba'alim Hashem,* "who is like you among the powers O God," – the battle cry of the rag tag Jewish resistance. The Maccabees who numbered under 12,000 with little to no training or equipment fought courageously against the Syrian armies who were highly trained, rode elephants and numbered over 40,000.

"But Judas said: "Many are easily hemmed in by a few; in the sight of Heaven there is no difference between deliverance by many or by few; for victory in war does not depend upon the size of the army, but on strength that comes from Heaven" (1 Maccabees 3:18-19).

After three years of fighting, tearing down pagan altars, circumcising uncircumcised boys, and rescuing Torah scrolls from the hands of the enemies, Judah Maccabee and his little army miraculously regained control over Jerusalem. They went to the Temple and saw its defilement. The courts had bushes and thickets, the gates were burned, and the priests chambers destroyed. Pigs had been sacrificed on the Altar and their blood sprinkled throughout the Holy Place. The Temple Menorah was missing, either stolen or melted down for its gold. A statue of Zeus sat in the Holy of Holies where the Ark of the Covenant should have been. They mourned the desecration and tore their clothing. They blew the shofar and cried out to God.

"Then said Judas and his brothers, "Behold, our enemies are crushed; let us go up to cleanse the sanctuary and dedicate it" (1 Maccabees 4:36).

This is what they did. Judah chose some men to fight against those remaining in the city. He chose priests who were devoted to the Torah to clean the Temple. They removed the defiled stones and replaced them with uncut ones, they tore down the Altar of Sacrifice and built a new one. They made new holy vessels and brought them into the Temple. They burned incense on the Altar, put bread on the Table of Presence and lighted the lamps on the Menorah.

Whether or not it's a true, a story is told in the Talmud about the Menorah. When the Levitical priests went to light the newly made Menorah in the Most Holy Place, they found only enough pure oil to last one day. To consecrate more oil would take eight days. Then, a miracle happened. The one vial of oil lasted eight days and the Menorah burned brightly and continuously just as God commanded for an eight day dedication.

"Early in the morning on the twenty-fifth day of the ninth month, which is the month of Chislev, in the one hundred and forty-eighth year, they rose and offered sacrifice, as the law directs, on the new altar of burnt offering which they had built. At the very season and on the very day that the Gentiles had profaned it, it was dedicated with songs and harps and lutes and cymbals. All the people fell on their faces and worshiped and blessed Heaven, who had prospered them. So they celebrated the dedication of the altar for eight days, and offered burnt offerings with gladness; they offered a sacrifice of deliverance and praise..." (1 Maccabees 4:52-56).

A Gambling Game

During the years of Greek persecution, unwanted and surprise visits by the Syrian soldiers often came when Jewish men were studying the Torah. If found, the Torah scroll would be shredded into pieces and those studying would be put to death. According to tradition, a way of protecting their scrolls and their lives during an invasion was invented with a gambling game played with a top. If suddenly disrupted by soldiers, they would hide their torah scrolls, pull out their tops and begin gambling. This tradition is remembered today with a top called a *dreidel* that has four letters: Nun, Gimel, Hey and Shin. The letters are symbolic for *Nes Gadol Hayah Sham* or "A Great Miracle Happened There." In Israel, however, the dreidels have one different letter, the Peh, signifying "A Great Miracle Happened HERE."

Yeshua and Hanukkah

Hanukkah is mentioned in the Gospels in John 10:22-39 as the Feast of Dedication. It was winter and Yeshua was walking in Solomon's Colonnade or porch. Though Hanukkah was a celebration about the re-dedication of the Altar in the Temple of Jerusalem, the focus of the Jews wasn't on sacrifices and offerings, but on the miracle of the oil and the light. They began asking Yeshua if he is the promised Messiah. Since they are celebrating miracles, Yeshua reminds them of all the miracles he has done 'in his Father's name.'

"I did tell you, but you do not believe. The miracles I do in my Father's name testify about me, but you do not believe because you are not my sheep. My sheep listen to my voice; I know them, and they follow me. I give them eternal life, and they shall never perish; no one will snatch them out of my hand. My Father, who has given them to me, is greater than all; no one can snatch them out of my Father's hand..." (John 10:25-29).

The greatest miracle stood in front of the Jewish people right there in the Temple. The golden Menorah had become flesh and blood. Just as the oil miraculously burned in the Menorah, the Spirit of God filled Yeshua and his light illuminated the Temple during the *Festival of Lights.* He no longer remained silent about his identity, but answered their question clearly giving them no doubt as to who he was: *"I and the Father are one."* They struggled with his declaration and picked up stones to kill him.

Hanukkah for Us

"I exhort you, therefore, brothers, in view of God's mercies, to offer yourselves as a sacrifice, living and set apart for God. This will please him; it is the logical "Temple worship" for you" (Romans 11:1).

Paul teaches that because we have been bought with price of Yeshua's blood, we are to honor God with our bodies because they are the temple of God's Spirit. (1 Corinthians 6:19-20). Our temple worship is to offer our lives as a holy sacrifice. This is the essence of the season of Hanukkah and cleansing the Altar of Sacrifice from everything that contaminated and defiled God's holy dwelling. On that same altar we are to offering ourselves.

"Therefore, my dear friends, since we have these promises [and miracles], let us purify ourselves from everything that can defile either body or spirit, and strive to be completely holy, out of reverence for God" (2 Corinthians 7:1).

The eight days of Hanukkah are the perfect time for believers in Messiah to do some temple house cleaning. In order to hear the voice of our Shepherd more clearly, we, like the Jewish people at the Temple, must turn from spiritual idolatry that perverts a pure worship of God. We must cleanse everything causes physical contamination to our temples in order to be completely holy and rededicated back to God.

Each night of Hanukkah Yeshua's light is present in the helper candle, the *shamash,* that kindles each individual wick on the hanukkiah. He is the golden Menorah from where the holy oil of God's Spirit flows and illuminates those hidden and not so hidden areas of our lives that need to be purged and burnt up on the altar of sacrifice. By the eighth evening of Hanukkah, our hearts and minds should be completely purified out of reverence for God reflecting each miracle that occurred during the days of Judah Maccabee: the rededication of the Temple, the Altar of Sacrifice, and Holy Oil in the Golden Menorah.

*The Septuagint is the Greek translation of the Hebrew Scriptures from 2 B.C.E. The two books of the Maccabees are found in this translation as well as the Apocrypha.

Chapter Photo: An oil menorah and Hanukkiahs burning in our home during the fourth night of Hanukkah.

Modern Maccabean Revolt

"What has been will be again; what has been done will be done again; there is nothing new under the sun" (Ecclesiastes 1:9).

In the days of Judah Maccabee, there was an attack on the Jewish people by the Greeks. Not just on the Jewish people themselves, but on everything the God of Israel had given them and promised them in the Scriptures. Everything ... Jewish.

Historically, every king, emperor or leader who has done these things has been considered an enemy to Israel and the Jewish people. The Pharaoh of Egypt, Haman in Persia, Caligula and Nero of Rome, Miguel de Morillo and Juan de San Martin of the Spanish Inquisitions, and all the way to Hitler of the modern era set themselves up as gods and tried to snuff out the lives of God's chosen people. Yet, there is still one more *man of lawlessness* to come, the one prophesied about in Daniel, spoken of by Yeshua, and explained by Paul.

"The people of the ruler who will come will destroy the city and the sanctuary. ... And at the temple he will set up an abomination that causes desolation, until the end that is decreed is poured out on him" (Daniel 9:26-27).

"So when you see standing in the holy place 'the abomination that causes desolation,' spoken of through the prophet Daniel—let the reader understand—then let those who are in Judea flee to the mountains" (Matthew 24:15-16).

"Don't let anyone deceive you in any way, for that day will not come until the rebellion occurs and the man of lawlessness is revealed, the man doomed to destruction. He will oppose and will exalt himself over everything that is called God or is worshiped, so that he sets himself up in God's temple, proclaiming himself to be God" (2 Thessalonians 2:3-4).

Today, the same deceptive battle rages. It's could be called the modern Maccabean revolt because it is a rebellion against modern-day Greek and Roman ideologies that have created a religious system contrary to Biblical commands. This system teaches that the Torah is nullified, the Temple is unnecessary, the Levitical priesthood is obsolete, the dietary laws are cancelled, circumcision is legalism, the Sabbath is changed, and the Jewish people are rejected by God. Everything ... Jewish.

These unBiblical doctrines transform the God of the Holy Scriptures into an institutionally designed god. Jesus is misrepresented as a Greek-based Roman triune godhead rather than the King of the Jews, the Messiah of Israel. Many who could come to know Yeshua are driven away from a deeper walk of faith with God through these false and misguided teachings. Those who represent these teachings are not giving the world the good news of salvation; they are twisting the truth and giving the father of lies a platform on which to present his message of lawlessness. This is nothing more than the work of the Adversary, the antichrist, or man of lawlessness prophesied by Daniel, Yeshua, and Paul.

There is nothing new under the heavens. There will always be lawless men who want to destroy the Jewish people along with their Biblical heritage. There will also be men and women, Jews and gentiles, like Judah Maccabee and his father, who fight against such destruction and assimilation. They will place a Hanukkah menorah in their window to show the Jewish people they stand with them and the God of Israel. They will light the eight festive candles each night to proclaim to the world that they, along with the Jewish people, will never assimilate into a Hellenized Roman religious system that advances the coming *man of lawlessness.*

The ancient Greeks didn't win against the small Maccabean army; Antiochus Epiphanes didn't destroy the Jews or the Torah they guarded for centuries. The modern-day Greeks won't win against a royal priesthood that has begun to stand against the lies and deceptions established over the centuries by the church and church fathers.   The modern-day Romans in Vatican City can't stop the *Torah from coming from Zion and the Word of the LORD from Jerusalem.* The battle is the LORD's and when Messiah of Israel returns all things will be restored and re-dedicated *hanukkah* to the LORD: the Torah's teachings and instructions, the eternal Levitical priesthood, the seventh-day Sabbath as the covenant sign between God and His people, circumcision for entrance into the Sanctuary, and the Temple as envisioned by Ezekiel with a *dedicated* altar of sacrifice. Everything ... Jewish.

Chapter Photo: View of the alAqsa Mosque where the Temple should be and eventually will be, Jerusalem, Israel.

The Cast of Purim

"Mordecai recorded these events and sent letters to all the Jews in all the provinces of King Ahasuerus, both near and far, instructing them to observe the fourteenth day of the month of Adar and the fifteenth day, every year, [to commemorate] the days on which the Jews obtained rest from their enemies and the month which for them was turned from sorrow into gladness and from mourning into a holiday; they were to make them days of celebrating and rejoicing, sending portions [of food] to each other and giving gifts to the poor" (Esther 9:20-22).

Purim is a memorial to the deliverance of the Jewish people from near destruction while they were in exile in Persia (modern-day Iran). During the reign of Ahasuerus (aka King Xerxes), a wicked anti-semitic man named Haman came to power. He wanted all Jews in kingdom destroyed because they had different customs that wouldn't allow them to obey the king's laws. *Purim* or 'lots' were cast to choose the day of their final destruction. A Jew named Mordecai along with his niece who had become Queen intercede for God's people and the annihilation was averted.

Purim celebrations are joyous and center around melodramas where the audience takes part. There are *groggers* or noisemakers used to either cheer for the heroes or drown out the name of the villan Haman. Cookies called *Hamentashen* are made to look like Haman's tricorn hat. Children dress in the costumes of their favorite *Purim* personality. Food is put in baskets and taken to the poor, the widow and the fatherless.

Within the account of Purim there are an array of characters. As you read one or two specific verses from the *megillah* or scroll of Esther about each of them, watch how power corrupts, faith overcomes and truth is revealed. More importantly, watch God work His hand of protection for the Jewish people, for without it, they would have been destroyed. As some have said, without *Purim*, there would have been no Jewish people. If there had been no Jewish people, there would have been no salvation from the Tribe of Judah.

In these last days, the Jewish people and the nation of Israel are under great attack from the nations around the world. As global events continue to unfold, everyone will have to choose a side: Israel and God's people or the world. Use the account of Esther to check your own heart regarding the Jewish people. Are you rebellious Queen Vashti, transformed King Ahasuerus, faithful Queen Esther, discerning Mordecai, vindictive Zeresh, or anti-semitic Haman?

Vashti
"Therefore, if it pleases the king, let him issue a royal decree and let it be written in the laws of Persia and Media, which cannot be repealed, that <u>Vashti is never again to enter the presence of King Xerxes</u>. Also let the king give her royal position to someone else who is better than she" (Esther 1:19).

Hadassah (Esther)
"Now there was in the citadel of Susa a Jew of the tribe of Benjamin, named Mordecai ... who had a cousin named Hadassah. This girl, who was also known as <u>Esther, was lovely in form and features</u>, and Mordecai had taken her as his own daughter when her father and mother died" (Esther 2:4-5).

Ahasuerus
"Now the king was attracted to Esther more than to any of the other women, and she won his favor and approval more than any of the other virgins. So he set a <u>royal crown on Esther's head </u>and made her queen instead of Vashti" (Esther 2:17).

Mordecai
"During the time <u>Mordecai was sitting at the king's gate</u>, two of the king's officers who guarded the doorway, became angry and conspired to assassinate King Xerxes. But Mordecai found out about the plot and told

Queen Esther, who in turn reported it to the king, giving credit to Mordecai" (Esther 2:21-22).

Haman

"Then Haman said to King Ahusuerus, "There is a certain people dispersed and scattered among the peoples in all the provinces of your kingdom whose customs are different from those of all other people and who do not obey the king's laws; it is not in the king's best interest to tolerate them. If it pleases the king, let a decree be issued to destroy them, and I will put ten thousand talents of silver into the royal treasury for the men who carry out this business" (Esther 3:8-9).

Haman's Wife

"His wife Zeresh and all his friends said to him, "Have a gallows built, seventy-five feet high, and ask the king in the morning to have Mordecai hanged on it. Then go with the king to the dinner and be happy" (Esther 5:14).

The Decree

"Letters were sent by courier to all the royal provinces "to destroy, kill and exterminate all Jews, from young to old, including small children and women, on a specific day, the thirteenth day of the twelfth month, the month of Adar, and to seize their goods as plunder" (Esther 3:13).

For Such a Time as This

"When Esther's words were reported to Mordecai, he sent back this answer: "Do not think that because you are in the king's house you alone of all the Jews will escape. For if you remain silent at this time, relief and deliverance for the Jews will arise from another place, but you and your father's family will perish. And who knows but that you have come to royal position for such a time as this?" (Esther 4:12-14).

The King

"Go at once," the king commanded Haman. "Get the robe and the horse and do just as you have suggested for Mordecai the Jew, who sits at the king's gate. Do not neglect anything you have recommended" (Esther 6:10).

The Queen

"Then Queen Esther answered, "If I have found favor with you, O king, and if it pleases your majesty, grant me my life—this is my petition. And spare my people—this is my request. For I and my people have been sold for destruction and slaughter and annihilation. If we had merely been sold as male and female slaves, I would have kept quiet, because no such distress would justify disturbing the king" (Esther 7:3-4).

The Jews
"The king's edict granted the Jews in every city the <u>right to assemble and protect themselves</u>; to destroy, kill and annihilate any armed force of any nationality or province that might attack them and their women and children; and to plunder the property of their enemies" (Esther 8:11).

Purim
"Mordecai recorded these events, and he sent letters to all the Jews throughout the provinces of King Ahasuerus, near and far, to have them celebrate annually the fourteenth and fifteenth days of the month of Adar as the time when the Jews got relief from their enemies, and as the month when their <u>sorrow was turned into joy and their mourning into a day of celebration</u>. He wrote them to observe the days as days of feasting and joy and giving presents of food to one another and gifts to the poor" (Esther 9:20-22).

Chapter Photo: My son, King Ahasuerus and my daughter, Queen Esther at Purim.

Part Three
Yielding Fruit

"Blessed is the man who trusts in Adonai;
Adonai will be his security.
He will be like a tree planted near water;
it spreads out its roots by the river;
it does not notice when heat comes;
and its foliage is luxuriant;
it is not anxious in a year of drought
but keeps on yielding fruit"
(Jeremiah 17:7-8).

Multiplying Loaves and Fish

 *"Taking the five loaves and the two fish and looking up to heaven, he gave thanks and broke the loaves. Then he gave them to the disciples, and the disciples gave them to the people"* (Matthew 14:19).

This is a simple study guide for those interested in learning about the Feasts of the LORD personally or with their family. Fully expect the Spirit of God to guide you into new and powerful truths about Yeshua, Israel, the nations, the coming Kingdom and Eternity. As the Spirit multiplies your loaves and fish, you *will* have 'ah-ha' moments.

1. Name of Festival

2. First time or two the command is given in Torah.

3. God's reason for giving the command.

4. Who was the command given to: priests, Israel, the nations, others? List the temple offerings sacrifices, responsibilities of priests, responsibilities of people affiliated with this festival.

5. What do each of these sacrifices represent? (It may be helpful to learn about the offerings and sacrifices in Leviticus 1-6.)

6. Find several Old Testament Scriptures where the festival is found. What is the significance of the verses? What was happening at the time? What was the teaching or instruction to be learned?

7. Using the New Testament answer the questions: Where is this festival found? What does Yeshua, the disciples, Paul, and the believers say or do about this festival?

8. From what you have gleaned, what are the shadows for this festival? How did or will Yeshua become the reality in these shadows? Consider his birth, his childhood, his life in Israel, his teachings as a Rabbi, his death, his resurrection, his return, his Kingdom, and his role in eternity.

9. Who are some other Biblical people and accounts that could also be a type and shadow of this festival? (Example: Noah, Enoch, Ruth, Esther, Joshua Deborah, the judges, priests and kings.)

10. How can you use this festival to *"declare the praises of him who called you out of darkness into his wonderful light?"* (1 Peter 2:9)

11. What are the sacrifices and offerings of those who are redeemed and have entered the new covenant? How do they relate to this festival? (1 Corinthians 6:19, Romans 12:1-2, Romans 15:16, 1 Peter 2:5).

12. Yeshua said *'true worshippers worship in Spirit and in Truth'* (John 4:24). How does this festival exemplify worship in Spirit? in Truth?

13. What are some Biblical commands you have learned through this festival that you can incorporate into a family celebration? What are some Jewish traditions that would enhance the Biblical observance of this festival?

14. Praise and worship are an integral part of celebrating God's 'appointed times'. Search the Psalms for those that were used during this festival.

16. How does learning about this festival change your view of God, Yeshua, the process of salvation, the power of the Holy Spirit, the Jewish people, Israel, and the unsaved?

17. Did you have a 'light bulb' or 'ah ha' moment while learning about this festival? If so, share it with your family or small fellowship group.

Chapter Photo: Armenian designed plate with loaves and fishes.

Celebrate Sabbath in Your Home

"Look, the LORD has given you the Shabbat. This is why he is providing bread for two days on the sixth day. Each of you, stay where you are; no one is to leave his place on the seventh day" (Exodus 16:29).

Our family along with the family of our daughter-in-law designed a Sabbath booklet to encourage those who are desiring to celebrate the Sabbath. It includes a simple outline incorporating some of the Friday evening Jewish traditions of candles, bread, wine, and blessings with Yeshua central to each. Print the PDF from our website and let it guide you and your family to *"Remember the Sabbath day to keep it holy."*

Website: www.tentstakeministries.net
This free booklet will be found under Biblical Calendar, Appointed Times, Sabbath.

Chapter Photo: Sabbath sunset over Pacific Ocean, Elk, California.

Challah Bread

Every Friday evening, two loaves of braided bread are placed on our Sabbath table and covered with a special cloth. This tradition came from the double portion of manna that was covered with dew and gathered for the Sabbath (Exodus 16).

Ingredients: 200 ml water, 2 eggs, 2 TBsp honey, 2 TBsp butter or oil, 2 cups unbleached white flour, 2 cups whole wheat flour, 1 tbsp yeast

Put all ingredients together in a bread machine.
Set on dough setting. OR

Knead by hand for about 10 minutes. Place in oiled bowl and cover. Allow to rise until it's double in size and punch down. Knead again. Divide into six small sections and roll into strips. Take three strips and braid. Make two loaves in this manner.

Egg Wash and Topping

1 egg, poppy seeds or sesame seeds, kosher salt

Mix the egg yolk and white together. Brush over the tops and sides of the loaves. Top with poppy or sesame seeds. Sprinkle with kosher salt. Let rise until nearly double the size.

Bake at 350˚ for 30 minutes.
Cool and put on the table covered with a cloth.

Passover Haggadah

"The living, the living—they praise you, as I am doing today; parents tell their children about your faithfulness" (Psalm 38:19).

Passover is a story that has been retold for thousands of years. It is the account of God's miraculous deliverance of His people from slavery to freedom, from despair to hope, from darkness to light. It encompasses the eternal truths of His character and personal involvement with His people. It endures as a testimony to His grace and merciful redemption because of the faithful who have told the story to their children from the time of ancient Egypt through the days of Messiah until this very day.

Our Passover Haggadah is a compilation from several different sources: the Covenant Community Church in McCook, Nebraska, two Messianic Haggadahs that were formatted from a traditional Jewish one, and our own personal insights from years of celebrating the memorial to the Lord's Passover.

Yeshua, the Messiah is the reality in the shadows of Passover and his last Passover seder is central to this Haggadah. From it you will learn more about your Savior and this 'appointed time' of God.

Copies for the Haggadah may be purchased on Amazon.com or from Tentstake Ministries.
Website: www.tentstakeministries.net
The Haggadah can be found under Biblical Calendar, Appointed Times, Passover.

Homemade Matzah

"The day after Passover they ate what the land produced, matzah and roasted ears of grain that day" (Joshua 5:11).

Unleavened bread or matzah is eaten at Passover and for the seven days of the Feast of Unleavened Bread. Matzah can be purchased or made at home. Homemade matzah gives a personal touch to the feasts and also makes tasty little peanut butter and jelly sandwiches.

Ingredients: 3 cups whole wheat flour, 2 tsp. salt, 3 TBsp. butter, 2 egg yolks, 2 tsp. olive oil, 1 cup water

To make the dough, add salt to the flour, then cut the butter into flour mixture as you would for a pie crust.

In another bowl, beat egg yolks adding oil slowly. Pour this mixture into the dough and stir with spoon or fork until it forms a ball that comes away from the sides of the bowl. Knead lightly on a floured board for about one minute to shape the dough into a soft ball.

Pinch off about 1/3 cup of dough and with your hands, pat it as thin as can easily be done. Roll it thinner with a rolling pin. Keep working the dough and rolling it until dough is so thin it just holds together without breaking when handled.

Place rolled dough on an un-greased cookie sheet. Cut into shapes - squares or circles - and pierce with a fork.

Bake at 400° for 8-12 minutes until puffed or very light brown.

Apostle People

"He is not here; he has risen, just as he said."

"Come and see the place where he lay. Then go quickly and tell his disciples:

'He has risen from the dead and is going ahead of you into Galilee..."(Matthew 28:6-8).

When my children were young, I wanted to find a way to celebrate the Feast of Firstfruits, the Resurrection of Jesus (Yeshua) that did not include hidden eggs and chocolate rabbits. I prayed for wisdom and a creative way to express what actually happened on that first day of the week when the women went to the tomb and found it empty.

Matthew 28 jumped out from the page in my Bible. The disciples were hiding. They were afraid. An angel appeared to the women at the tomb and said, *"Go tell the disciples, 'He is risen.'* The concept of the Apostle People was born.

The Apostle People are made from paint-stir sticks with heads cut from poster board. Each head is labeled with one of the names of the Apostles: Thaddeus (An Overseas Traveler), Andrew (A Fisherman), John (Cared for Yeshua's mother), Simon (Yeshua made him a man of peace), Peter (A Fisherman, the Rock), Bartholomew (Yeshua found him under a fig tree), Thomas (The Doubter), James (A Fisherman), Matthew (A Tax Collector), James (The Lesser, Short One), Philip (Fed the Apostles), Judas (Betrayer, Sold Yeshua for 30 pieces of silver).

There are two more people: Yeshua (Salvation) who wears a talit or prayer shawl and an Angel (Messenger) that wears white.

During the week of Passover, we would read of the events in Yeshua's life from his arrival in Jerusalem until Passover. On Passover day, we would wrap Yeshua in a white cloth and put him in a tomb made from a box. Then we would place a rock in front of the tomb.

On the night before the Resurrection, I would remove the rock and Yeshua from the tomb and place an angel by it. I would remove Yeshua's linens and hide him somewhere in the house. In the morning when my children got up, they saw the angel and the empty tomb. It was a perfect moment to say as the angel did, *"Why do you look for the living among the dead?"*

They would search the house for Yeshua and when they found him, there would be a special gift to encourage their spiritual growth. Over the years we gave them Bible character dolls, the armor of God, books about Esther or Jonah, Bible dictionaries, necklaces, T-shirts, concordances, or devotionals. Because Yeshua is the Word of God, the gifts always reflected the Word and growing in that Word.

They would also notice that the Apostle People were missing. They were no longer in the place they were kept. These men were hidden outside in the yard. My children would get excited to go outside to 'find the disciples'. When each one was found, the child would exclaim, *"He is Risen."* A few pieces of candy or a small treat was placed with each apostle to make the announcement a little 'sweeter'.

"How sweet are your words to my taste, sweeter than honey to my mouth!" (Psalm 119:103).

Shavuot Barley Stew

"Then all the people went away to eat and drink, to send portions of food and to celebrate with great joy, because they now understood the words that had been made known to them" (Nehemiah 8:12).

The 50 days of counting the omer began with the firstfruits of the barley harvest. If you want, buy some barley and put a kernel or two in a jar for each of the 50 days. On Shavuot use the collected barley along with some lamb and lentils to make this stew as a harvest offering.

Ingredients: 1 pound ground lamb, 2 stalks thinly sliced celery, 1 cup thinly sliced carrots, 1 medium onion, chopped; 2 tbsp butter, 6 cups chicken brother, 1 can diced tomatoes, ¾ cup lentils, ¾ cup barley, ½ tsp oregano, ½ tsp dried rosemary leaves, 1 cup Swiss cheese.

Directions: Cook the lentils and barley in water according to directions on the package or use a pressure cooker for less time. Brown the lamb and then remove from the pan and put into a stew pot. Sauté celery, carrots, and onion in butter.

When lentils and barley are cooked, drain and add the chicken broth with seasonings, the sautéed vegetables and the lamb. Simmer for ½ hour. Serve with Swiss cheese melted on top.

Dance the Hora

The Hora is considered the Israeli National Dance. It is easily danced by men, women and children. A simple, but joyful dance, the Hora and can be done anywhere, anytime from wedding celebrations, to festival days, to Sabbath at the Western Wall.

This traditional dance is done in a circle with a moderate to quick tempo with everyone holding hands. It is only 6 counts.

Part I (Holding hands)

Left foot steps Left and Right foot kicks Left;

Right foot steps Right and Left foot kicks Right.

Left foot steps Left, Right Foot steps behind Left foot and

Left foot steps Left to begin the kicking sequence again. Repeat.

Chapter Photo: Dancing the hora during Sukkot, Sterling, Colorado.

Memorial Candle

"A good name is better than fine perfume, and the day of death better than the day of birth" (Ecclesiastes 7:1).

There is a Jewish tradition on the Day of Atonement that involves lighting a 24-hour memorial candle called the *Yahrzeit.* It is also known as the *ner neshama* or 'soul candle'. It is also lit on the death anniversary of a loved one and on *Yom HaShoah,* the memorial of the Holocaust, and on *Yom Kippur.*

Though Yeshua did not die on the Yom Kippur, he did die as the *kapparah* for the sins of Israel and ultimately, the world. On the day he returns, Israel will look on him and mourn. Light a candle to remember to pray for the nation of Israel that the veil might be removed and they would see their salvation, their High Priest, Yeshua.

Sukkah of Study

"He raised up a testimony in Jacob and established a Torah in Israel. He commanded our ancestors to make this known to their children, so that the next generation would know it, the children not yet born, who would themselves arise and tell their own children, who could then put their confidence in God, not forgetting God's deeds, but obeying his commandments" (Psalm 78:1-7).

The Feast of Tabernacles is 'our season of joy'. It is the time of Yeshua's birth, the time to remember the Tabernacle in the wilderness, the time for celebrating the ingathering (of Israel) and a time to look forward to the coming eternal Kingdom of God.

When my children were young, we had no place of fellowship so we made our sukkah that place. Everyday we would run outside to read our Bibles and do an activity in the sukkah that helped all of us learn the deeper meaning to our 'temporary dwelling.'

This list of activities is for those who are wanting to learn more about the Feast of Tabernacles. As with all study guides, use them them as a springboard for your own personal study or teaching your own children. There are no right or wrong answers as all Scripture is divinely inspired for our training in righteousness. Some of the activities will take the entire week while others are just a single day activity. Depending on how you use it, it could even be eight years of teachings for your family. Whatever you do, do it all for the glory of God and give your children wonderful memories of 'our season of joy' that focuses on Yeshua, the living Tabernacle of God.

Preparation Day

The Day before the Feast of Tabernacles begins.

"You are to live in sukkot for seven days ... so that generation after generation of you will know that I made the children of Israel live in sukkot when I brought them out of the land of Egypt; I am the LORD your God" (Leviticus 23:42).

Build a sukkah inside or outside. Make sure it is a 'temporary structure'. You can use anything from sheets to wood, but its roof should be covered with branches or left open. Decorate it with pictures, fruit, and lights. Put pillows, chairs and tables inside if it is big enough. Make it a welcoming place for Bible study, eating snacks or meals, and inviting friends. Learn the Hebrew words sukkah and sukkot.

Read about Abraham living in a tent in a tent in Hebrews 11:9-10. Have your children draw a picture of his tent and hang them in your sukkah.

First day of Tabernacles

"On the first day you are to take branches from luxuriant trees—from palms, willows and other leafy trees—and rejoice before the Lord your God for seven days" (Leviticus 23:40).

Make some *lulavs* with branches and fruit. Gather some palm branches or buy some silk/plastic ones along with some lemons.

In Luke 8:4-15, Yeshua taught about the four heart conditions of men in the Parable of the Sower. Compare and contrast the spiritual *lulav* found in the Feast of Tabernacles chapter with the Parable.

Yeshua the Living Tabernacle

"The Word became flesh and tabernacled with us, we saw his glory, the glory of the Father's only Son, full of grace and truth" (John 1:14).

Read about Yeshua's birth in Luke chapters 1 and 2. Yeshua means 'salvation' in Hebrew. Look up Scriptures that have the word 'salvation.' Write them out on 3x5 cards replacing the word 'salvation' with 'Yeshua'. Put them in a basket in your sukkah and read several each day.

Play some praise and worship music and dance with your *lulavs* to celebrate the birth of Yeshua.

Second Day of Tabernacles

"...'Celebrate the Feast of Ingathering at the end of the year, when you gather in your crops from the field" (Exodus 23:16).

Using yellow, red, orange and brown construction paper, cut out autumn leaf shapes. On each leaf write a Scripture about the harvest or ingathering. Hang your leaves in your sukkah. Some examples can be found in Isaiah 11:12, 55:10, Matthew 13, Mark 4, John 4, Jeremiah 16:14-15, and Ezekiel 23:13.

Learn about *aliyah* and the modern-day ingathering of Jewish people from around the world. Seek out a ministry in Israel that encourages *aliyah* or helps new immigrants to adjust to life in the land of promise.

Third Day of Tabernacles

"I think it is right to refresh your memory as long as I live in the tent of this body ... (2 Peter 1:13).

Search for Scriptures about our bodies being 'tents' and 'temples'. Have children draw a self portrait and hang it in your sukkah.

Learn about the Holy Spirit or the *Ruach haKodesh* in Hebrew. Look up Scriptures that tell what he Holy Spirit does in a believer's life. What does it mean to be convicted of sin or comforted? What is the difference between the fruits of the Spirit and the gifts of the Spirit?

Fourth Day of Tabernacles

"But we have this treasure in jars of clay to show that this all-surpassing power is from God and not from us" (2 Corinthians 4:7).

What does it mean that we are clay jars that hold a treasure? Using some clay, make a jar that represents you. Paint your name on the outside. Write your favorite Scriptures on pieces of paper and put them inside the jar.

Learn about the Dead Sea Scrolls. They were found in 1948 by a bedouin shepherd in some caves near Qumran. The scrolls had been hidden in clay jars since the time of the revolt about 70 A.D. The scroll of Isaiah was found completely in tact. How would you consider the Dead Sea Scrolls as 'treasures in clay jars'.

Fifth Day of Tabernacles

"Then the cloud covered the tent of meeting, and the glory of the Lord filled the tabernacle" (Exodus 40:34).

Do a little study on the glory of the LORD. In Hebrew the word is *kavod.* What is significant about *kavod*?

Put a menorah in your sukkah. If you don't have a menorah, draw one or make a simple one with clay and seven birthday candles. If you are really creative glue seven spools on a piece of wood and paint it with gold paint.

"May my prayer be set before you like incense; may the lifting up of my hands be like the evening sacrifice" (Psalm 141:2).

Burn some incense in your sukkah. Frankincense and myrrh can be bought where most incense is sold.

Sixth Day of Tabernacles

"These are a shadow of things that are coming, but the body is of the Messiah" (Colossians 9:17).

Shine a light on your child and make a silhouette of them. Then take a photograph of them. Discuss the difference between a shadow and a reality. How does Yeshua become realities in shadows?

Read about the Tabernacle in Hebrews and Revelation. Find similarities and differences between the shadow of the Tabernacle in the wilderness and the Tabernacle in heaven.

Build a small Ark of the Covenant using a box. Spray paint it gold and put some dowels on the sides. From some poster board, make two cherubim and paint them gold. Attach them to the top of the Ark. Find two rocks and put them in the Ark for the stone tablets. Find a stick with leaves and put it in as Aaron's rod that budded. In a small container, put some oatmeal as manna. Put your Ark of the Covenant inside your sukkah.

What are the shadows of the Ark, the stone tablets, Aaron's rod, and manna fulfilled in Messiah Yeshua? the new covenant? the royal priesthood? the bread of life?

Seventh Day of Tabernacles

"For I will pour water on the thirsty land, and streams on dry ground; I will pour out my Spirit on your offspring and my blessing on your descendants" (Isaiah 44:2-4).

On this day, Yeshua attended the Feast of Tabernacles. Read about the events of that day in John chapter 7.

Fill a pitcher of water and pour it out as you read and discuss living water (Jeremiah 2:13, Jeremiah 17:13, Zechariah 14:8, John Chapter 4, Revelation 7:17).

Exodus 17:1-7 describes the account of the water coming from the rock. 1 Corinthians 10:3-4 explains the rock. How is this 'water from the rock' visible to the people on the last and greatest day of the Feast of Tabernacles?

Eighth Day of Tabernacles

"Blessed is the man who does not walk in the counsel of the wicked or stand in the way of sinners or sit in the seat of mockers. But his delight is in the Torah of the Lord, and on his Torah he meditates day and night. He is like a tree planted by streams of water, which yields its fruit in season and whose leaf does not wither. Whatever he does prospers" (Psalm 1:1-3).

This day is known as *Simchat Torah* or 'Rejoicing in the Torah'. Learn what the Hebrew word *torah* actually means and how it can be used with both the testaments of the Bible (2 Timothy 3:16).

Read Psalm 19 aloud. Notice that each section begins with a Hebrew letter. Learn the Hebrew Aleph-Bet along with their word pictures.

Make flags from dowels and small pieces of felt for celebrating Simchat Torah. Our little flags say, "Yeshua", "I Love God's Torah", "Rejoice in the Bible" and "Be Joyful". Wave the flags, play music and dance praising God for giving us this 'appointed time' to learn about His Tabernacle, His Son, and our earthly temples.

On the eighth day of Tabernacles, Yeshua was circumcised and given his name of 'salvation'. Learn about circumcision and discuss Romans 2:28-29.

It is traditional to begin a yearly cycle of reading Torah on Simchat Torah. Begin a Torah cycle for the next year so the Scriptures are planted in your heart, mind and soul.

Have children write a short poem, story, or paragraph about something that made their 'Season of Rejoicing' special.

Take pictures of your sukkah and begin a family scrapbook of the Feast of Tabernacles.

Spin the Dreidel

A dreidel is a four-sided top with a different Hebrew letter on each side.

Outside of the Land of Israel, the letters are: Nun - נ Gimel - ג Hay - ה Shin - ש

When the letters are put together, they stand for Nes Gadol Hayah Sham or "A Miracle Happened There."

Within the Land of Israel, the letters are: Nun - נ Gimel - ג Hay - ה Peh - פ

When these letters are put together, they stand for Nes Gadol Hayah Peh or "A Miracle Happened HERE."

The 'here or there' refers to the miracles of Hanukkah that occurred in Jerusalem about 165 B.C.E.

The first miracle is the victory of the Jewish people over the Greek armies who had taken control of the Temple in Jerusalem and desecrated the altar by sacrificing a pig and pouring out its blood, along with erecting a statue of Zeus in the Holy of Holies.

The second miracle is one that has grown over the centuries regarding the menorah and the oil. When the Temple was restored, there was only one sealed jar of consecrated oil for the Temple menorah. It would take eight days to consecrate more oil. Miraculously, the one jar lasted the entire eight days.

The third and greatest miracle is Yeshua, the Light of the World who stood in Solomon's Colonade as the true menorah of the Temple (John 8:12). .

The fourth miracle is that the Jewish people survived the persecution of Antiochus Epiphanes. If anyone was found the reading Torah, they and their families would be put to death. According to the tradition, when the soldiers came to a home, if the family was reading Torah, they would their scrolls, pull out their tops and begin playing the gambling game, Dreidel.

The Game of Dreidel:

1. Each player begins with 10 pennies, MnMs, buttons, toothpicks or gelt. Gelt is chocolate coins wrapped in gold foil.

2. Each person puts one of their gelt into the center 'pot.'

3. One person goes first by spinning their dreidel. The letter that falls face up determines what the player will do.

Nun - נ - The player does nothing, takes nothing.

Gimel - ג - The player takes all the coins, candy, items in the 'pot.'

Hey - ה - The player takes half of the coins, candy, items in the 'pot.'

Shin - ש - The player will put another coin, candy, item in the 'pot.'

One through three is repeated again with another person spinning their dreidel.

Hamantashen

Hamantaschen are special cookies made for Purim. They are filled with jam and the edges are pinched together to look like Haman's tri-corn hat.

Ingredients: 1 ½ cups butter, softened; 2 ¼ cups sugar, 3 large eggs, ¾ tsp. baking soda, 6 ½ cups unbleached flour, and your favorite jam or date paste.

⅓ cup cold water for pinching sides together

Mix the ingredients together until it forms a soft ball that is easily rolled. With a rolling pin, roll out dough until it's between ⅛ and ¼ inch thick. Using the top of a glass or jar, cut out circles.

Place a teaspoon of jam or date paste in the center of the circle.

Wetting your fingers with the water, pinch the sides together to form a triangle or tri-corn hat making them stick together.

Bake at 350˚ for 8-10 minutes or until fully cooked and light brown in color.

Acknowledgements

Several people were integral to the writing of this book. Dawnita Carlson took me under her wing when I was new to this walk of faith. She, along with her husband Bill, discipled our family and challenged us to dig deeper into the Word of God for answers to our questions. Dillard Griffith, through much support and encouragement, gave me the confidence to step out in faith and teach others about praise and worship dancing and God's 'appointed times'. Michael Gonzalez of Front Range Messianic blessed me by putting a link to my blog on his website from which I have received comments from people around the world who use the insights for personal as well as congregational study.

I am grateful for each of my children who helped create traditions and memories for our family. They dressed up as Hamans and Esthers, searched for afikomens, built sukkahs, lit menorahs, molded clay pots, learned to dance, played dreidel, tasted horseradish, smelled incense, sang Hebrew blessings and learned the sounds of the shofar. My husband has always been supportive and encouraging in our unique walk of faith by blowing the shofar at festival celebrations, leading seders and Sabbath meals for innumerable guests, and baptizing (immersing) our children. He has given his insights over the years when I asked at inopportune moments and was always patient when I needed his skill and advice with layout and design in Photoshop. Finally, without the tech services and expertise of my son Jesse, there would be no Tentstake Ministries website.

I am just one very tiny cell in the Body of Messiah growing in this Messianic faith. I am thankful for the Spirit of God that continues to guide me in the Scriptures and allows the Living Water to flow from the root of the Olive Tree to this 'fruity' wild olive.

About the Author

Julie Almanrode received a B.A. in English from Millersville University, Pennsylvania in 1980. She grew up in a traditional church setting always asking the question, "Why are there no Jews in church?" Even after writing a high school research paper comparing Christianity and Judaism, her search continued. On January 19, 1991 at a *Lamb* concert at Roeh Israel in Denver, Colorado, her question was answered. Jews and gentiles were worshipping Jesus together; something she had never  witnessed before. She asked a young Jewish man what it was like to be a 'completed Jew' to which he responded, "What is it like to be grafted into the Olive Tree of Israel?" Thus began the *Journey of Jeremiah*.

Julie maintains a website, Tent Stake Ministries, that chronicles her non-Jewish family's journey into the realm of being part a wild olive branch grafted into the Olive Tree of Israel. She home educated her four children who are now adults and continues to be a homemaker enjoying her chickens and guineas, as well as dancing with the Inner Court Dancers. She has been married for 30 years to a loving and supportive husband and lives in what she refers to as podunk, nowhere, Nebraska. Julie is available to teach dance seminars during the Feast days, and her husband John can lead Feast celebrations in your home or congregation. They can be contacted through Tent Stake Ministries, www.tentstakeministries.net.

Made in the USA
San Bernardino, CA
23 March 2015